PUBLIC EXPENDITURE ANALYSIS

Introduction to the Public Sector Governance and Accountability Series

Anwar Shah, Series Editor

A well-functioning public sector that delivers quality public services consistent with citizen preferences and that fosters private market-led growth while managing fiscal resources prudently is considered critical to the World Bank's mission of poverty alleviation and the achievement of Millennium Development Goals. This important new series aims to advance those objectives by disseminating conceptual guidance and lessons from practices and by facilitating learning from each others' experiences on ideas and practices that promote *responsive* (by matching public services with citizens' preferences), *responsible* (through efficiency and equity in service provision without undue fiscal and social risk), and *accountable* (to citizens for all actions) public governance in developing countries.

This series represents a response to several independent evaluations in recent years that have argued that development practitioners and policy makers dealing with public sector reforms in developing countries and, indeed, anyone with a concern for effective public governance could benefit from a synthesis of newer perspectives on public sector reforms. This series distills current wisdom and presents tools of analysis for improving the efficiency, equity, and efficacy of the public sector. Leading public policy experts and practitioners have contributed to the series.

The first seven volumes in the series (*Fiscal Management, Public Services Delivery, Public Expenditure Analysis, Tools for Public Sector Evaluations, Macrofederalism* and *Local Finances, International Practices in Local Governance,* and *Citizen-Centered Governance*) are concerned with public sector accountability for prudent fiscal management; efficiency and equity in public service provision; safeguards for the protection of the poor, women, minorities, and other disadvantaged groups; ways of strengthening institutional arrangements for voice and exit; methods of evaluating public sector programs, fiscal federalism, and local finances; international practices in local governance; and a framework for responsive and accountable governance.

Fiscal Management

Edited by Anwar Shah

Public Services Delivery

Edited by Anwar Shah

Tools for Public Sector Evaluations

Edited by Anwar Shah

Macrofederalism and Local Finances

Edited by Anwar Shah

International Practices in Local Governance

Edited by Anwar Shah

Citizen-Centered Governance

Matthew Andrews and Anwar Shah

PUBLIC SECTOR
GOVERNANCE AND
ACCOUNTABILITY SERIES

PUBLIC EXPENDITURE ANALYSIS

Edited by ANWAR SHAH

THE WORLD BANK
Washington, D.C.

ISBN-10: 0-8213-6144-9
ISBN-13: 978-0-8213-6144-3
eISBN: 978-0-8213-6145-0
DOI: 1596/978-0-8213-6144-3

Library of Congress Cataloging-in-Publications Data

Public expenditure analysis for citizen-centered governance / edited by Anwar Shah.
    p. cm.—(Public sector, governance, and accountability series)
  Includes bibliographical references and index.
  ISBN 0-8213-6144-9 (pbk.)
    1. Local government—Citizen participation. 2. Municipal services—Evaluation. 3. Local budgets. 4. Expenditures, Public. I. Shah, Anwar. II. World Bank. III. Series.

JS211.P827 2005
352.4'6214—dc22

2005043248

Contents

**Other Forthcoming Books
of Related Interest**   ii

Foreword   xi

Preface   xiii

Acknowledgments   xv

Contributors   xvi

Overview   xix
by Anwar Shah

CHAPTER

1   **Public Expenditure Incidence Analysis**   1
by Giuseppe Ruggeri
General Issues   2
The Allocation of Public Expenditures   15
Distributional Effects   25
Conclusions   29

2 On Measures of Inequality and Poverty with Welfare Implications 33
by Nanak Kakwani and Hyun Son
The Lorenz Curve and Social Welfare 34
Gini Index 36
Calculations of the Gini Index 37
Generalized Gini Index 38
Entropy Measures of Inequality 39
Atkinson's Inequality Measures 40
Measuring Poverty 42
An Illustration Using Lao PDR Data 44
Some Concluding Remarks 47

3 On Assessing the Equity of Governments' Fiscal Policies, with Application to the Philippines 49
by Hyun Son
Welfare Measures 50
Welfare and Income Components 52
Welfare Reform Index 55
Indirect Taxes and Subsidies 56
An Overview of the Philippines' Fiscal System 57
Basis for Measuring Distributional Effects 61
Analysis of Empirical Results 62
Some Concluding Remarks 67

4 Evaluating Public Pensions 69
by Robin Boadway and Katherine Cuff
The Imperative for Public Pension Reform
and Development 69
The Rationale for Government Intervention 72
Transfers to the Elderly 88
Contributory Pension Schemes 99
Encouragement of Voluntary Provision
for Retirement 125
Conclusion: Issues for Evaluation 128

5

Gender in Public Expenditure Reviews   135
by *Barbara Bergmann*
Choice and Range of Topics   137
Methodology of Analysis   139
Provision of Data   141
Remedies and Changes in Policy and Budget   142
Examples of Gender-Sensitive Budgetary Analysis   144
Summary   151

6

**Citizen-Centered Governance: A New Approach
to Public Sector Reform**   153
by *Matthew Andrews and Anwar Shah*
The Public Sector Reform Challenge in
    Developing Countries   154
Conventional Reform Approaches, the Legacy They Leave, and
    Their Problems   156
A New Citizen-Centered Framework to Guide Reform   165
Conclusion   175

7

**Toward Citizen-Centered Local-Level Budgets
in Developing Countries**   183
by *Matthew Andrews and Anwar Shah*
Citizens and the Common Approaches to Budgeting in Local
    Developing Countries   184
Citizens Analyzing Municipal Finances in Developing Countries:
    A New Approach   190
Conclusion   215

8

**Voice Mechanisms and Local Government Fiscal
Outcomes: How Do Civic Pressure and Participation
Influence Public Accountability?**   217
by *Matthew Andrews*
Background   218
The Link between Public Sector Accountability
    and Civic Voice   219

Reforms Focused on Enhancing Voice and
   Accountability   220
A Research Approach   222
Observations about the Link between Voice, Voice Mechanisms,
   and Accountability   223
Conclusion   241

BOXES

1.1   Components of Various Income Concepts   12
1.2   A Classification of Government Expenditures   18
1.3   Selected Groupings of Government Expenditures   26

FIGURES

2.1   Lorenz Curve   35
6.1   The Process Bias of Common Reform Combinations   161
6.2   The Top-Down, Centralizing Nature of Common
       Reform Combinations   164
6.3(a) A Roadmap for Citizen-Centered Governance   169
6.3(b) Citizen-Centered Reform—Formalizing the Results Focus   169
6.4   Citizen-Centered Reform Influences on Governance   170
6.5   Tools for Results-Oriented Management—External Citizen
       Focus   173
8.1   Voice Mechanisms, Voice Expression, and Accountability   221
8.2   Voice Expression and Accountability Effects
       of Mechanism Adoption   235
8.3   Voice Mechanisms, Voice Expression, and Accountability
       (Observed Experience)   242

TABLES

1.1   Global Indexes of Redistribution Based on Comparisons
       of Gini Coefficients   29
2.1   Calculation of the Gini Index   38
2.2   Inequality in Lao PDR   45
2.3   Poverty Measures: Lao PDR   46
3.1   Fiscal System in the Philippines: 1998   58
3.2   Government Expenditures by Functional Classification   60
3.3   Welfare Reform Index for Income Components:
       Philippines, 1998   63
3.4   Welfare Reform Index for Expenditures: Philippines, 1998   66

5.1 Summary of South African Gender Budget Document 146
5.2 Summary of Gender Budget Document for Barbados 149
6.1 Common Governance and Administrative Weaknesses in Developing Countries 154
6.2 Major Themes and Elements of Reform in the Development World 157
6.3 Key Elements of Citizen-Centered Governance Reforms 166
6.4 Citizen-Centered Budgeting 173
7.1 A Typical Budget Process and Time Line for Local Governments in Developing Countries 185
7.2 A Typical Local Government Budget and Financial Statement in Developing Countries 189
7.3 Institutions Facilities A Move toward Citizen-Oriented Budgeting Processes 191
7.4 Citizen-Oriented Revelation Records: An Example 196
7.5 Citizen-Oriented Reflection and Resolution Records: An Example 200
7.6 Citizen-Oriented Reporting Records: An Example 205
7.7 A Citizen-Oriented Budget Format 210

Foreword

In Western democracies systems of checks and balances built into government structures have formed the core of good governance and have helped empower citizens for more than two hundred years. The incentives that motivate public servants and policy makers— the rewards and sanctions linked to results that help shape public sector performance—are rooted in a country's accountability frameworks. Sound public sector management and government spending help determine the course of economic development and social equity, especially for the poor and other disadvantaged groups such as women and the elderly.

Many developing countries, however, continue to suffer from unsatisfactory and often dysfunctional governance systems including rent-seeking and malfeasance, inappropriate allocation of resources, inefficient revenue systems, and weak delivery of vital public services. Such poor governance leads to unwelcome outcomes for access to public services by the poor and other disadvantaged members of the society such as women, children, and minorities. In dealing with these concerns, the development assistance community in general, and the World Bank in particular, are continuously striving to learn lessons from practices around the world to achieve a better understanding of what works and what does not work in improving public sector governance, especially with respect to combating corruption and making services work for poor people.

This series advances our knowledge by providing tools and lessons from practices in improving efficiency and equity of public services provision and strengthening institutions of accountability in governance. The series highlights frameworks to create incentive environments and pressures for good governance from within and beyond governments. It outlines institutional mechanisms to empower citizens to demand accountability for results from their governments. It provides practical guidance on managing for results and prudent fiscal management. It outlines approaches to dealing with corruption and malfeasance. It provides conceptual and practical guidance on alternative service delivery frameworks for extending the reach and access of public services. The series also covers safeguards for the protection of the poor, women, minorities, and other disadvantaged groups; strengthening institutional arrangements for voice and exit; methods of evaluating public sector programs; frameworks for responsive and accountable governance; and fiscal federalism and local governance.

The *Public Sector Governance and Accountability Series* will be of interest to public officials, development practitioners, students of development, and those interested in public governance in developing countries.

Frannie A. Léautier
Vice President, World Bank Institute

Preface

Fairness or equity in public spending remains an area of major concern as the public sector in developing countries fails to provide services and to protect the poor, women, minorities, and other disadvantaged members of society. Instead, it is seen to serve the interests of an elite minority with little concern for the well-being of citizens at large.

This book provides tools of analysis for discovering equity in tax burdens as well as in public spending and judging government performance in its role in safeguarding the interests of the poor and those otherwise disadvantaged members of society, such as women, children, and minorities. The book further provides a framework for a rights-based approach to citizen empowerment—in other words, creating an institutional design with appropriate rules, restraints, and incentives to make the public sector responsive and accountable to an average voter. Various chapters in this book provide tools of analysis for addressing the following questions:

- *Public burden test:* Are public sector tax burdens and program benefits being equitably shared?
- *Poverty reduction test:* Are the programs appropriately targeted to the poor? Will these make any difference to their well-being?
- *Social protection test:* Do the elderly and the poor have some measure of income security?
- *Gender safeguard test:* Do programs ensure equality of access to women?
- *Responsiveness test:* Do citizen preferences matter for the design and delivery of public services?

■ *Accountability test:* Are citizens empowered to demand accountability from elected and appointed officials?

Applications of the above mentioned tests are expected to yield a better understanding of the civility of governance in developing countries. Such an understanding will hopefully lead to a reform of public governance to strengthen safeguards and protection of the poor and other vulnerable groups.

I am grateful to the Swiss Development Cooperation Agency for their support and to the leading experts who contributed papers, for making this series possible.

Roumeen Islam
Manager, Poverty Reduction and Economic Management
World Bank Institute

Acknowledgments

The completion of this book has been made possible through a grant from the Swiss Development Cooperation Agency and further support from the Swedish International Development Agency. The editor is grateful to their staff for guidance on the contents of the book. In particular, he owes a great deal of intellectual debt to Walter Hofer, Werner Thut, Pietro Veglio, Gerolf Weigel, Alexandre Widmer, and Hanspeter Wyss. The editor is also grateful to senior management of the Operations Evaluation Department of the World Bank, the World Bank Institute, and CEPAL (the United Nations Economic Commission for Latin American and the Caribbean) for their support. Thanks are due to Juan Carlos Lerda, CEPAL and Roumeen Islam, World Bank for their guidance and support.

The book has also benefited from comments received from senior policy makers at the CEPAL/World Bank joint workshop held in Santiago, Chile, in January 2001 and PREM (poverty reduction and economic management) seminars held at the World Bank. In addition, senior finance and budget officials from a large number of countries offered advice on the contents of the book. The editor is also grateful to leading academics who contributed chapters and Bank and external peer reviewers for their comments. Matthew Andrews, Azam Chaudhry, Neil Hepburn, and Theresa Thompson helped during various stages of preparation of this book and provided comments and contributed summaries. Agnes Santos prepared the book for publication.

Contributors

MATTHEW ANDREWS, a public sector management specialist at the World Bank, is a South African with a doctorate in public administration from the Maxwell School, Syracuse University. He has worked at all levels of government in South Africa and has published on topics such as public budgeting and management, evaluation, and institutional economics.

BARBARA BERGMANN is professor emerita of economics at the University of Maryland and at American University in Washington, D.C. She is the author of *America's Child Care Problem: The Way Out, Is Social Security Broke?, In Defense of Affirmative Action, Saving Our Children From Poverty: What the United States Can Learn From France,* and *The Economic Emergence of Women.* She served as a senior staff member of the President's Council of Economic Advisers during the Kennedy Administration, as senior economic adviser with the U.S. Agency for International Development, as an economist with the Bureau of Labor Statistics, and on advisory committees to the Congressional Budget Office and the Bureau of the Census. She has served as president of the Eastern Economic Association, the Society for the Advancement of Socio-Economics, the American Association of University Professors, and the International Association for Feminist Economics.

ROBIN BOADWAY is Sir Edward Peacock Professor of economic theory at Queen's University, Kingston, Ontario, Canada. He was editor of the *Canadian Journal of Economics* from 1987 to 1993 and president of the Canadian Economics Association in 1996–97. He is currently co-editor of the *Journal of Public Economics* and the

German Economic Review, and editorial advisor for the *Canadian Tax Journal.* He serves on the Executive Committee of the International Seminar on Public Economics and the Management Board of the International Institute of Public Finance. He works in the areas of public sector economics and welfare economics, with special emphasis on tax-transfer policies, fiscal federalism, and cost-benefit analysis. His books and monographs include *Public Sector Economics, Welfare Economics, Canadian Tax Policy,* and *Economics and the Canadian Economy; Taxes and Savings in Canada, The Constitutional Division of Powers: An Economic Perspective, Equalization in a Federal State: An Economic Analysis,* and *Intergovernmental Fiscal Relations in Canada,* as well as several articles in academic journals.

KATHERINE CUFF is an assistant professor of economics at McMaster University in Hamilton, Ontario, Canada. She holds a Ph.D. in economics from Queen's University, Kingston, Ontario, Canada. Her main research interests are redistributive theory and policy, optimal taxation, and fiscal federalism.

NANAK KAKWANI was appointed as the foundation professor of statistics at the University of New South Wales (Australia) in December 1970. Before joining UNSW, he was a lecturer at the University of Birmingham, England, Reader in Econometrics at Punjabi University and Professor of Econometrics at Kurukshetra University in India. He has published extensively (about seventy articles, and two major books published by Oxford and Cambridge Universities). His research includes econometrics theory, welfare economics— inequality and poverty, public finance and development economics. Nanak was elected a Fellow of the Academy of Social Sciences in Australia 1979 and was awarded the prestigious Mahalanobis Memorial Gold Medal in 1985 for outstanding research in quantitative economics.

GIUSEPPE RUGGERI is Vaughan Chair in regional economics and director of the policy studies center at the University of New Brunswick, Canada. Dr. Ruggeri did his undergraduate studies at the University of Messina, Italy, and Union College, Schenectady, New York. He received an M.A. in economics from the University of Michigan and a Ph.D. in economics from the State University of New York at Albany. Dr. Ruggeri has taught at the college and university level in the United States, Mexico, and Canada. He has also held senior positions with the federal government in Canada and the governments of New Brunswick and Alberta. Dr. Ruggeri is the author of four books and has published extensively in the areas of public finance, intergovernmental relations, public policy, and human capital.

ANWAR SHAH is the lead economist and the program/team leader for Public Sector Governance with the World Bank Institute and a Fellow of the Institute for Public Economics, Edmonton, Canada. He has previously served in the Ministry of Finance, Government of Canada and Government of Alberta, Canada, holding responsibilities for federal-provincial and provincial-local fiscal relations, respectively. He has advised the governments of Argentina, Australia, Brazil, Canada, China, Indonesia, Malaysia, Mexico, Pakistan, the Philippines, Poland, South Africa, and Turkey on fiscal federalism issues. He has lectured at the University of Ottawa, Canada; Peking University, Wuhan University, Quaid-i-Azam University, Islamabad, Pakistan; Harvard University; Duke University, Massachusetts Institute of Technology; and the University of Southern California. His current research interests are in the areas of governance, fiscal federalism, fiscal reform, and global environment. He has published several books and monographs on these subjects including *The Reform of Intergovernmental Fiscal Relations in Developing and Transition Economies* (World Bank 1994) and a 1995 Oxford University Press book on *Fiscal Incentives for Investment and Innovation*. His articles have appeared in leading economic and policy journals. He also serves as a referee and on editorial advisory boards for leading economic journals.

HYUN HWA SON holds her Ph.D. in economics from the University of New South Wales, Sydney, Australia. Her research interests are in the areas of poverty and income distribution. She is currently an associate lecturer at Macquarie University in Australia.

Overview

ANWAR SHAH

While the performance of the public sector in delivering public services in developing countries is generally considered less than satisfactory, its performance in providing services and protecting the poor and other disadvantaged groups such as women and the elderly is particularly disconcerting. Nor is the public sector generally responsive to the preferences of citizens at large. Instead, it serves the interests of a narrow, elite group of people to whom it is accountable.

This book provides tools of analysis for discovering the orientation of the public sector and creating a scorecard on its role in safeguarding the interests of the poor and those otherwise disadvantaged. The book further provides a framework for citizen-centered governance—in other words, creating an institutional design with appropriate incentives to make the public sector responsive and accountable to a median (or average) voter. Chapters in this book provide tools of analysis for addressing the following questions:

- *Public burden test:* Who bears the burden of taxes and who benefits from public programs?
- *Poverty reduction test:* Are existing public programs intended to reduce poverty? Are they likely to do so?
- *Social protection test:* Are there adequate safeguards for income security for the elderly and the poor?
- *Gender safeguard test:* Do programs ensure equality of access to women?

- *Responsiveness test:* Are public programs responsive to citizen preferences?
- *Accountability test:* Are citizens empowered to demand accountability from elected and appointed officials?

Public Burden Test

In chapter 1, Giuseppe Ruggeri examines the question of who benefits from public programs. The literature on fiscal incidence has traditionally focused on tax incidence—who pays taxes—and neglected the issue of expenditure incidence. This chapter attempts to fill in the gap and examines the major methodological issues arising in the measurement of expenditure incidence, or how government spending affects the economic position of families and individuals.

The estimation of expenditure incidence requires three major steps:

1. *Select time period, analytical framework, unit of analysis, and an appropriate income measure:* An important distinction should be made between the direct effects of public expenditure (partial equilibrium analysis) and the indirect effects through changes in relative prices (general equilibrium analysis). Measurement of the indirect effects may not be captured by conventional expenditure incidence analysis; therefore an appropriate counterfactual should be used—one with which the existing distribution of income can be compared. The author proposes that the appropriate counterfactual is a concept of income that assumes that the benefits of government spending are allocated in a distributionally neutral manner, rather than a counterfactual that assumes no government expenditure. In terms of the unit of analysis, there are different definitions of family that can used, as well equivalence scales to adjust for different family sizes. When the focus of incidence analysis is the distributional effect of the entire fiscal system, the most appropriate concept of income is comprehensive income, which includes private income plus income from government spending (transfers, government wages, government purchases of goods and services, and interest on public debt) minus taxes. An additional methodological consideration is whether to do annual or lifetime incidence analysis, because annual incidence cannot account appropriately for the multiyear benefits derived from investment spending.
2. *Allocate government expenditures to the selected family unit:* In theory, the value of benefits provided by public expenditures other than cash transfers is the dollar amount that individuals are willing to pay. However, will-

ingness to pay is not known in the case of publicly provided goods when there is no market for them; therefore, the cost to the government is used as an approximation. Government expenditures can be classified by the ease of identifying the beneficiaries. Specific expenditures such as transfers and purchases of some government services (such as health and education) can be assigned to specific individuals, and the costs of these programs can be added to the household income. General expenditures (such as defense, law and order, and administration) benefit society as a whole and are difficult to assign to individual beneficiaries. The incidence of interest payments on the national debt is a particularly difficult issue to tackle. Progress can be made, though, in assigning benefits when general expenditures are disaggregated, which may help identify beneficiaries for portions of spending programs that may otherwise be considered general expenditures. For instance, administrative costs of transfer programs can be assigned to beneficiaries of the program.

3. *Select and apply indexes of redistribution:* The final step in expenditure incidence is to summarize the results using some indexes of redistribution. These indexes can be applied to total government expenditures or to selected components. Local indexes (such as relative share adjustment, or RSA) measure the degree of redistribution for each income group. Global indexes measuring redistribution, such as a single index for the country, are based on comparisons of Gini coefficients. Several examples of suggested measures from the literature are included in the chapter.

Poverty Reduction Test

In chapter 2 (Nanak Kakwani and Hyun Son) and chapter 3 (Hyun Son) present a discussion of various empirical concepts that can be used to examine whether existing public programs have a positive effect in reducing poverty. These analytical approaches are then applied to the Lao People's Democratic Republic (PDR) and the Philippines to demonstrate their usefulness for policy purposes.

Chapter 2 provides a brief review of measures of inequality and poverty and their welfare implications. Major measures of inequality and poverty discussed in this chapter include Lorenz curve analysis, the Gini index, the Generalized Gini index, entropy measures of inequality, and Atkinson's inequality measures. The Lorenz curve is defined as the relationship between the proportion of people with income less than or equal to a specified amount, and the proportion of total national income received by those people. The Lorenz curve portrays the deviation of income distribution from perfect equality, where perfect equality is represented by the egalitarian line—the 45-degree angle line. The nearer the Lorenz curve is to the egalitarian line, the more equal is the distribution of income. Consequently, the Lorenz curve can be used as a criterion for ranking alternative government policies or programs.

The Gini index measures the extent to which the Lorenz curve departs from the egalitarian line. It assumes a value of zero for perfect equality and one for perfect inequality. The Gini index gives maximum weight to the people who are clustered around the mode of an income distribution. Under the Generalized Gini index, transfers received by different segments of the income distribution can be assigned different weights. The weight given to an individual with a certain income level is a measure of his or her relative deprivation, and the more people above him or her in society, the greater is his or her sense of deprivation. This index essentially measures the average deprivation suffered by all individuals in the society. The entropy measures of inequality proposed by Theil enable a researcher to decompose total inequality in the society into between-group and within-group income inequality.

Although these measures were derived without regard to the social welfare function, they do relate to it implicitly. For example, under certain conditions, the ranking of distributions according to the Lorenz curve is identical to the ranking implied by the social welfare function. If the social welfare function is defined as the sum of individual utilities and every individual has an identical, concave utility function that is increasing in income, then the ranking of distributions according to the Lorenz curve criterion is identical to the ranking implied by the social welfare function—provided that the distributions have the same mean income and their Lorenz curves do not intersect. Atkinson derived inequality measures directly from an assumed social welfare function. His measures are based on the concept of "equally distributed equivalent level of income," which is the level of per capita income that if received by everyone, would make the total welfare exactly equal to the total welfare generated by the actual income distribution. Atkinson's inequality measures embody a measure of degree of inequality aversion or an indicator of relative sensitivity to income transfers at different income levels. If this parameter is zero, society does not care about inequality and if it approaches infinity, society is concerned only about the poorest person.

The empirical results of a study of Lao PDR show that whichever way inequality is measured, rapid economic growth has led to a substantial increase in inequality. The magnitude of increase in inequality increases monotonically with the parameters of relative risk aversion, and it can be concluded that the relative benefits to the very poor have been less than the relative benefits to those who are not so poor. However, during the same period, all indicators of poverty reveal a remarkable reduction in poverty—implying that although the rich benefited much more than the poor, the benefits of economic growth did trickle down to the poor.

Chapter 3 makes two major contributions. First, it develops a general methodology to assess the equity implications of fiscal policies. Second, it uses this methodology to assess the overall equity of the fiscal system in the Philippines.

As a methodological tool, a welfare reform index (based on the class of homothetic social welfare functions) is derived and applied to poverty data gathered in the Philippines to rank policy changes in terms of their impact on social welfare. In this analysis, social welfare depends on both mean income and inequality. The author derives measures of welfare elasticities and a welfare reform index for two categories of fiscal policies: (a) policies that affect components of income (for example, income from manufacturing, services, and crop farming) and (b) policies that change prices. Once these measures are calculated, the two types of policies are evaluated for their relative impacts on poor and rich households.

1. *Policies that affect income:* Using data from the Philippines, the author found that a policy that raises family sustenance income (for example, income from subsistence farming) is the type of policy that will have the greatest impact on the poor. Policies that raise wages and salaries, and pensions and social security benefit the rich more than the poor.
2. *Policies that affect expenditures:* The author concludes that taxes on food as well as some nonfood items (such as alcohol and tobacco) are highly regressive. Private expenditures on health and education were found to be regressive in that the poor spend proportionately more than the rich. That suggests a need for better targeting of government expenditures on education and health to the poor. Finally, personal income taxes were found to be progressive and taxes on corporate income (the burden of which will also be shared by labor) to be only mildly progressive.

The author concludes that there is considerable room to make the Philippines' fiscal policies more equitable, as the current system is mostly regressive and benefits the rich more than it benefits the poor.

Social Protection Test

In chapter 4, Robin Boadway and Katherine Cuff provide a framework for assessing public pension plans as safeguards for income security for the elderly and the poor.

Public policies to ensure that the retired have secure and adequate incomes are among the most important that governments implement. In most countries in the Organisation for Economic Co-operation and Development (OECD), public pensions, and transfers to the elderly constitute a significant proportion of total government spending. They are bound to become increasingly important in developing countries for political, economic, and demographic reasons. Higher incomes increase the demand for income security and social insurance programs. The development of the market economy, especially the increase in flexibility and mobility in the labor market, tends to weaken traditional ties and reduce the traditional support mechanisms on which the retired previously relied. In addition, predicted growth in the elderly population, leading to higher dependency ratios, makes the delivery of an adequate level of care both more urgent and more costly. Thus, review and revision of pension systems is an important item on the policy agenda.

This chapter summarizes the main issues in the development and reform of pension systems. It does so by first identifying the objective of such policies, in particular the reason why the public sector needed to become involved in what was perceived as an economic issue. The chapter examines the rationale for government intervention in the pension area and identifies three main purposes: (a) to redistribute toward less well-off retired persons, whose needs are often uniquely associated with their age; (b) to facilitate savings for retirement, both to compensate for the tendency of persons not to save adequately for their own retirement and to increase the aggregate savings rate itself; and (c) to insure elderly individuals against various risks that the private sector is unable to cover. This threefold set of purposes was used to focus on the sets of policies that would be appropriate to address each of the three broad issues, recognizing that there is, necessarily, overlap of policies and objectives. For each of the roles of the public sector, the chapter identifies the various economic costs and the potential benefits of alternative pension plan design and reform options available to the government.

The benefits of pension reform include reduction in inequality, increase in self-sufficiency of the elderly, encouragement of economic growth, reduction of individual risks, and development of capital markets. The costs include fiscal burdens, adverse incentive effects on the efficiency of the market economy, administrative costs, public sector inefficiency, and unintended redistributional effects.

The chapter argues that the most important policy or design issues to be addressed in selecting a suitable pension system are as follows:

- *Public versus private role:* Some functions, such as delivering transfers to the needy elderly, can be provided only by the public sector. However, for many aspects of pension policy, there is a choice between public and private provision. Pension and retirement savings schemes can be provided by employers or private financial institutions or they can be administered by the public sector. In either case, there can also be a role for the other sector. Accumulated public pension funds can be managed by private investment firms, and occupational pension schemes can be mandated by the public sector. The extent of the government's role as regulator of private pension schemes, capital markets, and financial institutions must also be decided upon.
- *Universality versus targeting:* Within the redistributive component of the public pension scheme, transfers to the elderly can be based on universal demographic factors or they can be targeted to varying degrees. Targeting can take a wide variety of forms, including the use of in-kind transfers. A large number of considerations go into this decision, including institutional delivery capacity and administrative costs, economic incentive effects, individual take-up rates, and political economy considerations.
- *Funded versus unfunded:* Public components of the pension system, including social insurance components, can be funded or unfunded. If funded, the funding can be at the aggregate or the individual level. The extent of funding affects the sustainability of the program, its effect on saving, and the extent to which it redistributes intergenerationally. The funding arrangements can also influence the extent to which the program is immune to political and bureaucratic manipulation.
- *Mandatory versus voluntary:* Pension policy can involve varying degrees of mandating compliance, as opposed to inducing voluntary compliance. The mandating can take effect at the individual level or the firm level.
- *The structure of pensions:* The level of pension or transfer payments must be decided, as well as the form of contributions and the rate structure applying to both. These will involve the classic trade-off between efficiency and equity effects.

Resolution of the design issues discussed here involve political decision making. The responsibility now rests with policy makers, in both developed and developing countries, to choose among the wide variety of alternatives to ensure the stability of their economies and the well-being of their populations.

Gender Safeguard Test

Dealing with gender inequity is important from the perspective of economic and social justice and the perspective of human rights. A number of development assistance practitioners are advising developing countries to prepare "gender budgets," in which all budget components are scrutinized for their implications for women's welfare and estimates are presented as to what extent women are the net beneficiaries of public taxing and spending decisions. There is no consensus as yet on the utility of such exercises to further the empowerment of women.

In chapter 5, Barbara Bergmann reviews the experience with the "gender budget" exercises that have been conducted in Barbados, Israel, South Africa, and Sri Lanka. She further reflects on the potential of the World Bank's Public Expenditure Reviews (PERs) as tools for advocating for more room in the country's budget for enhancing women's access to public services and their participation in economic activities. The author suggests that the PER process might be used to advocate for creating space in the budget for programs that promote women's employment, education, and health and providing gender-neutral infrastructure (such as clean water) that facilitates household operations.

While gender analysis should not be restricted to programs that are directed specifically toward women, an "all sectors" approach that looks at every aspect of budgeting and policy (and in particular assesses taxation and trade and broader macroeconomic policies for gender effects) would be neither desirable nor feasible. Instead, a selective, country-focused approach would be more useful for policy purposes. Such a selective approach would concentrate on areas of government functioning where program changes have the maximum potential for reducing gender inequality. Major areas for such examinations could include public utilities, health care, education and training, personal safety, the needs of single parents, access to credit, legal and traditional barriers to women's ownership of land, and government employment of women.

Various tools that have been advocated for use in gender-sensitive budget analysis include (a) gender-disaggregated beneficiary assessments (such as surveys), (b) gender-disaggregated public expenditure incidence analysis, (c) gender-aware policy appraisal (how policies will affect gender inequality), and (d) gender-aware budget statements. A gender-aware budget statement would include gender equality–targeted expenditures, women's priority public services, a gender management system in government, women's priority income transfers, gender balance in public sector contracts employment, gender balance in business support, and gender balance in public sector contracts.

From a review of "women's budgets" prepared for the Bahamas, Barbados, South Africa, and Sri Lanka, the author concluded that such documents, while quite comprehensive, lack specific proposals for making budgets more responsive to women's needs. A short and highly selective gender-sensitive budget analysis brief prepared by a women's advocacy group in Israel, however, was timely and effective for the legislative debates. The author recommends a selective approach, with concrete policy suggestions for use in World Bank PERs to enhance their impact on gender inequality.

Responsiveness and Accountability Tests

In chapter 6, Matthew Andrews and Anwar Shah present a framework for responsive and accountable governance. The implications of this framework for local budgeting are drawn in chapter 7. Chapter 8, by Andrews, examines worldwide experiences with voice mechanisms, giving special emphasis to the South African experience with participatory budgeting.

The public sector continues to face a crisis of public confidence in developing countries. Vigorous and sustained civil service reforms carried out during the past several decades aimed at enhancing technical skills and capacity, introducing meritocracy, increasing public sector wages, simplifying salary structure, decompressing wages, and improving financial management and monitoring and evaluation have failed to restore public confidence in governments. In chapter 6, Matthew Andrews and Anwar Shah attribute the failure of these reforms to their focus on a hierarchical model of public sector governance. They argue that these top-down technocratic solutions do not build an incentive structure that facilitates responsiveness to citizen preferences and taxpayer accountability. Further, top-down approaches do not encourage responsible public management because public managers do not face any competitive pressures and are not answerable to their clients. To overcome these perverse incentives and to create an enabling environment for responsive, responsible, and accountable governance, Andrews and Shah propose a new institutional model of public governance. The citizen-centered governance approach they articulate has the following distinguishing elements:

- *Client's charter and sunshine laws:* Citizens are empowered through a client's charter to demand accountability from the public sector. The client's charter specifies service standards and triggers and processes of redress in the event of noncompliance. Sunshine laws establish citizens' right to know and media's right to tell.
- *Decentralized public management:* The division of responsibility among various levels of government is based on the subsidiarity principle; in other words, all public services are to be assigned locally unless a convincing case can be made for higher-level assignment. Local governments enjoy home rule in their spheres of responsibility.
- *Democratic participation:* Citizens influence governance by revealing their preferences for services to their elected representatives and holding these representatives accountable for ensuring that governments respect these preferences.
- *Direct democracy:* Major public programs should be subjected to popular referenda.
- *Legislative mandate:* The legislatures set budgetary priorities, authorize budgets, and specify output contracts for various government administrations and provide expectations on quality of life outcomes.
- *Service delivery contracts:* The executive enters into service delivery contracts with program managers and provides financing.
- *Managerial flexibility but accountability for results:* Managers are bound by few rules but are held accountable for results in service delivery performance. They may contract out services to nonpublic providers. Thus, citizen-centered governance provides an incentive structure for innovative and competitive service delivery.
- *Citizen-friendly budgets and report cards on government performance:* Annual budgets use citizen-friendly formats and report on the past year's service delivery performance while benchmarking against competitors.
- *Bottom-up accountability:* Citizens provide feedback on government performance. This feedback has a bearing on government programs. Civil society groups and media help citizens reach informed judgments on government performance.

The governance model proposed by Andrews and Shah represents a major departure from the current focus of public sector reform programs. It argues for a flexible, competitive, results-based, and citizen-centered public governance, as opposed to the top-down input controls driven management supported by most reform programs.

In chapter 7, Andrews and Shah ask how well budgets and financial management processes at the local level serve citizens and how they could be restructured to serve citizens better.

In the first section, the authors examine ways in which conventional budget processes and formats in developing countries frustrate citizens' abilities to contribute to the governance process or demand accountability for government performance. They argue that, although services provided locally tend to be highly visible (with citizens able to see whether roads are built or maintained, clinics are well staffed, and water delivery is reliable), citizens lack sufficient access to the budgeting and financial management process in such settings to contribute to the public debate—for instance, regarding what roads are built, informing representatives when clinics are not effectively staffed, or seeking redress when water is unsafe to drink. Citizens are generally excluded from most stages of the budget process completely, and where they have access it is usually symbolic, not substantive. Furthermore, the typical line-item format of budgets and financial statements by local governments fails to provide information relevant to the basic questions that citizens ask of their governing authorities: Is the government delivering services consistent with mandates from elected councils? Is it delivering these services efficiently? Is it making the best use of taxpayers' monies? How does its performance compare with other local jurisdictions? Is it collecting the taxes efficiently and fairly? Is the burden of taxes equitably shared? Is it keeping its debt within sustainable levels?

Andrews and Shah argue that a move toward citizen-oriented local-level budgeting and financial management in developing countries calls for a reform of the budgetary institutions and processes and the budget or financial statement format. In terms of the institutional reforms related to the budget process itself, they argue that citizen-oriented budget processes require institutions that facilitate citizen demand revelation, citizen reflection and resolution opportunity (in the budget decision or approval stage), citizen reporting abilities (regarding budget implementation), and citizen response and redress avenues (that influence the incentives administrative and political officials face). These reforms to reorient the local public sector to citizen's concerns are best done using existing institutions of local participation and accountability, as opposed to creating specialized institutions and processes outside the local government system as is generally advocated and practiced in developing countries.

Andrews and Shah propose that a citizen-oriented budget must satisfy several principles—relevance, readability, responsibility, and reportability.

The relevance principle requires that budgets be classified in meaningful ways, with budget formats and financial reports answering the major questions citizens ask (such as information about the entities receiving funds, the actual allocations received and targeted outputs, performance against such targets, and the official responsible for managing funds and producing results). The readability principle asserts that budgets should be formatted in a way that it is comprehensible to elementary school graduates, allowing easy understanding of the information and easy comparison of targets and performance. The principle of responsibility is simply that the format must communicate a responsibility by officials to citizens for things that matter to citizens (fiscal probity and service results). The reportability principle requires that the budget document facilitate citizen monitoring of government performance, feedback, and redress. The authors provide an illustration of such a citizen-friendly budget process and the format.

A large number of initiatives have been undertaken worldwide to facilitate citizen voice expression to promote greater public sector accountability. In chapter 8, Andrews examines the impact of these initiatives on local governance through a review of more than 50 cases of reforms involving voice-based mechanisms adopted by local and regional governments in developing countries, with a special emphasis on the South African experience.

This review shows that in only a small number of cases did the new voice mechanism improve public sector accountability to citizens at large. For voice mechanisms to promote accountability, citizens must be empowered to have a say in (a) who governs them, (b) how they are governed (the governance process), (c) what the public mandate is (the governance agenda), and (d) what is produced (outputs and outcomes). Where voice mechanisms facilitate broader participation and high levels of voice influence, the government is made more responsive and accountable to citizens. Where only a narrow social segment is given voice through a mechanism (for example, focus groups), accountability will be narrow and there is a risk of government capture by elites.

Andrews' review findings suggest that built-in evaluation devices, whereby the voice mechanism's effect is monitored and evaluated, can stimulate voice influence but that such influence is often constrained by the absence of a voice transmission medium. (A voice transmission medium is a device that transmits ideas, feedback, and criticism voiced by citizens.) Further, it is shown that centralized political structures and closed administrative structures limit broader participation and voice influence. The review concludes that participatory voice mechanisms typically work less well in poor areas because the voices of the poor are ignored or captured by special interest groups.

The author concludes that in South Africa, a few local governments that had a strong commitment to citizen voice effectively used voice mechanisms to improve local government performance. A large majority of local governments, however, simply considered voice mechanisms as unnecessary and burdensome processes and these mechanisms had no impact on local government performance.

1

Public Expenditure Incidence Analysis

GIUSEPPE RUGGERI

Governments collect revenues through taxes, fees and charges, royalties on natural resources, and the sale of goods and services. They also receive income from investments and often from borrowing. These revenues are used to make transfer payments to individuals and businesses, pay interest on accumulated debt, and finance general expenditures. Both spending and revenue-raising activities of governments tend to alter the relative economic position of individuals and families—often by design, because income redistribution is one of the main functions of government activity.[1] Economists have paid more attention to the distributional effects of the revenue side of the government budget, and the relevant literature contains numerous studies on the incidence of the tax system as a whole and of individual taxes (see, for example, Colm and Tarasov 1940; Musgrave and others 1951; Pechman and Okner 1980; Browning and Johnson 1979; Ruggeri, Van Wart, and Howard 1994a; Vermaeten, Gillespie, and Vermaeten 1994). The number of separate studies of expenditure incidence is rather limited, however, because the incidence of public expenditures has usually been measured as part of analyses of total fiscal incidence.[2] As a result, there are more details on the methodological issues faced in analyzing tax incidence analysis[3] than the issues faced in analyzing public expenditure incidence.[4]

This chapter expands on the fiscal incidence literature. It focuses on public spending and on the major methodological issues arising in the measurement of expenditure incidence. Estimating expenditure incidence requires three major steps. The first step deals with issues such as selecting the time period, the analytical framework, the unit of analysis, and the appropriate income measure. The second step involves allocating government expenditures to the selected family unit. The final step deals with selecting and applying indexes of redistribution. We will revisit the first step in the next section.

This section explores the concept of expenditure incidence, identifies the suitable data sources, discusses the timeframe for the analysis (annual versus lifetime incidence) and the analytical framework (partial versus general equilibrium analysis), evaluates the choice of the unit of analysis (individual versus household or family unit), and develops a variety of income concepts that may be used in the measurement of expenditure incidence. The following section deals with the second step. It focuses on the measurement of government expenditures, the relationship between costs incurred by the government and benefits received by individuals, and the allocation of the estimated benefits to households or families in different economic circumstances. The final step is analyzed in the next section, which discusses a variety of indexes of redistribution, separated into two major groups: global and local. The final section provides some concluding comments.

General Issues

The general issues discussed in this section include the concept of incidence, the government universe, the database, the unit of analysis, the concept of income, and annual versus lifetime incidence.

The Concept of Incidence

Government spending affects the economic position of individuals and families through two main channels: changes in earnings and changes in gross income. When government alters the level or mix of its expenditures, relative factor income and the relative prices of goods and services produced in the private sector are affected. For example, if production in the public sector is more labor intensive than production in the private sector, an increase in public spending will raise the returns to labor relative to the returns to capital. This, in turn, will raise the prices of labor-intensive goods and services relative to capital-intensive ones. Musgrave (1959) used the term *expenditure incidence* to identify those effects on relative factor and product prices that alter the distribution of earnings. Government expenditures also affect the well-being of individuals and families through direct cash transfers and the benefits generated by the public provision of goods and services. McClure (1974) calls this type of distributional change *benefit incidence.*

This distinction between expenditure incidence and benefit incidence reflects the differentiation between general equilibrium and partial equilibrium analyses. The direct effects of government spending on the distribution of gross income, which includes the benefits from such spending, are measured by partial equilibrium analysis. This approach takes private income as given and allocates public spending to individuals and families in different economic circumstances according to certain assumptions. The relative price effects of public spending can be captured only through computable general equilibrium (CGE) models that incorporate assumptions about the behavioral response of economic agents to changes in public policy. Empirical studies of the distributional effects of government spending, such as those listed in endnote 3, have focused on benefit incidence measured by partial equilibrium analysis, but they are commonly known as expenditure incidence studies. It may be worth emphasizing that the commonly used term *expenditure incidence* really refers to benefit incidence and that this partial equilibrium approach measures only one component of the distributional effect of public spending. In the rest of this chapter, the partial equilibrium effects of government spending on the distribution of income will be called *direct effects.* All other effects will be called *indirect effects.*

How much does the exclusion of indirect effects bias the estimates of expenditure incidence? This question cannot be fully answered because not all indirect effects can be accurately measured. In the case of transfer payments to persons, those effects can be estimated from suitable CGE models that incorporate behavioral responses to public expenditures as well as taxation. For example, transfers to persons over 65 years of age, such as social security pensions, are not expected to affect the choice between work and leisure. However, they may affect the saving behavior of younger people, who may save less during their working years if they can count on government transfers in their postretirement years. For seniors, the distributional effects of those transfers will be fully captured by the commonly used partial equilibrium analysis, applied to a given year. In theory, government transfer payments targeted to children should have no indirect effects because children make neither a work-leisure choice nor a consumption-saving choice. However, because these transfers are received by parents, they may affect parents' economic behavior.

The measurement of indirect effects becomes more complex in the case of in-kind transfers such as public spending on education and health care. For example, expenditures on public education are made for the benefit of children and adolescents, but they are assigned to the family unit. Education contributes to the acquisition of human capital, which is becoming an increasingly important contributor to economic growth in knowledge-based economies. Public spending on education, therefore, provides benefits to society as well as reducing the cost of human capital to those enrolled in public education programs. The spillover of benefits to other members of society may also occur in the case of health care, because everyone gains from a healthier human environment. Only a portion of these special effects—which need not be distributed equally to all members of society—may be captured in models of endogenous growth, and their measurement may involve the use of largely arbitrary assumptions. In the case of public spending for general administration and the protection of persons and property (which includes national defense and the entire justice system), indirect effects cannot be measured even with sophisticated computable general equilibrium (CGE) models. Market economies rest on the foundation of enforceable property rights. Expenditures on the institutions of government that protect property rights are a form of social overhead that allows market economies to function.[5] Therefore, their effect is indirect and pervasive and may be impossible to fully capture, even with the most sophisticated models.

In conclusion, public expenditures may have large indirect effects that are not captured by expenditure incidence analysis. The magnitude of these indirect effects can be minimized by selecting an appropriate situation (called a *counterfactual*) to which we compare the existing distribution of income. Two major types of exercises are usually performed in expenditure incidence studies: (a) the introduction of small changes in the level of public spending for selected programs or for the entire spending side of the budget, and (b) comparisons between spending that does not redistribute income and spending that does. In the first case, there is an increase or decrease in the level of public spending; in the second case, there is simply a reallocation of a given level of spending. In either exercise, the indirect effects incorporated in the counterfactual are also present in the actual situation. Therefore, what traditional expenditure incidence analysis fails to capture are the indirect effects of small changes in either the level of public spending or in its distribution, for a given level of spending. Although the magnitude of indirect effects may be minimized through the selection of the counterfactual, this discussion serves as a reminder that government spending generates both equity and efficiency effects and that these two effects are interconnected.

The separation of equity and efficiency often found in theoretical analysis may be seldom warranted in practice.

The Government Universe

Identifying the government universe raises two issues: (a) what should be included in government expenditures and (b) how should these expenditures be aggregated.

What is included in government expenditures

Government activity affects the economic dimensions of peoples' lives through a variety of channels: public spending, taxation, borrowing, monetary policy, foreign policy, competition policy, regulatory activities, and ownership or control of business enterprises. By concentrating on public spending, analysis of government expenditure incidence focuses on only one of the channels through which government activity affects the relative well-being of individuals and families. The coverage of even this component in expenditure incidence studies is often incomplete.

The government uses four major vehicles for delivering its spending programs: (a) direct spending through its departments and agencies as recorded in budgetary transactions, (b) direct spending through funds that are not included in the budget, (c) indirect spending through the business enterprises it owns or controls, and (d) spending programs delivered through the tax system, commonly known as tax expenditures. Only the first two items are usually included in expenditure incidence analysis, partly because those are the items that define the government sector in official statistical publications. For example, in the *National Accounts* published by the Organisation for Economic Co-operation and Development (OECD 1998, 643) the government sector is defined as

> all departments, offices, organizations and other bodies which are agencies or instruments of the central, state or local public authorities, whether accounted for, or financed in, ordinary or extraordinary budgets or extrabudgetary funds. Included are nonprofit institutions which while not an integral part of a government are wholly, or mainly, financed and controlled by the public authorities or primarily serve government bodies; all social security arrangements for large sections of the population imposed, controlled or financed by a government; and government enterprises which mainly produce goods and services for government itself or primarily sell goods and services to the public on a small scale. Excluded are other government enterprises and public corporations.

Expenditure incidence analysis also omits the spending programs that are delivered through the tax system. Treating these indirect expenditures as part of the tax system does not affect the overall incidence of the government budget, but doing so does alter the relative contribution of spending and taxation. For example, if those tax expenditures are distributed in a regressive manner—that is, if they benefit high-income families relatively more than low-income families—their inclusion in tax incidence analysis will reduce the estimated progressivity of the tax system and increase the progressivity of public expenditures.

Disaggregation by level of government

In unitary states, all the spending decisions are made by the central government, although the delivery of programs may be delegated to other administrative units. In federal states, spending decisions may be made independently by different levels of government. Often, spending responsibilities of each level of government are not perfectly matched with their respective revenue-raising capacities. These differences are usually bridged through the use of intergovernmental transfers. In the presence of such transfers, the allocation of revenues and expenditures by level of government is not uniquely determined and one must choose among a number of approaches.

One approach is to assign revenues to the level of government that actually raises them and expenditures to the level of government that spends the funds directly. Under this approach, grants from the federal government to state and local governments are treated as expenditures of the recipient governments. In another approach, all revenues collected and expenditures made by the federal government, including intergovernmental transfers, are assigned to the federal government. State and local governments are treated largely as administrative units with respect to intergovernmental transfers. Finally, the recipient governments may be assigned both the expenditures financed through intergovernmental grants and the associated revenues. In this case the federal government is treated as a tax collector for a portion of state and local government revenue.

The Database

Three main sources of information on public expenditures can be used to estimate their redistributional impact (the Canadian terminology will be used as an example): public accounts, the system of national accounts, and the financial management system. The public accounts are financial statements produced by each level of government to provide a record of their fiscal transactions during a given fiscal year. They provide a wealth of details but are not well suited for incidence analysis because they do not always follow the same accounting practices. Standardization of accounting procedures is used in the financial management system. In these sets of accounts, financial information for all levels of government in a given fiscal year is presented on a consistent basis, which allows for consolidation of data and for comparisons between different levels of government.

These accounts have two additional advantages: they provide a breakdown of government expenditures by function and incorporate a broad definition of government by including agencies that perform governmental functions. Standardization of accounts is also used in the national accounts, which provide public expenditure data on a calendar year basis. Unlike the financial management system, however, the system of national accounts presents largely aggregated data and does not provide a detailed classification of government expenditures. Therefore, it can be used in studies analyzing the incidence of government spending as a whole, but it is not suitable for measuring the redistributional effect of selected government spending programs.

The Unit of Analysis

Selecting the unit of analysis requires a choice between individuals, households, and families; an adjustment for family size; and grouping by age, income level, or both.

Individuals, households, and families

The major concern of fiscal redistribution studies is with the well-being of individuals and how it is affected by government spending and taxation. Individuals, however, do not exist as separate entities but spend most of their lives as part of larger socioeconomic groups. Even hermits spend part of their lives in a group during their early years. The most common pattern is for individuals to move through a variety of such groups throughout their lives: the family that nurtures them in their childhood and adolescence and the family or families they form during their adult lives. Placing individuals within larger units raises two methodological issues: (a) economies of scale associated with common housekeeping and (b) income sharing among members of the same unit. The formation of a larger unit generates economic benefits for its members because additional individuals share existing facilities and equipment. As a result, providing a given level of well-being to a second individual living in the same dwelling does not cost twice as much as providing it to one individual. In empirical studies, well-being is usually approximated by some measure of income. However, some individuals have no income during part of their lives; their well-being depends on the income generated by other members of the group to which they belong. This is the case of dependent children and spouses in one-income families. These people share the resources of the entire family and use a portion of the family's income, although officially no income is assigned to them.

To take into account the diversity of economic arrangements among individuals, it is important to use units of analysis that capture economies of scale and income sharing that may take place among groups of individuals living together. Four types of such units are most commonly used in income distribution studies: the household, the economic family, the census family, and the nuclear family.

- A household comprises a group of individuals living in the same dwelling. Its focus is on common dwelling rather than blood or marital relationships.
- An economic family includes any number of individuals related by blood, marriage (including common-law marriages), or adoption who live together as an economic unit in the same dwelling. This definition of family captures not only common housekeeping, but also blood or marital relationships and shared spending decisions.
- A census family differs from an economic family by restricting membership of dependent children to never-married children living in the same dwelling.
- A nuclear family is even more restrictive because it excludes never-married children older than a specified age, usually 18 years.

The household is the broadest of the four units because it imposes only the restriction of common housekeeping. The nuclear family is the narrowest unit because it imposes the restrictions of marriage and blood relationships as well as a constraint on the age of dependent children. The household tries to capture only the economies of scale associated with common housekeeping among unrelated individuals. Two unrelated single people living together in the same dwelling are treated as two separate families but as a single household. In extending its net, however, the household imposes the assumption that there is also income sharing within the household, when often there is not any.

The choice between household and some concept of family in studies of income distribution depends largely on (a) the purpose of the study, (b) the national or international nature of the study, and (c) the availability of data. If we are concerned primarily with the issue of income sharing, then a family concept is the more appropriate choice. If we want to capture economies of scale even among unrelated individuals, then the household concept is the more suitable choice. The full range of choice of which larger unit to use may not be available when conducting multicountry studies because there may be consistency of definitions for one grouping and not for others. Therefore, one is forced to choose a larger unit that has the least degree of inconsistency among countries. Finally, one can choose only among larger units for which reliable data are available.

Adjustment for size

Placing individuals in a family context (from now on the term *family* will include households) automatically reduces the degree of income dispersion because of income sharing. Under all definitions of the larger unit, it is assumed that income is pooled and is divided equally among its members. If no economies of scale were generated by common housekeeping, then each family unit would be represented by the simple average of the family income because each member would be assigned an equal share of income. It is assumed that equal levels of income generate equal levels of well-being. In the presence of economies of scale, we need a weighting scheme to account for additional members' share of the use of existing facilities and durable goods.

The weights attached to each family member in deriving a measure of average family well-being are called *equivalence scales*. They indicate the cost added by an additional member in order to obtain the same well-being as the first member. They are expressed as fractions of one, where this value represents the income required by an unattached individual. For example, a value of 0.6 for the second family member means that only 60 percent of the income required to maintain the standard of living of the first member is needed to provide the same standard of living for the second member. Because individual requirements may differ by age, equivalence scales are sometimes adjusted to take into account differences in age. For example, it may cost more to provide a given standard of living to an additional adult than to an additional child and, correspondingly, the equivalence scale may be higher for an adult than for a child.

There is no consensus in the literature on the correct value of equivalence scales. In a survey of studies using equivalence scales, Buhmann and others (1988) found a range between 0.3 and 0.6, indicating that an additional family member adds 30 percent to 60 percent of the costs of the first member. Smeeding and others (1993) assigned a weight of 1.0 to the first adult, 0.4 to each additional adult, and 0.3 to each child. In its calculations of low-income measures, Statistics Canada (2002) assigns a value of 1.0 to the first member,

0.4 to the second member, and 0.3 to each additional member. The choice of equivalence scales depends partly on whether the study is confined to a single country or involves a number of countries. In the first case, it may be advisable to use the same scales used in the calculation of poverty measures. This approach will facilitate comparisons with published statistics. In the second case, a compromise approach may be to use equivalence scales that minimize the differences in the scales used in the official statistics of each country.

Grouping by age and by income levels

The income of different size families is standardized by dividing total family income by the equivalent number of adults. For example, if a family of two adults receives income of $30,000 and the equivalence scale for the second adult is 0.6, the well-being of each family member is measured by the average income of $18,750 ($30,000/1.6). Through this procedure we are effectively moving back from the family to the individual. However, instead of an individual as a separate entity we now have an individual within the proper family context, taking into account both economies of scale and actual or assumed income sharing.

When the purpose of a study is to measure fiscally induced changes in the economic position of individuals or families with different income levels (vertical redistribution), the total number of families is disaggregated into selected income groups, usually in ascending order of average income per adult equivalent. The selection of the groups depends on the focus of the analysis. For example, if the focus is on various dimensions of poverty, the disaggregation will include an income class that represents a measure of the poverty line and also income classes below that line, to evaluate the effect of fiscal activity on other dimensions of poverty.

Equivalence scales facilitate the identification of different families belonging to these selected income groups. For example, if the absolute poverty line for an individual is $10,000 and equivalence scales are 0.4 and 0.3 for the second and third members of the family, the poverty line is $14,000 for a two-person family and $17,000 for a three-person family. In some studies, the poverty line is determined in relation to average income, say, one-half of median income. In this case, the dollar value of the poverty line is determined by ranking all families in ascending order of income per adult equivalent, finding the income level that is exceeded by 50 percent of adult equivalents, and then taking half of that value. When the focus is on the relationship between the rich and the poor, a generally used approach is to divide the distribution of adult equivalents into 10 parts (deciles) and then express the income per adult equivalent in each decile as a percentage of the median. The changes in the ratio of the top decile to the bottom decile serve as measures of the changes in the relative distribution of income caused by government spending or taxation.

Researchers may also be interested in the effect of government spending and taxation on the economic position of individuals and families in similar economic circumstances (horizontal redistribution). In this case, the focus shifts to noneconomic characteristics such as age and family composition. With respect to age, a useful distinction is that between families in which income earners are actively engaged in the labor market and families in which they are not. The latter group comprises families in which one or both members are more than 65 years of age. Because of the recent trend toward early retirement, this demographic group is sometimes extended to those in the 55–64 years age range. With respect to family characteristics, a useful way to disaggregate them is as unattached individuals, single parents, two-parent families without children, and two-parent families with children. The first group is a pure group in the sense that the calculations are not affected by assumptions about income sharing and economies of scale. Single parents are a large component of low-income families, and their separate identification is useful in studies of the fiscal effects on poverty. A comparison between the last two categories helps identify the redistributional effects of the fiscal treatment of dependent children.

The Concept of Income

The main purpose of expenditure incidence is to measure the effect of government spending on the well-being of individuals in different economic circumstances. Since well-being in practice is measured by some concept of income, the selection of the income measure is crucial in the distributional analysis of government expenditures.[6] A useful approach to the evaluation of these different income measures is to identify the major building blocks and then find the combinations of building blocks used in each income measure (box 1.1).

The selection of the appropriate income concept depends on the purpose of the analysis. When the focus is on the distributional effect of the entire fiscal system, the most appropriate concept of income is comprehensive income. Despite the methodological difficulties of allocating the benefits of government spending and the unresolved issues in the distribution of the tax burden, they must also be included in the measure of income when all components of the fiscal system are analyzed. This concept of income has also been used often in studies of expenditure incidence, because this type of exercise is usually performed as part of an analysis of total fiscal incidence.

BOX 1.1 Components of Various Income Concepts

I. **Income components**
    A. *Private money income*
        1. Wages and salaries from the private sector
        2. Net income of farm operators
        3. Net income of nonfarm unincorporated business (excluding rent)
        4. Paid net rent
        5. Dividends and miscellaneous investment income
        6. Interest received from the private sector
        7. Income received from nonresidents
        8. Income from private pensions
    B. *Nonmoney additions to private income*
        1. Imputed interest
        2. Imputed rent
        3. Investment income of life insurance companies
        4. In-kind farm income
    C. *Adjustments to private income*
        1. Supplementary labor income
        2. Employer's portion of payroll taxes
        3. Transfers from corporations to individuals
        4. Retained earnings
        5. Corporate taxes, real property taxes, resource taxes, and sales taxes assigned to labor or capital income
    D. *Income from government spending*
        1. Government transfers to persons including public pensions and transfers to charitable and nonprofit organizations
        2. Government transfers to businesses
        3. Government wages and salaries
        4. Government purchases of goods and services (excluding wages)
        5. Interest on the public debt
    E. *Direct taxes on individuals*
    F. *Total taxes*
II. **Income concepts**
        1. Private income
            Private money income (A) plus nonmoney additions to private income (B) and adjustments to private income (C).
        2. money income
            Private money income (A) plus government transfers to persons (D.1) plus government wages and salaries (D.3).
        3. Disposable income
            Money income (II.2) minus direct taxes on individuals (E)
        4. Comprehensive income
            Private income (II.1) plus income from government spending (D) minus total taxes (F)

In the case of tax incidence, a more limited concept of income—that is, money income—is often used. Three main reasons are generally offered to justify the use of a partial income concept: (a) it serves as an approximation of tax bases; (b) it is the concept of income most familiar to policy makers; and (c) it avoids the complexities of allocating the benefits of government expenditures.

Convenient as it may be in empirical studies, this income concept has a major shortcoming. It covers only a portion of the government budget, that is, transfers to persons. As a result, it yields different patterns of tax or expenditure incidence for a given level of public spending or tax level, depending on the mix between transfers to persons and other government expenditures. Since transfers to persons are part of money income while other government expenditures are not, an increase in transfers associated with an offsetting reduction in other spending will raise the level of money income, although the level of well-being may not have changed. The reasons for choosing a limited income concept are even less valid in the case of expenditure incidence. In this case, there is no approximation of a tax base and the allocation of the benefits of public expenditures is already part of the exercise. Since the most difficult methodological issues are already addressed in the allocation of government expenditures, there is no justification for using a limited concept of income in the case of expenditure incidence.

After the appropriate concept of income for the period under investigation has been selected, we need to choose the measure of income that will be used for comparison purposes (the counterfactual). Two approaches to this hypothetical income measure may be used. Under one approach, it is assumed that the counterfactual represents the situation in which there are no government expenditures. It addresses the following question: how is the distribution of income altered by the addition of government spending? In this case, we start with the distribution of income in the absence of government expenditures and then measure the changes that occur when we add the benefits of government spending.

This approach has a major shortcoming: it involves a measure of counterfactual income that may be inconsistent with the conceptual framework of the incidence analysis. Since counterfactual income does not contain government spending, the appropriate income measure is private income, as defined in box 1.1. However, the addition of a large spending component such as government expenditures is likely to generate substantial indirect effects. One may even argue that there is no such thing as private income in the absence of government activity, because without government there is no properly functioning market economy. In any event, the values of private income with and without government expenditures may be quite different and the comparison of the income distribution before and after government expenditures is a poor measure of expenditure incidence.

This shortcoming is avoided when we use as the counterfactual a concept of income that assumes that the benefits of government spending are allocated in a distributionally neutral manner. This approach addresses the following question: how is the distribution of income altered when the current pattern of government expenditures is replaced by distributionally neutral spending? This approach has a number of desirable features. First, it involves a balanced-budget exercise in which both the level of expenditures and the revenues used to finance them are kept constant. Therefore, it bypasses the thorny issues associated with comparisons of income with and without government spending. Second, it minimizes the potential indirect effects because it confines them to the changes in the distribution of a given level of government expenditures. These indirect effects would arise only when these distributional changes affect the behavior of economic agents. Third, the inclusion of both cash transfers and transfers in kind (the allocated benefits from government purchases of goods and services) provides a more meaningful concept of economic well-being.

Annual versus Lifetime Analysis

The measurement of expenditure incidence is usually performed by grouping households into income classes according to a measure of annual income. Each class is then assigned a share of government expenditures for the same year, based on a chosen set of assumptions. The redistributional impact of government spending is then determined by comparing the benefits of government spending received by households in each class with their respective incomes. This approach is useful when government spending is analyzed from the perspective of vertical equity—that is, the fiscally induced changes in the economic position of individuals and families in different economic circumstances. One may also be interested in the pattern of government benefits received by the same individual during his or her lifetime. For example, one may want to find out whether government spending redistributes the income of a given individual from his or her working years to the postretirement years. These issues can be addressed through an analysis of lifetime incidence.

Annual and lifetime incidence differ with respect to data requirements, incidence methodology, and the interpretation of the results. Annual incidence studies use actual data on each source of income for each income class, while lifetime incidence studies must use data derived from models that simulate the income of each individual through his or her lifetime. In annual incidence studies, the unit of analysis is a household or a family. There is no equivalent "lifetime household" because individuals are usually members of different households during their lifetimes. Therefore, in lifetime incidence studies, the appropriate unit of analysis is the individual. Since nearly all individuals are members of multiperson households for most of their lives, and their standard of living depends to a large extent on the economic position of the household to which they belong, the separation of the individual from the household eliminates important information on the distributional effect of government spending. The two approaches, however, are complementary. Lifetime expenditure incidence depends on the profile of income through time as well as the level of lifetime income. Therefore, the correct measurement of lifetime expenditure incidence requires the separate calculation of annual incidence for each year of an individual's life.

Compared with lifetime incidence, annual incidence has the potential shortcoming of dealing inaccurately with public investment spending. Government purchases of goods and services include both current expenditures, such as the payments of wages and utility bills, and capital expenditures, such as building roads, schools, and hospitals. Annual expenditure incidence treats capital spending as current spending and allocates the full amount of these expenditures in the year they are made, although they provide a stream of benefits throughout their useful life. If public investment involves a steady flow of equal annual spending, the allocation under the annual incidence approach may provide a good approximation of annual benefits. Since capital spending is uneven over time, the allocation of the benefits of public investment under annual incidence may be inaccurate. A more accurate allocation of those benefits can be achieved through lifetime incidence because, under this approach, public investment spending can be replaced by the stream of the annual benefits it provides—which, in turn, can be allocated to the selected beneficiaries.

The Allocation of Public Expenditures

After selecting the unit of analysis and the income measure, the next step in expenditure incidence exercises is to allocate the benefits of government spending. Before going into the details of this allocation, a number of conceptual issues must be addressed.

Costs to Government versus Benefits to Individuals

Because the purpose of expenditure incidence is to determine how government spending affects the economic well-being of individuals and families, ideally what should be allocated are the benefits received by these economic agents. Those benefits must be measured in dollar terms either as direct increases in income or indirect increases generated by the consumption of publicly provided goods and services. However, all we can measure with certainty are the costs incurred by the government in delivering its spending programs. How are these costs related to the benefits received? There is no unique answer to this question because the relationship between costs and benefits depends on the characteristics of each spending program. In the case of cash transfers to individuals, there is a one-to-one correspondence between the two values: one dollar of transfer costs the government one dollar and increases by one dollar the income of the recipient. Such correspondence is not found in the case of purchases of goods and services. In theory, the value of the benefits provided by public expenditures other than cash transfers is the dollar amount that individuals are willing to pay. However, this willingness to pay is not known in the case of publicly provided goods and services, because there is no market for them. Because they are provided free of charge and financed through compulsory taxation, individuals are not forced to reveal how much they value these goods and services.

Lacking reliable estimates of how much individuals value government-provided goods and services, researchers studying expenditure incidence have used their costs as an approximation of the benefits they deliver. The same assumption is made in national account statistics, which record government goods and services at cost on both the expenditure and the income sides. It is important to stress, therefore, that what is being allocated in expenditure incidence studies are the expenditures actually incurred by government in making cash transfers and in providing goods and services.

"Cost Incurred on Behalf of" Approach

Some analysts have tried to circumvent the difficulties in estimating and allocating the benefits of government spending by changing the focus of their inquiry (see, for example, Ruggles and O'Higgins 1981). They do not attempt to estimate benefits; they simply determine what expenditures the government makes on behalf of different income groups. They address the question, "On whose behalf was a certain government expenditure made?" rather than "Who benefits from that expenditure and how much?" This shift of emphasis fails to solve the problem because, in practice, the calculations are the same under both approaches. Under either approach, the same amount of expenditures would be allocated to different individuals and families.

In its attempt to bypass the explicit assumption that benefits equal costs, the "cost incurred" approach does not allow a meaningful interpretation of the results in terms of income redistribution. The income concept in expenditure incidence serves as an indicator of well-being. To measure redistribution we must add to private income a dollar value for the income received from government or the consumption of publicly provided goods and services. Costs incurred can be given a redistributional interpretation only when they become a component of the income of individuals, and this happens only when they are assigned a dollar value as benefits received.

Externalities

Publicly provided goods and services may generate benefits to the individuals to whom the benefits are targeted (direct benefits) as well as to the population at large. The latter are usually called externalities or communitywide benefits. For example, publicly funded education increases the potential earning capacity of students. It may also raise the standard of living of the population as a whole if it contributes to higher productivity of all workers. Similarly, the direct benefits of publicly funded health care accrue to patients, but everyone benefits from a healthier human environment.

Obvious as these external benefits may be, it is extremely difficult to assign a dollar value to them. Moreover, government spending is financed by compulsory taxation and it is well known that taxes may distort private choices, creating costs in excess of the revenues they raise. If we followed the practice of including expenditure externalities in expenditure incidence analysis, then we should include the excess burden of taxation in tax incidence analysis. Because of the difficulties in measuring expenditure externalities and, to a lesser extent, excess burdens of taxation, analysts confine their attention to the direct benefits and the actual revenue collected. Eliminating the indirect components from both revenues and expenditures may be interpreted as assuming that there is a functioning political market in which public spending on each program is carried to the point that the total benefits of the last dollar spent equal the total cost to society of raising that dollar through taxation.

A Classification of Government Expenditures

Government expenditures can be grouped in a variety of ways. For the purpose of expenditure incidence, which focuses on the allocation of the benefits of these expenditures to different income groups, it is useful to classify the various programs of government spending in a manner that highlights the relationship between costs to government and benefits to individuals. This classification effectively presents a ranking of government expenditures with respect to the difficulties of making the allocation of benefits (box 1.2). It also helps determine the proportion of government expenditures whose allocation does not require arbitrary assumptions.

The major breakdown in box 1.2 is between specific and general expenditures. Interest on the public debt is placed in a separate category because it does not share the main features of either transfers or purchases. The difference between specific and general expenditures is based on the ease with which beneficiaries of government spending can be identified. It is also related to the closeness of the relationship between costs to government and benefits to individuals. Specific expenditures involve programs delivered to beneficiaries that can be identified through selected criteria such as those described below:

- Are there eligibility criteria? For example, old-age security pensions are paid to eligible individuals over 65 years of age. Therefore, the beneficiaries of these programs can be identified on the basis of age.
- Does the benefit from a program depend on individual utilization rates? For example, the benefits received from public health care depend on the frequency of admittance to hospitals or to physicians' care. Therefore, beneficiaries can be identified by the use they make of a public program.

BOX 1.2 A Classification of Government Expenditures

I. **Specific expenditures**
    A. *Transfer payments*
       1. To persons including public pensions and transfers to charitable and nonprofit organizations
       2. To business
    B. *Purchases of goods and services*
       1. Education
       2. Health care
       3. Other
II. **General expenditures**
    A. *Purchases of goods and services*
       1. General administration
       2. National defense
       3. Protection of persons and property
       4. Other
III. **Interest on the public debt**

- Are benefits specifically targeted to certain income groups? Some programs are strictly targeted to certain income groups and the beneficiaries can be identified by their income. For example, the public provision of low-income housing is aimed at benefiting only those individuals and families that meet a target low-income requirement.
- Are benefits related to some components of private consumption? For example, the benefits from public highways depend largely on the use of privately owned motor vehicles.

When individuals or selected groups of beneficiaries cannot be identified through criteria such as the ones described above because government spending programs provide benefits to the population as a whole, those programs are classified as general expenditures. As shown in box 1.2, such public spending is largely in the form of a "social overhead," because it represents the necessary foundations on which the entire economic system rests.

Within the two major categories of government spending—specific and general expenditures—there are large differences in the relationship between costs to government and benefits to individuals and in the ease of identification of beneficiaries. Therefore, the detailed allocation of the various components of government spending requires a review of each major program.

Allocation of Specific Expenditures

For incidence analysis, government expenditures may be separated into four major categories: transfer payments, purchases of goods and services, general expenditures, and interest on the public debt.

Transfer payments

Transfer payments may be separated into transfers to persons and transfers to business.

TRANSFERS TO PERSONS. Transfers to persons are made up of two major components: direct transfers to individuals and indirect transfers. The first component includes all the cash payments the government makes directly to individuals. The second component includes all the cash grants to nonbusiness institutions, such as charitable and nonprofit institutions, which use these funds to deliver cash and noncash benefits to targeted groups of individuals and families.

Direct transfers to individuals are the easiest category of expenditures to allocate. They involve a direct relationship between cost to government and benefit to individuals because a dollar spent by the government adds a dollar of income to the individual. In addition, the beneficiaries of these transfers are easily identifiable because these programs are usually targeted to select groups. For example, transfers to seniors are allocated to individuals 65 years of age and older. Similarly, transfers to children are allocated to the family units to which they belong.

The allocation is more complex in the case of indirect transfers because, in this case, private sector institutions serve as intermediaries between the government and the intended beneficiaries and because the benefits received may be in the form of goods and services instead of income. Consider, as an example, grants to cultural organizations that sponsor theatre or music performances. If those performances are made possible by government grants, those expenditures are likely to benefit both patrons and performers, who otherwise would have to seek alternative employment. Ideally, the allocation of these indirect transfers requires a distribution between performers and patrons and the identification of patrons according to their income levels. In practice, a rougher approximation may be used, depending on the type of data available and the details of the expenditure incidence analysis.

TRANSFERS TO BUSINESS. These transfers are government subsidies to firms in selected economic sectors. Their allocation raises the same issues as those for indirect transfers to persons. The government wants to deliver special benefits to individuals who consume certain private goods and services, and it uses the producers as intermediaries. These subsidies are effectively negative taxes and are treated as such in the national accounts. The allocation of subsidies is facilitated by the selective use of these government transfers, which allows identification of the targeted sectors. One can identify the beneficiaries as the producers or the consumers of the subsidized products. Whether the benefits of these subsidies are retained by their recipients or are passed on to consumers depends largely on the degree of price flexibility for the products being subsidized. For example, in small, open economies or in countries that make heavy use of marketing boards for the purpose of stabilizing farm prices, agricultural subsidies are likely to benefit farmers as producers because, in those cases, farmers would be price takers.

Purchases of goods and services

Purchases of goods and services are often called *in-kind transfers* because the beneficiaries are identifiable but the benefits they receive are in the form of free goods and services rather than cash. The relationship between cash and in-kind transfers is best explained by the case of education. The government may provide school vouchers to each child of school age to pay for the full cost of education. Alternatively, the government may build schools and pay teachers to provide free education services to children of school age. Aside from the issues associated with comparisons between private and public schools, the students receive the same benefits from these two public spending programs; only the delivery mechanisms differ. In the first case there is a direct transfer payment, while in the second case there is a noncash transfer of equivalent value. As mentioned earlier, the items included in this category meet the necessary criteria for identification of the beneficiaries. The specific allocation procedure, however, may differ among those items. In this section we will discuss the two largest components of this category of public spending: education and health care. Their beneficiaries can be identified by the criterion of utilization rates.

EDUCATION. For the purpose of expenditure incidence, it is useful to separate elementary and secondary school students from postsecondary students for two reasons: (a) costs per student vary for each level of education; and (b) while the first group includes entirely dependent children, the second group may contain separate household or family units.

The allocation of government expenditures on elementary and postsecondary education involves two steps. First, the average expenditure per student in each education level is estimated by dividing the respective total spending by the number of students enrolled. This is done both for direct spending on public schools and for subsidies to private schools. This average expenditure is then treated as a benefit and is added to the income of the families to which the students belong. The same procedure can be applied to spending on postsecondary education. The difference in this case is that postsecondary students may not be dependents. They may live as a separate household or may be members of their own family rather than the family that raised them. As a result, even if all these different families can be identified, the interpretation of the results is not clear-cut. For example, if all postsecondary students are dependent children, then public spending on postsecondary education will be allocated on the basis of the income distribution of their families, which may be similar to the income distribution of all families. If, however, all postsecondary students are unattached individuals, most of them will be classified as poor even if their parents are rich. In this case, public spending on postsecondary education will appear to be very redistributive, even when only a minority of students comes from poor families.

The allocation of education spending highlights a major shortcoming of annual expenditure incidence when the benefits of public spending extend beyond the period in which the expenditures were made. The main purpose of public education is to equip young people with the skills necessary to be productive members of the labor force. The intended effect is to increase the potential earning power of students over their working lives. Ideally, therefore, the benefits of education spending should be allocated directly to the students and on the basis of their lifetime incomes. The redistributional effect of public spending on education, therefore, is captured more accurately through lifetime expenditure incidence. In this case, annual incidence exercises may lead to misleading conclusions about redistribution through public spending. Assigning the benefits of elementary and secondary education to the families of students implicitly assumes that the lifetime incomes of the students will have the same distribution as that of their parents. Treating postsecondary students as separate households disregards entirely their potential earning power. In annual incidence, these students will be categorized as poor although they may receive high lifetime income, and publicly funded postsecondary education may appear to be pro-poor when in effect it may be pro-rich.

HEALTH CARE. Public spending on health care can be viewed as an insurance benefit provided to all those covered by public health care plans. The value of this benefit will differ among individuals as health care needs may differ by age, gender, or even income level. As in the case of education, the allocation of these benefits requires two steps. In the first step, the average benefit for each selected group is calculated by dividing the costs of selected health care services by the number of people in each age-gender group. This cost, which is equated to the average benefit received, is then allocated to the household or family unit to which the members of a group belong. What is being allocated under this approach is the average benefit for the representative member in each age-gender group, independently of the actual utilization rate of each individual member. The more detailed is the breakdown of health care expenditures into their components and the disaggregation of the population, the more accurate is the allocation of the benefits of public spending on health care. Similar procedures are used in the allocation of all government purchases of goods and services for which specific beneficiaries can be identified.

General Expenditures

This category of public spending includes all expenditures for which specific beneficiaries cannot be identified. Its major components are central administrative expenditures, spending on the executive and legislative branches of government, spending on environmental protection, national defense spending, and expenditures on the protection of persons and property, which includes spending on the police, the court system, and correctional facilities. The main problem created by this category of public spending in expenditure incidence studies is that it contains mainly public goods. Because the benefits of these goods are enjoyed by the population at large and the benefits received by individual A do not affect the benefits received by individual B, it is not possible to allocate these expenditures to specific beneficiaries. Therefore, one must find some general rules for distributing these expenditures to all members of society. Because the choice of allocation approach for general expenditures is largely arbitrary, expenditure incidence studies often present results derived from the use of more than one allocation procedure.

Two bases for allocating general expenditures have been used in empirical studies: demographic units and some measure of income. In the first case, general expenditures are allocated in equal amounts to each member of society (per capita basis) or to each family, independently of size. Income bases used include capital income, factor income, money income, and disposable income. A departure from these two sets of bases is represented by Musgrave, Case, and Leonard (1974) who, in one of his alternatives, allocated general expenditures in proportion to tax burdens. The equal per capita allocation is consistent with the treatment of general expenditures as public goods indivisible in consumption. The allocation to capital income or total income is more consistent with the concept of insurance. For example, in the case of protection of persons and property, including defense spending, one may argue that what are protected are the assets of individuals and families. These include physical assets, financial assets, and human capital incorporated in the potential earnings of a person.

Aaron and McGuire (1970) have argued that the different approaches to the allocation of general expenditures are associated with implicit or explicit utility functions. They show that allocating the benefits of general expenditures on an equal basis to each family or each individual assumes implicitly that the marginal utility of income remains constant as income increases. Alternatively, allocating general expenditures on the basis of total income implicitly assumes that the marginal utility of income declines as income increases, which in turn implies that the relative utility of public goods will rise with income.

From a practical perspective, useful improvements in the allocation of general expenditures will come from the greatest possible disaggregation. Such disaggregation would serve two main purposes: (a) it may allow the identification of components for which specific beneficiaries may be identified; and (b) it allows the application of the allocation procedure most suitable for each component of general expenditures. For example, the administrative costs of transfer payment programs can be assigned to the recipients of those programs rather than to all the population on the basis of family status or income. Similarly, the educational and health care expenditures by national defense organizations can be allocated as part of health care and education spending. The costs of maintaining the legislative and executive branches may be appropriately allocated on a per capita or per family basis, but the costs of protection of persons and property may be more appropriately allocated to some concept of income on the basis of the insurance principle.

Allocation of Interest Payments on the Public Debt

Expenditures on servicing the public debt raise both conceptual and methodological issues. They are cash payments to individuals or institutions; unlike direct transfers to individuals, however, they involve a quid pro quo. They are paid to those who hold government bonds. Because they are conditional payments, one may argue that they do not provide benefits to the recipients and, therefore, should not be included in expenditure incidence. After all, the owners of government bonds might have purchased private securities if government bonds were not available. Excluding interest on the debt from expenditure incidence, however, would create an inconsistency in the treatment of revenues and expenditures. The costs of servicing the public debt in a given year are financed through current taxation. That tax revenue is fully allocated to those who bear its burden. To maintain consistency, all the expenditures that are financed through current taxation must also be allocated. The relevant issue in expenditure incidence is how this component of public spending should be allocated.

Public debt accumulates because taxpayers, through the political process, decide to receive in a given year public services for which they are not willing to pay immediately. The interest on the debt may be considered a measure of the benefit from consuming public goods and services before they are fully paid. The allocation of the interest on the public debt, therefore, raises the issue of intergenerational equity. In theory, these payments should be allocated to those who benefit from public expenditures financed through borrowing. In practice, the identification of these beneficiaries is an impossible task. Therefore, one is left with the choice of somewhat arbitrary allocation rules. One can allocate these payments to those who receive interest income.

Alternatively, one can assume that borrowing benefited those who gained from government spending and allocate the interest on the debt in proportion to the allocated amounts of all other government expenditures. One may also argue that, given the level of government spending that is fully recorded in the government accounts, the beneficiaries of debt financing are the taxpayers who did not pay the full cost of the benefits received. Therefore, the interest on the debt should be allocated on the basis of tax payments.

The allocation of the interest on the debt is further complicated by the fact that the borrowed funds may be used to finance both current and capital expenditures. If the borrowed funds are used to finance public investment, the benefits of those expenditures will benefit future generations including, perhaps, those who are paying through taxation the costs of servicing the debt in the year covered by the expenditure incidence analysis. In this case, there is no intergenerational shift of tax burdens. If public borrowing finances current expenditures, there is a shift of tax burden to future generations. The situation becomes even more complicated during periods of persistent government deficits. In that case, we have a combination of benefits from current expenditures that are not fully paid and benefits from the postponement of full payment of past expenditures.

Distributional Effects

Presenting the estimates of the distributional effects of public expenditure incidence requires a choice of the categories of government spending and the selection of the appropriate indices of redistribution.

Presenting the Results

The final step in the expenditure incidence exercise is to summarize the results using some indexes of redistribution. These indexes can be applied to total government expenditures or to selected components. A short list of suggested groupings of the components of government spending is presented in box 1.3.

The first group includes all expenditures and provides an overall picture of the redistributional impact of government spending. This type of information by itself provides little guide to policy makers because it does not identify the programs that deliver the measured redistribution. Therefore, it must be complemented by a more disaggregated analysis. The most detailed approach is to present indexes of redistribution for each of the spending programs for which a separate allocation was made. If the expenditure incidence study involved a detailed disaggregation of government spending, presenting

BOX 1.3   Selected Groupings of Government Expenditures

1. The sum of all expenditures
2. A detailed disaggregation of expenditures
3. All expenditures minus military spending
4. Civilian expenditures excluding the interest on the debt
5. Separation between transfer payments, purchases, and interest on the debt
6. Separation between transfers, specific purchases, general purchases and the interest on the debt

redistributional indexes for each program may add excessive and perhaps unnecessary details. It may be preferable, as an alternative, to group the spending programs in categories that are meaningful for policy analysis.

One useful disaggregation of government expenditures is between transfer payments and purchases. Conventional wisdom holds that transfers are more redistributive than purchases because transfers are usually targeted to low-income individuals and families. Disaggregating these two major groups of public spending would help put this view to the test. Another useful category is total government spending net of military expenditures. As mentioned earlier, military spending is part of the group of government expenditures for which specific beneficiaries cannot be found and whose allocation is based on largely arbitrary assumptions. If military spending represents a large share of total government spending, it may have a strong effect on the measured degree of redistribution, depending on the manner in which it is allocated. When comparing expenditure incidence among countries with widely different shares of military spending it is advisable to leave those expenditures out of the results.

We may go one step further and eliminate also the interest on the public debt. This approach would focus on public spending aimed at civilians and bypass the intergenerational issues raised by the interest on the debt. It would also provide more reliable estimates of expenditure incidence because it would exclude two potentially major items whose allocation involves arbitrary assumptions. A final desegregation would separate the four major groups of public spending: transfer payments, specific purchases, general purchases, and interest on the debt. This approach would not only single out the interest on the debt but would also allow a comparison of transfer payments and purchases and, for purchases, a comparison between specific and general purchases. Of course, other groupings can be devised, depending on the focus of the analysis.

Indexes of Expenditure Incidence

The results of the expenditure incidence exercise can now be summarized. Two sets of indexes may be used: disaggregated and global. The first provides details according to the distribution of income used in the exercise, while the second provides a summary measure for the entire population.

Disaggregated indexes

The simplest and most widely used index of expenditure incidence is the ratio (g) of benefits (G) to some measure of income (Y); that is, $g = G/Y$. This ratio is calculated for each income group selected in the study; it is often presented in graphical form, with income classes on the horizontal axis and the benefit ratio on the vertical axis. The situation in which public spending does not redistribute income is represented by a constant value of the benefit ratio for all classes and is shown graphically as a straight horizontal line. A pattern of increasing benefit ratios, approximated by a positively sloping line, indicates a regressive pattern of incidence, which means that public spending benefits high-income families relatively more than low-income families. The opposite conclusion applies when the benefit ratios decline as income increases, a situation known as progressive incidence and portrayed graphically by a downward-sloping line.

This ratio has been used in different combinations in what are called *local measures of redistribution*. They are called *local* because each value measures the degree of redistribution for each income group. They possess the special property of forming the building blocks for the global measures of redistribution. Presenting estimates of both the local indexes and the associated global indexes provides a consistent picture of the overall degree of redistribution and its pattern among various income groups.

A local index that provides a direct interpretation in terms of redistribution is the relative share adjustment (RSA) which, in the case of public spending, can be defined for each income group as the share of actual income divided by the share of income under the assumption that government expenditures do not affect the distribution of income (Baum 1987). The value of this index for the ith income group can also be calculated as

$$\text{RSA}_i = (1 + g_i)/(1 + g) \tag{1.1}$$

Expression 1.1 shows that this index effectively compares the actual benefit ratio g_i to the benefit ratio under the assumption that government expenditures do not redistribute income. If government spending does not improve the relative economic position of a selected income group—say, low-income families—the estimated value of RSA_i is 1. A net gain (loss) by the selected group is represented by an RSA_i value greater (less than) than 1. For example, an estimated RSA_i value of 1.04 indicates that the ith income group would lose 4 percent of current income if government expenditures were distributed in proportion to income for all families. The pattern of RSA1 values provides an indication of the overall redistributional impact of government spending. If the RSA_i has values of 1 for all income classes, government spending does not redistribute income. If the values of RSA_i increase with the level of income, the incidence of public spending is regressive (pro-rich); if they decline with income, the incidence is progressive (pro-poor).

Global indexes

The degree of income inequality is often shown graphically through what is commonly known as the Lorenz curve. This diagram relates the cumulative proportion of income, measured on the vertical axis, to the cumulative proportion of individuals or family units, measured on the horizontal axis. Perfect equality of income is represented by the diagonal from the bottom left corner to the top right corner. Unequal income distributions are represented by curves to the right of the diagonal. The area between these curves and the diagonal provides a graphical indication of the degree of income inequality. Comparing the curve for income under distributionally neutral public spending with the curve under the actual distribution of government expenditures provides an indication of redistribution.

The Lorenz curve can be transformed into a single index, a widely used global measure of income concentration called the Gini coefficient. This index is calculated as the area between an income curve and the diagonal divided by the total area below the diagonal. If income is equally distributed, the income curve coincides with the diagonal, the numerator equals 0 and the Gini coefficient takes the value of 0. If the distribution of income is perfectly unequal, the area between the income curve and the diagonal coincides with the total area below the diagonal, the numerator equals the denominator and the Gini coefficient takes the value of 1. The redistributional effect of government spending can be measured by comparing Gini coefficients estimated under different assumptions. A variety of global indexes based on comparisons of Gini coefficients is shown in table 1.1, where Gn stands for the Gini coefficient for income under distributionally neutral government spending, Gy indicates the Gini coefficient for the income under the actual distribution of public spending, and Gg refers to the Gini coefficient of the distribution of government expenditures.

TABLE 1.1   Global Indexes of Redistribution Based on Comparisons
of Gini Coefficients

Author	Global Index of Redistribution
Kakwani (1976)	$Gg - Gy$
Reynolds and Smolensky (1977)	$Gn - Gy$
Musgrave and Thin (1948)	$(1 - Gn)\backslash(1 - Gy)$
Pechman and Okner (1980)	$(Gn - Gy)\backslash Gy$
Khetan and Poddar (1976)	$(1 - Gy)\backslash(1\backslash Gg)$

A global index of redistribution that does not depend on a direct relationship between Gini coefficients is the global relative share adjustment
(RSAg), which is derived as a weighted average of the local RSA discussed
earlier (Cassady, Ruggeri, and Van Wart 1996). The weights are based on the
distribution of income under the neutral public spending assumption and
decline monotonically from low- to high-income classes. RSAg ranges from
0 to 2. A value of RSAg of 1 indicates that a given spending program, or public spending as a whole, does not redistribute income. A value greater (less)
than 1 indicates that public expenditures redistribute income from higher
(lower) to lower (higher) income classes.

Conclusions

Government spending may alter the distribution of income and may affect
economic efficiency by influencing private choices. The term *expenditure
incidence* is commonly used in connection with the first set of effects, which
are measured through partial equilibrium analysis. Measuring expenditure
incidence involves three major steps and each step raises difficult methodological issues.

In the first step the analyst must identify the government universe by
selecting the types of public spending that will be included in the analysis,
choose the appropriate databases, and select the unit of analysis and the
income concept to be used in measuring the distribution of income that may
be affected by government spending. The second step requires the allocation
of the benefits from the various public spending programs to the selected
income groups. Since it is impossible to measure directly the benefits of public spending received by individuals, because there is no market for publicly
provided goods and services financed through compulsory taxation, benefits are usually approximated as the costs incurred by government.

The major difficulties encountered in this step are created by general expenditures on goods and services. Because these expenditures are largely of the public goods type it is not possible to identify specific beneficiaries. Therefore, one is left with the option of making somewhat arbitrary assumptions in allocating these expenditures. This problem can be minimized through a fine disaggregation of government purchases, which may help identify specific beneficiaries for portions of spending programs that may otherwise be considered general expenditures. The final step involves the presentation of the results through the use of indexes of redistribution. In order to provide as much useful information for policy analysis as possible, it is desirable that both local and global indexes be presented and that they be applied to total public expenditures as well as selected groupings.

Notes

1. A detailed analysis of the functions of government is found in Musgrave (1959).
2. Examples of separate studies are Smeeding and others (1993) and Ruggeri, Van Wart, and Howard (1994b). Examples of overall fiscal studies are Gillespie (1965); Dodge (1975); Musgrave, Case, and Leonard (1974); Reynolds and Smolensky (1977); Ruggles and O'Higgins (1981); O'Higgins and Ruggles (1981); and Ruggeri, Van Wart, and Howard (1996).
3. Examples of such studies are Rolph (1954), Musgrave (1959), Harberger (1962), Mieszkowsky (1967), and McClure (1970).
4. Examples of such studies are Aaron and McGuire (1970), Thurow (1971), McClure (1972), and Schwab (1985).
5. A discussion of these issues is found in Meerman (1978, 1980) and DeWulf (1981).
6. A discussion of a variety of income concepts is found in Simons (1938), Meerman (1974), Peskin and Peskin (1978), Ellwood and Summers (1986), and Oxley and others (1997).

References

Aaron, Henry, and Martin McGuire. 1970. "Public Goods and Income Distribution." *Econometrica* 38: 907–18.

Baum, Sandra R. 1987. "On the Measurement of Tax Progressivity: Relative Share Adjustment." *Public Finance Quarterly* 15: 166–87.

Browning, Edgar K., and William R. Johnson. 1979. "The Distribution of the Tax Burden." American Enterprise Institute, Washington, DC.

Buhmann, Brigitte, Lee Rainwater, Guenther Schmaus, and Timothy Smeeding. 1988. "Equivalence Scales, Well-Being, Inequality, and Poverty: Sensitivity Estimates across 10 Countries Using the Luxemburg Income Study (LIS) Database." *Review of Income and Wealth* 34: 115–42.

Cassady, Kim, Giuseppe C. Ruggeri, and Don Van Wart. 1996. "On the Classification and Interpretation of Global Progressivity Measures." *Public Finance* 51: 1–22.

Colm, Gerhard, and Helen Tarasov. 1940. "Who Pays Taxes?" Study prepared for the Temporary National Economic Committee, Monograph 3, 76th Congress, *Congressional Record—Appendix Extension of Remarks* 84: 3336.

DeWulf, Luc H. 1981. "Incidence of Budgetary Outlays: Where Do We Go From Here?" *Public Finance* 36: 55–76.

Dodge, David A. 1975. "Impact of Tax, Transfer, and Expenditure Policies of Government on the Distribution of Personal Income in Canada." *Review of Income and Wealth* 21: 1–52.

Ellwood, David, and Lawrence Summers. 1986. "Measuring Income: What Kind Should Be In?" Discussion Paper 1248, Harvard Institute of Economic Research, Harvard University, Cambridge, MA.

Gillespie, W. Irwin. 1965. "The Effect of Public Expenditures on the Distribution of Income." In Richard A. Musgrave, ed., *Essays in Fiscal Federalism,* 122–86. Washington: DC, Brookings Institution.

Harberger, Arnold C. 1962. "The Incidence of the Corporation Income Tax." *Journal of Political Economy* 70: 215–40.

Kakwani, Nanok C. 1976. "Measurement of Tax Progressivity: An International Comparison." *Economic Journal* 87: 71–80.

Khetan, C. P., and Satya N. Poddar. 1976. "Measurement of Income Tax Progression in a Growing Economy: The Canadian Experience." *Canadian Journal of Economics* 9: 613–29.

McClure, Charles E. 1970. "Tax Incidence, Macroeconomic Policy, and Absolute Prices." *Quarterly Journal of Economic* 84: 254–67.

———. 1972. "The Theory of Expenditure Incidence." *Finanzarchiv* 30: 432–53.

———. 1974. "On the Theory and Methodology of Estimating Benefit and Expenditure Incidence." Unpublished manuscript, Rice University, Houston, TX.

Meerman, Jacob. 1974. "The Definition of Income in Studies of Budget Incidence and Income Distribution." *Review of Income and Wealth* 20: 515–22.

———. 1978. "Do Empirical Studies of Budget Incidence Make Sense?" *Public Finance* 33: 295–312.

———. 1980. "Are Public Goods Public Goods?" *Public Choice* 35: 45–57.

Mieszkowsky, Peter M. 1967. "On the Theory of Tax Incidence." *Journal of Political Economy* 75: 250–62.

Musgrave, Richard A. 1959. *The Theory of Public Finance.* New York: McGraw-Hill.

Musgrave, Richard A., and Tun Thin. 1948. "Income Tax Progression, 1929–48." *Journal of Political Economy* 56: 498–514.

Musgrave, Richard A., Karl Case, and Herman Leonard. 1974. "The Distribution of Fiscal Burdens and Benefits." *Public Finance Quarterly* 2: 299–311.

Musgrave, Richard A., John J. Carroll, Lorne D. Cook, and Lenore Frane. 1951. "Distribution of Tax Payments by Income Groups: A Case Study for 1948." *National Tax Journal* 4: 1–54.

OECD (Organisation for Economic Co-operation and Development). 1998. *National Accounts, Detailed Tables, 2, 1982–96.* Paris: OECD.

O'Higgins, Michael, and Patricia Ruggles. 1981. "The Distribution of Expenditures and Taxes among Households in the United Kingdom." *Review of Income and Wealth* 27: 298–326.

Oxley, Harvard, Jean-Marc Burniaux, Thai-Thanh Dang, and Marco Mira d'Ercole. 1997. "Income Distribution and Poverty in 13 OECD Countries." *OECD Economic Studies* 29: 55–94.

Pechman, Joseph A., and Benjamin Okner. 1980. "Who Bears the Tax Burden?" Brookings Institution, Washington, DC.

Peskin, Henry M., and Janice Peskin. 1978. "The Valuation of Non-Market Activities in Income Accounting." *Review of Income and Wealth* 24: 71–92.

Reynolds, Morgan, and Eugene Smolensky. 1977. "Public Expenditures, Taxes, and the Distribution of Income." New York: Academic Press.

Rolph, Earl R. 1954. *The Theory of Fiscal Economics.* Berkeley: University of California Press.

Ruggeri, Giuseppe C., Don Van Wart, and Robert Howard. 1994a. "The Redistributional Impact of Taxation in Canada." *Canadian Tax Journal* 42: 417–51.

———. 1994b. "The Redistributional Impact of Government Spending in Canada." *Public Finance* 49: 212–43.

———. 1996. *The Government as Robin Hood: Exploring the Myth.* Kingston, ON: School of Policy Studies, Queen's University.

Ruggles, Patricia, and Michael O'Higgins. 1981. "The Distribution of Public Expenditures and Taxes among Households in the United States." *Review of Income and Wealth* 27: 137–64.

Schwab, Robert. 1985. "The Benefits of In-Kind Government Programs." *Journal of Public Economics* 27: 195–210.

Simons, Henry. 1938. *Personal Income Taxation.* Chicago: University of Chicago Press.

Smeeding, Timothy M., Peter Saunders, John Cody, Stephen Jenkins, Johan Fritzell, Aldi J. M. Hagenaars, Richard Hauser, and Michael Wolfson. 1993. "Poverty, Inequality, and Family Living Standards Impacts across Seven Nations: The Effect of Noncash Subsidies for Health, Education, and Housing." *Review of Income and Wealth* 39: 229–56.

Statistics Canada. 2002. *Income in Canada.* Cat. No. 75-202. Ottawa: Supply and Services Canada.

Thurow, Lester C. 1971. "The Income Distribution as a Pure Public Good." *Quarterly Journal of Economics* 85: 326–36.

Vermaeten, Frank, W. Irwin Gillespie, and Arndt Vermaeten. 1994. "Tax Incidence in Canada." *Canadian Tax Journal* 42: 348–416.

2

On Measures of Inequality and Poverty with Welfare Implications

NANAK KAKWANI AND HYUN SON

In the 1950s and 1960s, growth in per capita gross domestic product (GDP) (or related income measures) was the principal yardstick for the measurement of economic development. The dominant ideology was that economic growth would create widespread prosperity by creating more jobs and more goods and services. The benefits of economic growth would eventually trickle down to the poor.

Yet despite high economic growth rates, many countries are still faced with problems of poverty and income inequality, with varying degrees of seriousness. An awareness of the existence of high levels of inequality and poverty has increased in recent times. It is being increasingly realized that policies that emphasize economic growth are not sufficient to protect vulnerable groups in the society. The fact that the government can play an important role in reducing inequality and poverty is increasingly recognized. The problem is measuring inequality and poverty so that policies can be devised to tackle these issues.

The main objective of this chapter is to provide a brief review of measures of inequality and poverty. In such measures, ethical evaluation and statistical measurement are not always clearly distinguishable. For this reason, this chapter attempts to bring out the welfare implications of various measures of poverty and inequality and at the same time explain the statistical measurement and analysis of inequality and poverty.

To illustrate how various measures can be used to analyze changes in inequality and poverty, the chapter provides an empirical illustration using the Lao Expenditure and Consumption Surveys conducted in 1992–93 and 1997–98. These were nationwide surveys of 2,937 and 8,882 households, respectively.

The Lorenz Curve and Social Welfare

The Lorenz curve is a simple device that has been widely used to describe and analyze income distribution data. This curve has become important in recent times because it provides a useful method of ranking income distributions from the welfare point of view. It is defined as the relationship between the proportion of people with income less than or equal to a specified amount and the proportion of total income received by those people. To explain the idea in a simple way, suppose there are five people whose incomes arranged in ascending order are 2, 3, 5, 6, and 8, which gives a total income of 24. The cumulative proportion of people whose incomes are less than or equal to 2, 3, 5, 6, and 8 is given by

$$p = \frac{1}{5}, \frac{2}{5}, \frac{3}{5}, \frac{4}{5}, \frac{5}{5}$$

and the cumulative proportion of incomes is given by

$$L(p) = \frac{2}{24}, \frac{5}{24}, \frac{10}{24}, \frac{16}{24}, \frac{24}{24}$$

The Lorenz curve is obtained by plotting the values of p on the horizontal axis with the corresponding values of $L(p)$ on the vertical axis.

More generally, the Lorenz curve is represented by a function $L(p)$, which is interpreted as the fraction of total income received by the bottom pth fraction of people, when the people are arranged in ascending order of income. The curve is drawn in a unit square (figure 2.1). Thus, if $p = 0$, $L(p) = 0$ and if $p = 1$, $L(p) = 1$. The slope of the curve is positive and increases monotonically; in other words, the curve is convex to the p axis. From this, it follows that $p \le L(p)$. The straight line represented by the equation, $L(p) = p$, is called the egalitarian line.

In figure 2.1, the egalitarian line is the diagonal OB through the origin of the unit square. The Lorenz curve lies below this line. If the curve coincides with the line, it means that each person in society receives the same income,

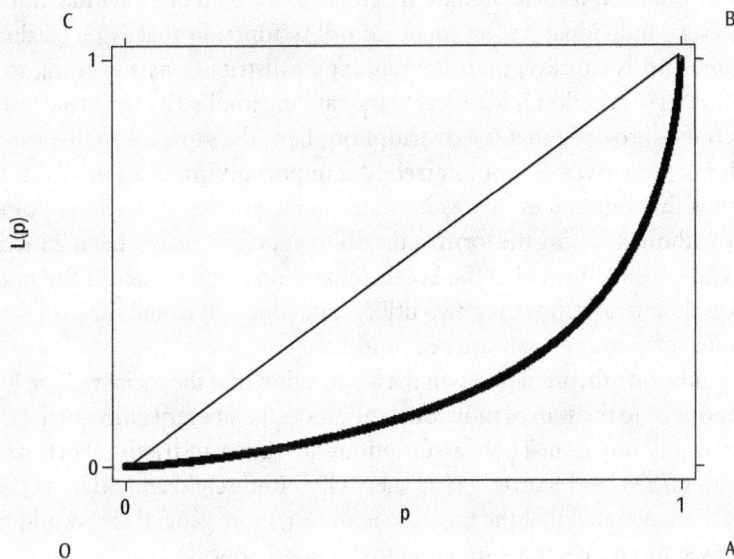

FIGURE 2.1 Lorenz Curve

which is the case of perfect equality of income. In the case of perfect inequality, the Lorenz curve coincides with OA and AB, implying that one person in society receives all the income that is generated in the economy.

Because the Lorenz curve displays the deviation of income distribution from perfect equality (represented by the egalitarian line), it captures, in a sense, the essence of inequality. The nearer the Lorenz curve is to the egalitarian line, the more equal will be the distribution of income. Consequently, the Lorenz curve can be used as a criterion for ranking government policies or programs. Suppose there are two alternative government policies, which result in two different income distributions, namely, X_1 and X_2. If the Lorenz curve of X_1 is above that of X_2 at all points then, from an equity point of view, the first policy is preferred over the second policy. However, if the two Lorenz curves intersect, neither policy can be said to be more equitable than the other. Thus, the Lorenz curve provides only a partial ranking of distribution.

Government policies should be judged on the basis of their impact on social welfare. According to this view, the first policy should be judged as superior to the second only when the social welfare derived from X_1 is greater than that derived from X_2. Fortunately, under certain conditions, the ranking of distributions according to the Lorenz curve is identical to the ranking implied by the social welfare function. In 1970, Anthony Atkinson proved a theorem that showed that if social welfare is defined as the sum of individual utilities, and every individual has an identical utility function that is increasing in income and is concave, then the ranking of distributions according to the Lorenz curve criterion is identical to the ranking implied by the social welfare function—provided that the distributions have the same mean income and their Lorenz curves do not intersect. An important implication of this theorem is that one can evaluate alternative policies from the welfare point of view without knowing the form of the utility function except that it is increasing and concave, provided the Lorenz curves do not intersect. If the Lorenz curves do intersect, however, two utility functions that would rank the distributions differently can always be found.

Atkinson's theorem relies on the assumption that the social welfare function is equal to the sum of individual utilities and that every individual has the same utility function. These assumptions are rather restrictive. Fortunately, Dasgupta, Sen, and Starrett (1973), as well as Rothschild and Stiglitz (1973), have demonstrated that the theorem is, in fact, more general and would hold for any symmetric welfare function that is quasi-concave.

Income shares of deciles and quintiles are frequently used to describe income inequality and are readily obtained from the Lorenz curve. These measures provide a useful description of inequality and can be used to identify which segment of income distribution will gain or lose from government policies.

Gini Index

Although the Lorenz curve is a powerful device for judging alternative government policies from the welfare point of view, its main limitation is that it works only if the Lorenz curves do not intersect. If the Lorenz curves intersect, then we need to consider single measures of inequality, each of which implies a different social welfare function. This implies that any analysis of inequality based on a single measure involves value judgments about the social welfare function. Thus, it becomes necessary to evaluate alternative inequality measures on the basis of their welfare implications.

Of all the inequality measures, the Gini index is the most widely used. It became popular because of its direct relationship with the Lorenz curve. It measures the extent to which the Lorenz curve departs from the egalitarian line. It is defined as twice the area between the Lorenz curve and the egalitarian line. This definition ensures that the value of the Gini index lies between zero (for complete equality) and one (for complete or most extreme inequality).

Inequality measures are generally computed from household income and expenditures surveys, which are now conducted by almost every country in the world. Inequality is computed on the basis of either per capita household income or per capita household expenditure. No consensus exists on whether one should use income or expenditure. Income is the major resource for each individual for consuming goods and services in the economy, whereas consumption indicates the actual standard of living enjoyed by an individual. The inequality of per capita income is generally larger than that of per capita consumption.

One of the important requirements of an inequality measure is that any transfer of income from a poorer person to a richer person should increase inequality. This requirement is known as the Pigou-Dalton condition in the inequality literature (Sen 1973). Although the Gini index satisfies this condition, it gives maximum weight to transfers near the mode of the distribution rather than at the tails. If society is most concerned about the poor, then the inequality measure should give maximum weight to the poorest member and weight should decrease monotonically with the level of income. Thus, the Gini index may not be considered desirable if society is most concerned about the poor.

Calculations of the Gini Index

The Gini index is not an easy measure to calculate from survey data. Suppose we have a hypothetical sample of 10 households, whose per capita incomes are given in column 2 (denoted by x_i) of table 2.1. Each sample household is generally associated with a population weight, which immediately gives the relative frequency of each household, shown in column 3 (denoted by f_i). This column shows, for instance, that 17 percent of the population lives in households whose per capita income is $400. In these calculations, it is assumed that each person in the household shares exactly the same income, so that the Gini index measures the inequality of income among individuals. The mean per capita income is obtained as

$$\mu = \sum_{i=1}^{10} f_i x_i, \qquad (2.1)$$

which is the weighted average of household per capita income, with weight proportionate to the households relative frequency. The mean per capita income is computed to be equal to 6,100.

Column 4 gives the income share of each household, which is obtained by multiplying income x_i by the relative frequency f_i and dividing by the

TABLE 2.1   Calculation of the Gini Index

Households	x_i	f_i	$f_i \times \dfrac{x_i}{\mu_i}$	q_i	d_i
1	0	0.03	0.00	0.00	1.00
2	1,000	0.03	0.01	0.01	0.99
3	2,000	0.03	0.01	0.02	0.98
4	3,000	0.07	0.03	0.05	0.93
5	4,000	0.17	0.11	0.16	0.79
6	5,000	0.20	0.16	0.32	0.52
7	6,000	0.20	0.20	0.52	0.16
8	10,000	0.17	0.27	0.79	−0.31
9	12,000	0.07	0.13	0.92	−0.72
10	14,000	0.03	0.08	1.00	−0.92
Total	6,100	1.00	1.00	—	0.30

mean per capita income of the whole population, denoted by μ. Column 5 gives the cumulative income share, which is denoted by q_i. This column, for instance, shows that 32 percent of all persons in the population have income less than equal to $5,000. Then the Gini index is obtained as (Kakwani 1980b):

$$G = \sum_{i=1}^{10} f_i d_i \qquad (2.2)$$

where $d_i = 1 - q_i - q_{i-1}$,
where $i = 1, 2, \ldots, 10$ and $q_{i-1} = 0$, if $i = 1$.

This gives a value for the Gini index equal to 0.30.

Generalized Gini Index

The Gini index is not a suitable measure of inequality when society wishes to give greater importance to the most poor. The Gini index gives maximum weight to the people who are clustered around the mode of an income distribution. In view of this drawback, Kakwani (1980b) proposed a generalization of the Gini index that makes it possible to alter the weight given to transfers at different segment of the income distribution.[1]

The general class of inequality measures can be described as

$$G(k) = (k + 1) \int_0^\infty g(x)[1 - F(x)]^k f(x) dx \qquad (2.3)$$

where $g(x) = \dfrac{\mu - x}{\mu}$ is the proportional income shortfall of the individual with income x from the mean income, $F(x)$ is the probability distribution function (the proportion of people with income less than or equal to x), $f(x)$ is the density function, and k is a parameter that can be given some assigned value. If $k = 0$, $G(k) = 0$ for any income distribution, implying an inequality-neutral attitude of society, which means that the society does not care about inequality, in which case government policies will be focused only on promoting economic growth. The question of who benefits from the growth will not be of much concern to policy makers.

When $k = 1$, $G(k)$ gives the Gini index. It can be demonstrated that the larger the value of k is, the greater is the weight attached to the lower end of the distribution and the less is the weight attached to the incomes of richer people. The value of k should be chosen according to society's preference: whether it is most concerned about the welfare of the poor or of those falling in the middle segment of income distribution.

Note that $G(k)$ has been defined as the weighted average of the proportional shortfalls of individual incomes from the mean. The greater is the shortfall, the larger is the weight attached to that individual. The weight given to an individual is proportional to $[1 - F(x)]^k$, where $[1 - F(x)]$ is proportional to the number of individuals who have income larger than that individual. It means that the weight given to an individual with income x is a measure of his or her relative deprivation: the greater the number of persons above him or her in society, the greater is his or her sense of deprivation. Thus, this class of measure captures the relative deprivation aspect of inequality (Sen 1973). The weight attached to the individual measures the share of deprivation suffered by that individual relative to others. Thus, the Kakwani (1980b) class of inequality measure, of which the Gini index is a particular member, essentially measures the average deprivation suffered by all individuals in society, which may be regarded as an attractive feature.

Entropy Measures of Inequality

Theil (1967) proposed two inequality measures based on the notion of entropy in information theory. These measures have gained popularity because they can be decomposed. If a population is divided into a number of groups according to certain socioeconomic characteristics of individuals, these measures can be decomposed into between-group and within-group income inequality. Thus,

$$TI = BGI + WGI \qquad (2.4)$$

which shows that the total inequality (TI) in the society is the sum of two components, between-group inequality (BGI) and within-group inequality (WGI). The BGI is the inequality that would exist if each observation were replaced by the mean income of the group sharing the same characteristics. The WGI is the weighted average of the inequality within each group. The ratio of BGI to TI indicates how much inequality is explained by the groups. For instance, if the population is divided according to age, then we can know the contribution of age to total inequality. If this contribution is large, then we can think of policies that would induce the disparity caused by the age of individuals.

The two entropy measures can be calculated using the formula:

$$I_0 = \log\mu - \sum_{i=1}^{n} f_i \log x_i \qquad (2.5)$$

$$I_1 = \frac{1}{\mu}\sum_{i=1}^{n} f_i x_i \log x_i - \log\mu \qquad (2.6)$$

where f_i is the proportion of all individuals who have income x_i and μ is per capita mean income. Both of these measures satisfy the Pigou-Dalton condition that any transfer from a rich to a poor person reduces inequality. In addition, they are more sensitive to income transfers at the lower incomes.

Unlike the Gini index, Theil's two measures take the form of an additive function of incomes or income shares. This means that the social welfare function implied by them is additive separable, suggesting that the satisfaction an individual derives is independent of the consumption of others. This assumption may be regarded as restrictive, because people do compare themselves with others and feel deprived when they see others enjoying higher consumption. The generalized Gini index is more attractive, because it takes into account the relative deprivation aspect of inequality. Unfortunately, the generalized Gini index is not decomposable into between-group and within-group inequality.

Atkinson's Inequality Measures

Although the inequality measures discussed in the previous sections were derived without any regard to social welfare function, they do have some implicit welfare function. Economists are primarily interested not in the distribution of income as such, but in the effect of policies on social welfare that is derived from incomes. Thus, it makes sense to derive the inequality measures directly from a social welfare function.

This approach was suggested by Dalton in 1920 but was revived by Atkinson in 1970. This section presents Atkinson's measures, which have the attractive feature of being invariant to any positive linear transformation of the utility function. His class of measures is derived based on the concept of the "equally distributed equivalent level of income," x^*, which is the level of per capita income that, if received by everyone, would make the total welfare exactly equal to the total welfare generated by the actual income distribution. Atkinson assumed that the social welfare function is utilitarian and every individual has exactly the same utility function. Under these conditions, x^* is given by

$$u(x^*) = \sum_{i=1}^{n} f_i u(x_i) \tag{2.7}$$

where f_i is the population share of the individuals with income x_i and $u(x_i)$ is the utility function.

The inequality measure proposed by Atkinson (1970) is

$$A = 1 - \frac{x^*}{\mu} \tag{2.8}$$

which is in fact a measure of the loss of welfare caused as a consequence of inequality.

The relative measures of inequality have the attribute that if everyone's income increased or decreased by the same proportion, inequality would not change. Such measures are said to be scale-independent. If Atkinson's measure is to be scale-independent, then the utility function has to be of the form

$$u(x) = A + B\frac{x^{1-\varepsilon}}{1-\varepsilon}, \varepsilon \neq 1 \tag{2.9}$$

$$= \log_e(x), \varepsilon = 1, \tag{2.10}$$

where $\varepsilon > 0$ is the measure of relative risk aversion. Under this utility function, which is homothetic, Atkinson's index is equal to

$$A(\varepsilon) = 1 - \frac{1}{\mu}\left(\sum_{i=1}^{n} f_i x_i^{1-\varepsilon}\right)^{\frac{1}{1-\varepsilon}}, \varepsilon \neq 1 \tag{2.11}$$

$$= 1 - \frac{\upsilon}{\mu}, \varepsilon = 1 \tag{2.12}$$

where υ is the geometric mean that can be calculated from

$$\log_e(\upsilon) = \sum_{i=1}^{n} f_i \log_e(x). \tag{2.13}$$

The variable ε is a measure of the degree of inequality version or the indicator of relative sensitivity to income transfers at different income levels. As ε rises, more and more weight is attached to income transfers at the lower end of the distribution and less weight to transfers at the top. If $\varepsilon = 0$, it reflects an inequality-neutral attitude, in which case society does not care about inequality at all. If ε approaches infinity, then society is concerned only about the poorest person.

This corresponds to Rawls' (1958) "maximum rule," whereby the social objective is to maximize the welfare level of the worst-off individual. It is indeed a very strong egalitarian criterion, in which case only the worst-off person in the society gets all the weight in the formulation of policies. Poverty measures, however, give all the weight to individuals who are considered poor. Thus, poverty measures provide a nice compromise between the highly inegalitarian criterion of giving equal weight to everyone in the society and the highly egalitarian criterion of giving all the weight to the worst-off person in the society.

Measuring Poverty

In the measurement of poverty, the focus is on the poor. The poor are those who lack the resources to obtain the minimum necessities of life. The poverty line is the level of income that is sufficient to buy the basic needs. A person is poor if his or her income falls below the poverty line. Once we have identified the poor among the total population in the society, then the next step is to measure the intensity of poverty suffered by those below the poverty line.

Let x_i be the per capita (or per equivalent adult) income of the ith household and z be the per capita poverty threshold. The ith household is classified as poor if $x_i < z$. Define

$$r_i = 1, \text{if } x_i < z$$

$$= 0, \text{ otherwise}$$

which implies that r_i takes a value of 1 for the poor households and 0 for the nonpoor households. To measure the poverty incidence for individuals, it is necessary to assume that all persons living in a household enjoy exactly the same standard of living, so all persons living in a poor household will be classified as poor with the same degree of poverty.

The most popular measure of poverty is the head-count ratio, which is defined as the proportion of the population that is poor. If f_i is the proportion of people living in the ith household, then the head-count ratio H is computed as

$$H = \sum_{i=1}^{n} f_i r_i \qquad (2.14)$$

where n is the total number of households sampled.

The percentage of the population below the poverty line (known as the head-count ratio) does not reflect the intensity of poverty suffered by the poor. The problem is identifying how poor the poor are. Their income may lie either near the poverty line or far below it. It seems natural then to take account of the shortfall of incomes of the poor from the poverty line. Thus, an alternative measure is the poverty gap ratio, which is defined as

$$G = \sum_{i=1}^{n} f_i r_i g_i \qquad (2.15)$$

where $g_i = \dfrac{z - x_i}{z}$ is the proportional income shortfall of the ith person (from the poverty line). This measure can also be written as

$$G = HI, \qquad (2.16)$$

$$I = \frac{z - x^*}{z}, \qquad (2.17)$$

x^* being the per capita mean income of the poor and I the aggregate income gap.

The poverty gap ratio provides adequate information about the intensity of poverty if all the poor have the same income. That is because this measure is derived on the assumption that the distribution of income among the poor is of no importance. This implies that all poor are treated alike. It is obvious that a person whose income is near the poverty line has a lower degree of suffering than one whose income is far below the poverty line. Thus, the weight given to the two must differ. This prompted Sen (1976) to propose a new measure of poverty, which is sensitive to the distribution of income among the poor. His new measure is given by

$$S = HI + H(1 - I)G^*, \tag{2.18}$$

where G^* is the Gini index of the poor. Sen derived this measure based on welfare-economic ideas, linking the weights on income shortfalls to the ordering of individual incomes. This measure takes account of the relative deprivation aspect of the inequality of income among the poor.

Kakwani (1980a) provided a generalization of Sen's measure, which was motivated by the capacity of Sen's measure to satisfy some transfer-sensitivity axioms. His class of measures can be described as

$$\eta(k) = HI + H(1 - I)G(k), \tag{2.19}$$

where $G(k)$ is the generalized Gini index of the poor. The larger the value of k is, the greater is the weight given to the very poor.

Sen and Kakwani's measures of poverty are based on interdependent utility functions—that is, the utility of a person depends on the utility enjoyed by other persons in the society. There are many poverty measures in the literature that are based on additive separable social welfare functions, in which the utility enjoyed by an individual is independent of that enjoyed by others.

Foster, Greer, and Thorbecke (1984) proposed a family of additive separable poverty measures

$$F_\alpha = \sum_{i=1}^{n} a_i r_i g_i^\alpha, \tag{2.20}$$

where $g_i = \dfrac{z - x_i}{z}$. When $\alpha = 0$, F_α is equal to the head-count ratio and when $\alpha = 1$, F_α is equal to the poverty gap ratio. In order to make the measure sensitive to inequality of income among the poor, α must be greater than 1. If the measure is to satisfy Kakwani's (1980a) transfer-sensitivity axioms, α must be greater than 2. Like Kakwani's measures, the larger the value of α is, the greater is the weight given to the very poor and the less is the weight given to the less poor.

An Illustration Using Lao PDR Data

This section provides empirical estimates of inequality and poverty in the Lao People's Democratic Republic (PDR), using the Lao Expenditure and

Consumption Surveys conducted in 1992–93 and 1997–98. These were nation-wide surveys of 2,937 and 8,882 households, respectively.

Lao PDR is located in the East Asian region that has been growing rapidly during the past three decades. Like the governments of its neighbors, the government of Lao PDR has given a high priority to economic growth that is deemed to enhance the welfare of the people. To accomplish this objective, the government has emphasized the importance of macroeconomic policy management such as maintaining stable, low inflation and promoting domestic and foreign investment.

Real GDP per capita in Lao PDR grew at an annual rate of 4.6 percent between 1992–93 and 1997–98. This impressive growth has been accompanied by a sharp increase in inequality, as can be seen from the inequality estimates presented in table 2.2.

The Gini index increased from 30 percent in 1992–93 to 36.5 percent in 1997–98. The income shares of the first four quintiles declined, while that of the top quintile increased quite substantially during the five-year period. Thus, the benefits of economic growth have gone proportionally more to the very rich (the top 20 percent of the population).

TABLE 2.2 Inequality in Lao PDR

Inequality Measure	1992–93	1997–98	Change
Generalized Gini index			
$k = 1$	30.0	36.5	6.5
$k = 1.5$	35.8	42.6	6.8
$k = 2$	39.9	46.7	6.8
Quintile shares			
1st quintile	9.0	7.7	−1.2
2nd quintile	13.2	11.6	−1.5
3rd quintile	16.6	15.2	−1.4
4th quintile	21.8	20.4	−1.4
5th quintile	39.5	45.0	5.6
Theil's inequality measures			
I_0	14.6	22.1	7.4
I_1	15.9	26.8	10.9
Atkinson's measures			
$e = 1$	13.6	19.8	6.2
$e = 1.5$	19.1	26.6	7.4
$e = 2$	24.1	32.4	8.3

The empirical results in table 2.2 clearly show that whatever way we measure inequality, the rapid economic growth has led to a substantial increase in inequality. However, the different measures give different magnitudes of the increase in inequality. The magnitude increases monotonically with the parameters of relative risk aversion. It may be recalled that the higher the inequality aversion parameter is, the larger is the weight that is given to the poorer persons. From these results we may conclude that the relative benefits of the very poor have been less than those of the less poor.

To estimate poverty, we need to know the poverty line, which is the income level below which one is regarded as poor. Lao PDR does not have an official poverty line. Recently, Kakwani (2000) developed a new poverty line for the country, which adequately takes into account regional price differences and the different needs of household members by using the energy requirements of household members of different ages and genders. The empirical estimates of poverty based on the new poverty line are presented in table 2.3.

In 1992–93, 62.7 percent of the population in Lao PDR was identified as poor, whereas in 1997–98 46.9 percent fell below the poverty line. Therefore, there was a remarkable reduction in poverty during those five years. Although the rich have benefited much more than the poor, the reduction of poverty by 15.8 percentage points does indeed indicate that the benefits of economic growth have effectively trickled down to the poor. All the measures presented in table 2.3 tell the same story. The poverty gap ratio declined from 20.3 percent in 1992–93 to 13.8 percent in 1997–98. It may be recalled that Sen's poverty measure is obtained when $k = 1$ in Kakwani's generalized poverty measures. Sen's measure shows a decline of poverty by 8.3 percentage points during the five-year period.

TABLE 2.3 Poverty Measures: Lao PDR

Measure	1992–93	1997–98	Change
Poverty measure			
Head-count ratio	62.7	46.9	−15.8
Poverty gap ratio	20.3	13.8	−6.5
FGT index	8.7	5.6	−3.0
Generalized poverty measures			
$k = 1$	26.9	18.7	−8.3
$k = 1.5$	28.9	20.2	−8.7
$k = 2$	30.4	21.3	−9.0

Note: FGT refers tp Foster, Greer, and Thorbecke.

Some Concluding Remarks

This chapter has provided only a partial review of inequality and poverty measures. The focus has been on those measures that are widely mentioned in the literature. There appears to be no reason to use all the measures in the analysis of poverty and inequality because, first, there are too many of them and, second, many of them tend to tell a similar story.

These measures play an important role in monitoring the progress made by countries in reducing inequality and poverty. However, the analysis of poverty and inequality should not stop here. Attempts should be made to identify the causes of changes, keeping in view the policies followed by the government. Our ultimate objective is to improve inequality and reduce poverty, so our focus should be on reforming existing government policies. The analysis of inequality and poverty should, therefore, extend to measuring the impact of different government policies on inequality and poverty and determining how these policies can be improved.

Note

1. Yitzhaki (1983) proposed exactly the same generalization of the Gini index but interestingly did not acknowledge that it was originally Kakwani's idea.

References

Atkinson, Anthony. B. 1970. "On the Measurement of Inequality." *Journal of Economic Theory* 2: 244–63.

Dalton, Hugh. 1920. "The Measurement of the Inequality of Incomes." *The Economic Journal* 30: 348-61.

Dasgupta, Partha, Amartya K. Sen, and David Starrett. 1973. "Notes on the Measurement of Inequality." *Journal of Economic Theory* 6: 180–87.

Foster, James, Joel Greer, and Erik Thorbecke. 1984. "A Class of Decomposable Poverty Measures." *Econometrica* 52: 761–65.

Kakwani, Nanak. 1980a. "On a Class of Poverty Measures." *Econometrica* 48 (2): 437–46.

———. 1980b. *Income Inequality and Poverty: Methods of Estimation and Policy Applications.* New York: Oxford University Press.

———. 2000. "Poverty in Lao PDR." Unpublished paper, Asian Development Bank, Manila.

Rawls, John. 1958. "Justice as Fairness." *Philosophical Review* 67 (2): 164–94.

Rothschild, Michael, and Joseph E. Stiglitz. 1973. "Some Further Results on the Measurement of Inequality." *Journal of Economic Theory* 6: 188–204.

Sen, Amartya. 1973. *On Economic Inequality.* Oxford, U.K.: Clarendon Press.

———. 1976. "Poverty: An Ordinal Approach to Measurement." *Econometrica* 44: 219–31.

Theil, Henri. 1967. *Economics and Information Theory.* Amsterdam: North-Holland.

Yitzhaki, Shlomo. 1983. "On an Extension of the Gini Coefficient." *Quarterly Journal of Economics* 24: 617–28.

On Assessing the Equity of Governments' Fiscal Policies, with Application to the Philippines

HYUN SON

A fiscal system may be defined as progressive if it redistributes income from the rich to the poor; it is regressive if it redistributes income from the poor to the rich. This redistribution can happen through the way the government collects and spends its revenue. Unfortunately, equity is generally not an overriding objective of government policies. Governments make policies while keeping in view a multiplicity of objectives. It is, therefore, important to know how equitable a government's fiscal systems are.

This chapter is concerned with the assessment of government fiscal policies from the equity point of view. This focus does not imply that efficiency should be completely ignored in analyzing government policies. However, if our main concern is with poverty reduction, then the social welfare function, which forms the basis for assessing policies, should give greater weight to those at the bottom of the income distribution and less weight to those at the middle or the top end of the income distribution. In such situations, the contribution of efficiency to social welfare will be small.

This article was published previously (2003) in *Public Finance/Finance Publiques* 53(3-4): 452-69. Permission to reprint was granted by the publisher.

To assess and reform government policies, we require a social welfare function that can be put in practice. It should also be flexible enough to allow—in a simple way—changing the weights given to individuals at different segments of income distribution. This chapter proposes to use a class of homothetic social welfare functions proposed earlier by Atkinson (1970) in connection with the measurement of inequality. This class of social welfare function depends on an inequality aversion parameter, through which one can change the weights given to individuals in different segments of the income distribution.

This chapter derives the welfare elasticity for the Atkinson's class of social welfare function. Using the idea of welfare elasticity, the chapter proposes a welfare reform index that can be used to assess fiscal policies with a view to bringing about marginal reforms. This index may be helpful in making a fiscal system more equitable through marginal reforms.

The methodology developed in the chapter is applied to the Philippines using the 1998 Annual Poverty Indicator Survey (APIS). This survey gathers detailed information on different sources of income and expenditures from 78 provinces and from all the cities and municipalities of Metro Manila.[1]

The chapter is organized as follows. The second section discusses the welfare measures. The welfare elasticity of income components is derived in the third section. The fourth section develops the welfare reform index. The fifth section deals with the indirect taxes and subsidies. An overview of the Philippines' fiscal system is presented in the sixth section. The seventh section presents the case study for the Philippines. Some concluding remarks are presented in the last section.

Welfare Measures

To derive a welfare measure, it is assumed that social welfare is the sum of individual utilities that are functions of their respective incomes, and that every individual has the same utility function. The social welfare function based on these assumptions will be additive, separable, and symmetric.

Suppose x is the per equivalent adult income of a household. Because households are selected randomly, we may assume that x is a random variable with probability density function $f(x)$. In addition, assume that $n(x)$ is the number of individuals in a household with per equivalent adult income x. Thus, the average number of individuals in the society will be given by

$$E(n(x)) = \int_0^\infty n(x)f(x)dx \qquad (3.1)$$

Because we generally do not know how the total household welfare is distributed among household members, it is reasonable to assume that every individual in a household enjoys exactly the same level of welfare irrespective of age and sex. Hence, the probability density function of individual income distribution can be defined as

$$g(x) = \frac{n(x)f(x)}{E(n(x))} \tag{3.2}$$

such that $\int_0^\infty g(x)dx = 1$. If $u(x)$ is the individual utility function, then the average welfare of the society will be given by

$$W = \int_0^\infty u(x)g(x)dx \tag{3.3}$$

Atkinson (1970) proposed a welfare measure that is invariant with respect to any positive linear transformation of individual utilities. It is derived from the concept of the equally distributed equivalent level of income, x^*, the level which, if received by every individual, would result in the same level of social welfare as the present distribution, that is,

$$u(x^*) = \int_0^\infty u(x)g(x)dx \tag{3.4}$$

where x^* is per person welfare measure of the society and a measure of social welfare in terms of income.

The inequality measure proposed by Atkinson is

$$I = 1 - \frac{x^*}{\mu} \tag{3.5}$$

Where μ, given by

$$\mu = \int_0^\infty xg(x)dx, \tag{3.6}$$

is adjusted (for the household composition) mean income of the society. Using (3.5), the social welfare, x^*, can be written as

$$x^* = \mu(1 - I) \tag{3.7}$$

which shows that the social welfare, x^*, depends on the two factors—mean income and inequality in the society. Because this welfare measure is sensitive to inequality, it allows us to evaluate the relative impact of government policies on the poor and the nonpoor.

If the inequality measure I is to be scale-independent, the utility function must be homothetic. A class of homothetic utility functions is given by

$$\mu(x) = A + B \frac{x^{1-\varepsilon}}{1-\varepsilon}, \varepsilon \neq 1$$

$$= A + B \log x, \varepsilon = 1 \tag{3.8}$$

where $B > 0$ and A and B are any two constants. Note that ε is a measure of the degree of inequality aversion. As ε rises, greater weight is given to transfers at the lower end of the distribution and less weight to transfers at the top. If $\varepsilon = 0$, it reflects an inequality-neutral attitude, in which case the social welfare is measured by the mean income of society. The larger the value of ε, the greater is the concern of the society about inequality. When ε approaches infinity, the society becomes most concerned about the poorest person. In this case, social welfare is measured by the income of the poorest person in the society. Thus, ε is a measure of society's concern about inequality, which is generally not estimated from the data. In our analysis of the equity of the fiscal system, we assume alternative values of ε equal to 0, 1, and 2.

Substituting (3.8) into (3.4) gives the average welfare level of the society as

$$x* = \left[\int_0^\infty x^{1-\varepsilon} g(x) dx \right]^{\frac{1}{(1-\varepsilon)}}, \varepsilon \neq 1$$

$$= \exp\left[\int_0^\infty \log xg(x) dx \right], \varepsilon = 1 \tag{3.9}$$

where exp stands for exponential. Note that $x*$ is independent of A and B, which implies that the social welfare measure $x*$ is invariant to any positive linear transformation of the utility functions. Substituting $x*$ into (3.5) gives Atkinson's measure of inequality for different values of the aversion parameter ε.

Welfare and Income Components

The total income of an individual is equal to the sum of all income components. Let $v_i(x)$ be equal to the ith income component of an individual having the total per equivalent adult income x. Thus,

$$x = \sum_{i=1}^{k} v_i(x) \qquad (3.10)$$

Suppose μ_i is the mean income of the ith income component. Therefore,

$$\mu_i = \int_0^\infty v_i(x)g(x)dx \qquad (3.11)$$

where $g(x)$ is the individual density function, as defined in (3.2). Combining (3.10) and (3.11) gives

$$\mu = \sum_{i=1}^{k} \mu_i \qquad (3.12)$$

If individuals (or households) are arranged in ascending order of their income x, one can construct the Lorenz function $L(p)$, which is the income share of the bottom $100 \times p$ percent of the individuals. Similarly, one may construct the concentration curve $C_i(p)$, which is the share of the ith income component of the bottom $100 \times p$ percent of individuals when individuals are arranged in ascending order of their total income x.

Using the properties of the Lorenz and concentration curves given in Kakwani (1977, 1980), we obtain

$$x = \mu L'(p) \qquad (3.13)$$

and

$$v_i(x) = \mu_i C'(p) \qquad (3.14)$$

where $L'(p)$ and $C'(p)$ are the first derivatives of $L(p)$ and $C_i(p)$ with respect to p, respectively. Substituting (3.13) and (3.14) into (3.10) gives

$$x = \mu L'(p) = \sum_{i=1}^{k} \mu_i C_i'(p) \qquad (3.15)$$

We may now write the welfare measure x^* defined in (3.4) as

$$u(x*) = \int_0^1 \mu \left[\sum_{i=1}^{k} \mu_i C_i'(p) \right] dp \qquad (3.16)$$

where $dp = g(x)dx$, $0 < p < 1$, and $0 < x < \infty$. This equation enables us to measure the effect on social welfare of a small change in the mean income of the ith component.

We assume that the mean of the ith income component changes without affecting its distribution across individuals: $C_i'(p)$ remains constant when μ_i changes. Differentiating (3.16) with respect to μ_i yields

$$u'(x^*)\frac{\partial x^*}{\partial \mu_i} = \int_0^1 u'\left[\sum_{i=1}^k \mu_i C_i'(p)\right]C_i'(p)dp,$$

which gives the elasticity of x^* with respect to μ_i as

$$\eta_i = \frac{\partial x^*}{\partial \mu_i}\frac{\mu_i}{x^*} = \frac{1}{x^* u'(x^*)}\int_0^\infty u'(x)v_i(x)g(x)dx, \tag{3.17}$$

where (3.13) and (3.14) are used. If the mean of the ith income component changes by 1 percent, the social welfare x^* will be changed by η_i percent.

Following similar reasoning, we can derive the elasticity of x^* with respect to μ as

$$\eta = \frac{1}{x^* u'(x^*)}\int_0^\infty u'(x)xg(x)dx, \tag{3.18}$$

It can be easily seen from (3.17) and (3.18) that

$$\eta = \sum_{i=1}^k \eta_i, \tag{3.19}$$

which always holds. This equation shows that if all income components change by 1 percent, the social welfare x^* changes by η percent.

Let us assume that the utility function is homothetic, as defined in (3.8). Thus, substituting (3.8) into (3.17) gives

$$\eta_i = \frac{\displaystyle\int_0^\infty x^{-\varepsilon}v_i(x)g(x)dx}{\displaystyle\int_0^\infty x^{1-\varepsilon}g(x)dx}, \varepsilon \neq 1$$

$$= \int_0^\infty \frac{v_i(x)}{x}g(x)dx, \varepsilon = 1 \tag{3.20}$$

and $\eta = 1$ for all values of ε, which from (3.20) implies that $\sum_{i=1}^k \eta_i = 1$. This result indicates that if η_i is greater than 1, we can say that the ith income component is welfare superior; if it is less than 1, the ith income component is welfare inferior. Thus, the welfare elasticity in (3.20) enables us to measure the effect on the society's total welfare of a small change in the ith income component: the higher the value of this elasticity is, the greater will be the welfare superiority of that income component.

Welfare Reform Index

This section derives a welfare reform index that may help bring about marginal reforms in governments' tax and expenditure policies. Atkinson's measure of inequality denoted by I is defined in (3.5). To measure the effect on inequality of a small change in μ_i, we derive the elasticity of I with respect to μ_i as

$$\delta_i = \frac{\partial I}{\partial \mu_i} \frac{\mu_i}{I} = -\frac{x^*}{(\mu - x^*)}\left[\eta_i - \frac{\mu_i}{\mu}\right],\tag{3.21}$$

where use has been made of (3.5) and (3.12). This equation can be written as

$$\eta_i = \frac{\mu_i}{\mu} - \frac{(\mu - x^*)}{x^*}\delta_i\tag{3.22}$$

The first term on the right-hand side of (3.22) is the share of the ith income component in total income. It may be called the *income effect*. It is the percentage change in the mean income of the society when the mean income of the ith component changes by 1 percent.[2] The second component on the right-hand side of (3.22) may be called the *inequality effect*: it is the percentage change in total welfare as a result of income redistribution caused by the change in the ith income component.

It is the inequality effect that tells us whether an increase in μ_i favors the rich or the poor. If this component is positive, it means that the redistribution effect of the ith income component increases social welfare; if it is negative, the redistribution effect decreases social welfare. This leads us to suggest a welfare reform index

$$\phi_i = \frac{\eta_i}{s_i} - 1,\tag{3.23}$$

where $s_i = \dfrac{\mu_i}{\mu}$

and is the share of the ith income component in total income. If ϕ_i is positive, it means that any increase in the ith income component will benefit the poor proportionally more than the rich; if it is negative, any increase will benefit the poor proportionally less than the rich. The term ϕ_i measures the marginal benefits in terms of increasing social welfare of an extra dollar spent on the ith income component.

Suppose i and j are two different government transfer programs. If $\phi_i > \phi_j$, then one dollar spent on the ith program will lead to a greater increase in social welfare than one dollar spent on the jth program. In other words, we can improve social welfare by cutting down the expenditure on the jth program and increasing the expenditure on the ith program by the same amount. Thus, ϕ_i can be usefully employed to bring about marginal reform in governments' tax and expenditure policies.

Indirect Taxes and Subsidies

To bring welfare reforms to indirect taxes and subsidies, we will need to measure the impact of price changes on social welfare. This task can be accomplished by deriving welfare elasticity with respect to the prices of individual commodities. To derive the elasticity, let us write the disposable income as

$$x = \sum_{i=1}^{m} p_i q_i(x) + S(x) \tag{3.24}$$

where p_i is the price of the ith commodity and $q_i(x)$ is the quantity of the ith commodity consumed by an individual whose disposable income is x, where $i = 1, 2, \ldots, m$. $S(x)$ is the saving of the individual with income x.

Suppose that, because of indirect taxes and subsidies, the price vector $\tilde{p}$ changes to $\tilde{p}^*$. How will this change affect the individual's real income? To answer this question, we consider the cost function $e(u, \tilde{p})$, which is the minimum cost required to obtain u level of utility when the price vector is $\tilde{p}$. The real income of the individual with income x will change by

$$\Delta x = -[e(u, p^*) - e(u, p)], \tag{3.25}$$

which, on using Taylor's expansion, gives

$$\Delta x = -\sum_{i=1}^{m} (p_i - p_i^*) q_i(x)$$

This equation immediately gives

$$\frac{\partial x}{\partial p_i} = -q_i(x) \tag{3.26}$$

Differentiating (3.4) with respect to p_i and utilizing (3.26) gives

$$u'(x^*)\frac{\partial x^*}{\partial p_i} = -\int_0^\infty u'(x)q_i(x)g(x)dx$$

This gives the elasticity of x^* with respect to p_i as

$$\varepsilon_i = \frac{\partial x^*}{\partial p_i}\frac{p_i}{x^*} = -\frac{p_i}{x^* u'(x^*)}\int_0^\infty u'(x)q_i(x)g(x)dx, \tag{3.27}$$

which will be negative because it is assumed that given other things, any price increase in goods and services will reduce individuals' real income, which will thus reduce social welfare.[3] It will be useful to write

$$\varepsilon_i = -\frac{p_i\bar{q}_i}{\mu} + \left(\varepsilon_i + \frac{p_i\bar{q}_i}{\mu}\right), \tag{3.28}$$

where μ is the mean income of the disposable income and $p_i\bar{q}_i$ is the mean expenditure of the ith commodity.

The first term in (3.28) is the income effect of the price increase, and the second term is the redistribution or inequality effect of price change. The redistribution effect tells us whether an increase in price p_i hurts the poor more than the rich. If this component is positive, it suggests that the ith price increase hurts the rich more than the poor. This leads us to suggest the price reform index:

$$\delta_i = \frac{\varepsilon_i\mu}{p_i\bar{q}_i} + 1 \tag{3.29}$$

If δ_i is positive, an increase in the ith price hurts the rich more than the poor; if it is negative, an increase hurts the poor more than the rich. Thus, if δ_i is negative, then the ith commodity should be subsidized so that the poor benefit more than the rich. On this account, δ_i can be used to improve the tax or subsidy systems so that the maximum improvement in social welfare is obtained with a given marginal reform.

An Overview of the Philippines' Fiscal System

Like many Asian countries, the Philippines' fiscal system is highly centralized. The national government collects most of the taxation revenue and also spends most of it. The local governments collect a very small share of revenue through taxation. Table 3.1 presents the overall revenue structure of

TABLE 3.1 Fiscal System in the Philippines: 1998

Different Types of Taxes	Actual Tax in Revenue (million pesos)	Distribution of Taxes (%)	Tax as % of GNP
Net income and profits	**183,914**	**39.76**	**6.58**
Individual income tax	61,755	13.35	2.21
Corporate income tax	75,153	16.25	2.69
Tax on T-bills	15,885	3.43	0.57
Commercial papers	2	0.00	0.00
Bank deposits	26,732	5.78	0.96
Capital gains tax	4,387	0.95	0.16
Excise taxes	**62,755**	**13.57**	**2.25**
Alcohol products	12,428	2.69	0.44
Tobacco products	16,768	3.63	0.60
Fuel and oil	30,758	6.65	1.10
Mining	124	0.03	0.00
Automobiles	2,629	0.57	0.09
Tobacco inspection fee	32	0.01	0.00
Miscellaneous	16	0.00	0.00
Sales tax, VAT and licenses	**67,865**	**14.67**	**2.43**
Banks/financial institutions	11,549	2.50	0.41
Insurance premium	481	0.10	0.02
Amusement	332	0.07	0.01
VAT	47,539	10.28	1.70
Franchise tax	2,261	0.49	0.08
Other percentage taxes[a]	4,037	0.87	0.14
O.W. stock transaction tax	1,666	0.36	0.06
Other domestic taxes	**22,641**	**4.90**	**0.81**
Documentary stamp tax	18,915	4.09	0.68
Tax on property	469	0.10	0.02
Travel tax	180	0.04	0.01
Miscellaneous	3,077	0.67	0.11
Import taxes	**76,005**	**16.43**	**2.72**
Import duties	48,792	10.55	1.75
VAT on imports	27,213	5.88	0.97
Other taxes	**3,405**	**0.74**	**0.12**
Total tax revenue	**416,585**	**90.07**	**14.91**
Nontax revenue	**45,931**	**9.93**	**1.64**
Total revenues	**462,516**	**100.00**	**16.55**

Source: National Statistical Office 1998.
Note: a. These are percentage taxes, which are applied at varying rates to sales of various services, including cars for rent or hire; domestic and international carriers; franchises; international communications services; banks and nonbanks intermediaries, and so on.

both the national and local governments. It can be seen that the major source of government revenue comes from taxation. Nontax revenue is only 9.93 percent of the total revenue. It is worth pointing out that in the past, tax collection in the Philippines has failed to harness its full potential. Although the revenue effort has been similar to that in Thailand and Indonesia, it has collected lower amounts than the efforts in Malaysia and Korea (Rodlauer and others 2000).

The revenue share of direct taxes is almost 40 percent in the Philippines, which is quite high compared with other East Asian countries such as Thailand. The individual income tax contributes only 13.35 percent to total government revenue. The corporate income tax, which is levied on the net income of companies, provides the major share—16.25 percent in 1998.

Within the indirect tax structure, three taxes dominate. They are import taxes (which include import duties and value added tax [VAT] on imports), VAT, and excise or selective sales taxes. The most dominant indirect tax is the VAT, which is a sales tax levied on the producers and importers of goods and services based on their gross sales receipts or import values. The share of VAT on domestically produced goods and services is 10.28 percent, while that on imports is 5.88 percent. The excise taxes in the Philippines are levied on a few sumptuary items such as tobacco and liquor, automobiles, and petroleum products. The contribution of these taxes to total revenue is 13.57 percent.

The property and capital gains taxes can be progressive but their combined share is only 1.05 percent, which is expected to have a very small impact on the total redistributive impact of taxes. The local governments collect the major share of their revenues from real property taxes. The administration of these taxes is rather weak and is based mostly on outdated property and land values. Thus, local government taxes have negligible impacts on equity.

Total government revenue as a percentage of gross national product (GNP) in the Philippines is 16.55, while government expenditure is 19.23 percent of GNP. Thus the government is running a budget deficit, which is 2.68 percent of GNP. This is not a large budget deficit, given that 1998 was the year most affected by the economic crisis, which would have adversely affected the tax revenue. It seems that policy makers responded appropriately to the regional financial crisis by allowing the fiscal deficit to rise in line with the slowing economy.

Table 3.2 shows the distribution of government expenditures classified by function. Of the five major functions—namely, economic services, social

TABLE 3.2 Government Expenditures by Functional Classification

Functional Classification	Actual Expenditure (million pesos)	Distribution of Expenditure (%)	Expenditure as % of GNP
Economic services	129,394	24.08	4.63
Social services	175,152	32.59	6.27
Education	106,850	19.88	3.82
Health	13,542	2.52	0.48
Social security and labor welfare	22,755	4.23	0.81
Housing and community development	2,792	0.52	0.10
Other social services	745	0.14	0.03
Subsidy to local governments	28,468	5.30	1.02
Defense	31,512	5.86	1.13
General public service	101,254	18.84	3.62
Net lending	329	0.06	0.01
Debt servicing	99,792	18.57	3.57
Total government expenditure	537,433	100.00	19.23

Source: National Statistical Office 1998.

services, defense, general public service, and debt servicing—social services ranks first in terms of its share of total expenditure (32.59 percent). Further breakdown of social services spending shows that education is the major item of expenditure, at 19.88 percent. The share of health expenditure is very small, only 2.52 percent of the total. This is because health services are provided on the basis of the user pays principle, so the poor may not be receiving adequate health services because they cannot afford to pay.

Economic service is the second biggest item of government expenditure. Almost one-fourth of the budget is devoted to this item, which includes spending on agricultural development and infrastructure. Surprisingly, the defense expenditure is only 5.86 percent of the total budget, which is quite small relative to its neighbors. For instance, the Thai government spends about 15 percent of its total budget on defense.

The government of the Philippines spends 99,792 million pesos—equivalent to 3.57 of its budget—on debt servicing, which is a very heavy burden for any government. These substantial debt service payments could have constrained policy choices, particularly by limiting much-needed outlays for infrastructure and social sectors, such as education and health. This in turn suggests that the government does not have enough resources to tackle the severe poverty that exists in the Philippines (Kakwani 2000).

Basis for Measuring Distributional Effects

To assess the distributional effects of various government policies we need a measure of individual welfare that can be used to measure the distribution. The most commonly used indicator of welfare is income. The concept of income must include all the components that have an impact on people's welfare. This chapter uses a fairly comprehensive income concept, which includes[4]

- wages and salary from employment
- imputed rent of owner-occupied dwelling
- value of home consumption goods
- income from entrepreneurial activities, including
  — family sustenance activities
  — crop farming and gardening
  — livestock and poultry raising
  — fishing
  — forestry and hunting
  — wholesale and retail
  — manufacturing
  — community, social, recreational, and personal services
  — transport, storage, and communication services
- other sources of income
  — transfers from abroad
  — transfers from domestic sources
  — rental income and imputed rent from owner-occupied house
  — interest
  — pensions, social security, and workers' compensation[5]
  — dividends
  — other incomes

Because taxes that people pay do not make a direct contribution to their welfare, we use the concept of disposable income, which is total income minus direct taxes.

The economic welfare of households is determined not only by their income but also by their needs. Because households differ in size, age composition, and other characteristics, it is expected that they will have different needs. In a recent study, Kakwani (2000) developed poverty thresholds that account for the different needs of people living in households.[6] Because these poverty thresholds adequately account for the different needs of households, it is appropriate to measure household welfare by the ratio of per capita disposable income of a household to the per capita poverty threshold of that household. This measure of welfare can be interpreted as the percentage of excess income a household has over its basic needs.

Once the welfare index of a household is constructed, the next step is to determine the welfare of the individuals in the household. In the study, individual welfare was derived by assigning every individual in a household a value equal to the per capita welfare level of that household. Thus, government fiscal policies are assessed with respect to the distribution of per capita welfare, which, in fact, is the needs-adjusted per capita disposable income derived from the households. Each income component and income tax paid by individuals was divided by the household-specific poverty line, so the total per capita welfare can be expressed as the sum of the individual income components minus income tax. The welfare elasticity of each income component and income tax was then calculated using the formula given in (3.20) for the alternative values of the inequality aversion parameter. Given the values of elasticity and income shares from the APIS data, the welfare reform index was computed using the formula given in (3.23).

Analysis of Empirical Results

Table 3.3 presents the values of welfare elasticity and the welfare reform index for different income components. Public policies can be assessed for different values of the inequality aversion parameter. When the inequality aversion parameter is zero, the society does not care about inequality and thus any improvement or deterioration in income distribution will have no impact on social welfare, in which case the welfare reform index will always be zero. Thus, the inequality aversion parameter should always be greater than zero.

As pointed out, the higher the value of the inequality aversion parameter, the greater is the weight given to the transfer of income at the lower end of the income distribution. If our concern were with the poor, then we would choose a higher value for the inequality aversion parameter. For our analysis we selected two values, namely, 1 and 2.[7]

It can be seen that welfare elasticity varies widely for different income components. If, for instance, wage and salary income increases by 1 percent, per capita welfare will increase by 0.45 and 0.375 percent when the values of the inequality parameter are 1 and 2. Thus, the elasticity of wage and salary income declines when the inequality aversion parameter is increased. This implies that wage and salary income is not concentrated much among the very poor. The welfare elasticity of income from family sustenance activities increases substantially, from 0.035 to 0.063, when the value of the inequality

TABLE 3.3 Welfare Reform Index for Income Components:
Philippines, 1998

Sources of Income	Percent Shares	Aversion Parameter = 1		Aversion Parameter = 2	
		Welfare Elasticity	Welfare Reform Index	Welfare Elasticity	Welfare Reform Index
Family sustenance	1.4	0.035	1.45	0.063	3.39
Crop by other households	0.8	0.008	0.06	0.009	0.13
Crop farming	3.7	0.074	1.01	0.108	1.94
Poultry	0.3	0.005	0.69	0.007	1.27
Fishing	0.5	0.011	1.14	0.014	1.73
Hunting	0.0	0.001	1.35	0.001	2.51
Wholesale and retail trade	2.4	0.019	−0.20	0.016	−0.34
Manufacturing	0.1	0.001	0.18	0.001	0.27
Services	0.4	0.003	−0.13	0.003	−0.32
Construction	0.0	0.000	−0.13	0.001	1.31
Transport	0.6	0.005	−0.06	0.004	−0.23
Mining	0.3	0.001	−0.84	0.000	−0.93
Entrepreneurial activity	0.1	0.001	−0.29	0.001	−0.31
Wages and salary	47.1	0.450	−0.04	0.375	−0.20
Overseas transfers	7.6	0.044	−0.43	0.023	−0.70
Domestic transfers	2.7	0.037	0.38	0.046	0.70
Rent from property	1.0	0.005	−0.56	0.002	−0.78
Interest	0.3	0.001	−0.68	0.000	−0.86
Pensions & social security	2.6	0.015	−0.44	0.008	−0.68
Dividends	0.2	0.000	−0.78	0.000	−0.90
Other sources	0.5	0.004	−0.27	0.005	−0.05
Imputed rent	28.3	0.286	0.01	0.318	0.12
Income Tax	−1.1	−0.006	0.44	−0.004	0.59
Total disposable income	**100.0**	**1.000**	**0.00**	**1.000**	**0.00**

Source: The author's calculations based on the 1998 APIS.

aversion parameter is increased from 1 to 2. This increase implies that the poor depend more heavily on family sustenance income than the nonpoor do.

As pointed out, the welfare reform index can be used to make government policies more equitable through marginal reforms. The positive value of ϕ_i indicates that any increase in the ith component redistributes income from the rich to the poor, resulting in a higher level of social welfare. Also, the higher the value of ϕ_i is, the greater will be the benefits to the poor. For instance, ϕ_i has the highest value of 3.39 for family sustenance income, which means that any subsidy given to households whose main income source is sustenance farming will help the poor much more than the rich.[8] Similarly, government subsidies given to households whose main income sources are hunting, crop farming, and crop farming by other households[9] will benefit the poor more than the rich. Since the shares of hunting and crop farming in total income are very small, they have negligible impacts on equity.

It is generally believed that the major source of income for the poor is wages and salary and that therefore any policy that increases wage and salary income will be pro-poor. This proposition is not supported by the empirical results. The welfare reform index for wage and salary income is −0.2, which means that any increase in wage and salary income will benefit the rich more than the poor. The income components that do not favor the poor are rent from property, interest, pensions and social security benefits, and dividends.

It is interesting to note that pensions and social security payments, which are mostly provided by the government, go more to the nonpoor than to the poor. The welfare reform index for this component is −0.68, indicating that pensions and social security payments are highly regressive.[10]

In the Philippines, overseas transfers contribute 7.6 percent to total disposable income. A general perception is that these transfers help poor families. This is not supported by the empirical results. The value of the welfare reform index for these transfers is −0.70, which shows that overseas transfers are highly regressive, supporting rich families more than poor families, indicating that remittances from overseas tend to increase inequality. By contrast, domestic transfers have the opposite effect. The value of the welfare reform index for domestic transfers is 0.70, which suggests that transfers within the country tend to reduce inequality.

The personal income tax is progressive, as indicated by the value of the welfare reform index, which is equal to 0.59. The magnitude of the index shows that the degree of progressivity is rather small. The government collects only about 13 percent of its revenue from income tax. Thus, there is scope to increase the revenue from income tax by increasing the tax rates on higher incomes, which will also increase the progressivity of income tax.

The Philippine government collects 16.25 percent of its revenue from corporate income tax. Due to international capital mobility, one can assume that the burden of corporate income tax falls on labor so that it is proportional to wage and salary income. The value of the welfare reform index for tax on wage and salary income is 0.20, which shows that corporate income tax is progressive but the degree of progressivity is very small. As a matter of fact, we may characterize it as being proportional.

Table 3.4 gives the values of welfare elasticity with respect to prices. Because increases in prices reduce people's real income, all values of welfare elasticity are negative. The price reform index can be either positive or negative. A negative value of the price reform index implies that the increase in prices hurts the poor more than the rich; a positive value implies that the increase hurts the poor less than the rich. The index is highly negative for roots and tubers and cereals, which indicates that subsidizing these items will benefit the poor much more than the rich. The value of the price reform index for all food items consumed at home is −1.80, suggesting that any indirect tax on food is highly regressive and will hurt the poor more than the rich. However, a tax on food consumed outside the home is mildly progressive, having a price reform index value equal to 0.16.

It is generally believed that the indirect tax system with a single uniform tax rate such as value added taxes can be made progressive by exempting food items. This belief is not supported by the empirical results, in view of the fact that the tax on nonfood items is also regressive, having a price reform index value equal to −0.57. However, an indirect tax can be made progressive if we have higher tax rates on luxuries, lower rates on necessities, and zero tax rates on most essential goods and services. Such a tax system can be designed using our proposed price reform index. The commodities with positive values of the price reform index would attract lower tax rates; those with negative values would attract higher tax rates. Unfortunately, as our empirical results in table 3.4 show, only a few commodities have positive values of the price reform index. This suggests that it will be difficult to design an indirect tax system that would be more progressive.

The values of the price reform index for alcohol and tobacco are −2.22 and −1.70, respectively, implying that the burden of taxation on these items is borne heavily by the poor. The Philippine government collects 6.32 percent of its total revenue through excise taxes on tobacco and alcohol products.

It is interesting to note that expenditures on education and health care are regressive; the poor spend proportionately more than the rich, as indicated by the negative values of the price reform index. Thus, there is a clear need to target government expenditure to the health and education of the poor.

It is also interesting to note that the price reform index for education is +0.05 when the aversion parameter is 1 but it decreases to −0.53 when the aversion parameter is 2. How can we explain this? One possible explanation is that tax on education is most detrimental to the ultra poor, who have to spend proportionally much higher shares of their income on education

TABLE 3.4 Price Reform Index for Expenditures: Philippines, 1998

Expenditure items	Percent Shares	Aversion Parameter = 1		Aversion Parameter = 2	
		Welfare Elasticity	Price Reform Index	Welfare Elasticity	Price Reform Index
Cereal	11.60	−0.217	−0.87	−0.393	−2.39
Fruit and vegetables	3.08	−0.043	−0.40	−0.088	−1.86
Meat	5.46	−0.063	−0.16	−0.107	−0.95
Fish	5.64	−0.088	−0.56	−0.159	−1.83
Dairy products and eggs	2.34	−0.027	−0.14	−0.040	−0.71
Drink	1.21	−0.014	−0.13	−0.032	−1.69
Coffee	1.23	−0.018	−0.50	−0.043	−2.52
Roots and tubers	0.76	−0.014	−0.78	−0.031	−3.12
Other food	3.03	−0.045	−0.47	−0.066	−1.18
Food consumed at home	34.34	−0.528	−0.54	−0.961	−1.80
Food consumed outside home	3.93	−0.037	0.05	−0.033	0.16
Alcohol	0.81	−0.012	−0.51	−0.026	−2.22
Clothing and footwear	1.93	−0.023	−0.21	−0.030	−0.58
Durable furnishings	0.59	−0.004	0.27	−0.003	0.41
Nondurable furnishings	0.19	−0.002	−0.04	−0.002	−0.23
Household operations	1.86	−0.021	−0.13	−0.036	−0.94
Personal care	1.84	−0.022	−0.22	−0.033	−0.77
House maintenance and repairs	1.10	−0.009	0.15	−0.008	0.25
Education	4.11	−0.039	0.05	−0.063	−0.53
Recreation	0.30	−0.002	0.23	−0.003	−0.05
Medical care	2.50	−0.025	−0.02	−0.030	−0.19
Gifts	0.57	−0.004	0.27	−0.006	0.01
Tobacco	1.33	−0.022	−0.64	−0.036	−1.70
Transport and communication	3.79	−0.036	0.06	−0.044	−0.17
Fuel, light and water	4.80	−0.060	−0.25	−0.092	−0.93
Special family occasions	1.66	−0.017	−0.05	−0.031	−0.87
Other expenditures	1.82	−0.011	0.39	−0.013	0.28
Imputed and actual rent	11.55	−0.098	0.15	−0.105	0.09
Food expenditure	38.26	−0.566	−0.48	−0.994	−1.60
Non-food excluding rent	29.22	−0.312	−0.07	−0.457	−0.57
Food and nonfood	67.48	−0.878	−0.30	−1.451	−1.15
Total expenditure	**79.03**	**−0.976**	**−0.23**	**−1.556**	**−0.97**
Savings	20.97	−0.024	0.89	0.556	3.65

Source: The author's calculations based on the 1998 APIS.

compared with the poor. This suggests that the government should particularly provide a subsidy on education to the ultra poor in order to achieve the maximum improvement in social welfare.

Some Concluding Remarks

This chapter makes two major contributions. First, it develops a general methodology to assess government fiscal policies from the point of view of equity. Second, it provides an analysis of the Philippines' fiscal system in view of making some marginal reforms. The study shows that there is considerable scope to make the Philippines' fiscal policies more equitable. The current system is regressive and benefits the rich proportionately more than the poor.

Notes

1. This study uses the unit record data from the Annual Poverty Indicator Survey (APIS), which consists of 38,000 sample households. The raw data were made available to us by the Philippine government's National Statistical Office in Manila.
2. The proof of this proposition is as follows: Differentiate (3.12) with respect to μ_i to obtain $\dfrac{\partial \mu}{\partial \mu_i} \dfrac{\mu_i}{\mu} = \dfrac{\mu_i}{\mu}$, which proves the proposition.
3. The indirect taxation reduces social welfare through price increases. However, if taxes are used as an instrument of public (social) expenditure, it is possible that social welfare may increase. Therefore, to see the ultimate effect of taxation on equity, we should also analyze how government expenditures affect the poor. The indicators presented in this chapter can deal with both issues.
4. The detailed listing of all income components is given in table 3.3.
5. The government of the Philippines provides pensions to its employees. Some very large companies also provide pensions to their executives, but such schemes are very limited. As for social security benefits, while public employees are covered under the Government Service Insurance System, private sector employees have to enroll at the Philippine Health Insurance Corporation and the Social Security System. Workers' compensation benefits are given to workers who became handicapped by accidents during employment.
6. The poverty threshold is set using the calorie requirements of individuals, which differs by age and gender within households. The poverty line also takes into account different costs of living between regions and areas in the Philippines. Kakwani (2000) provides a good discussion on how to construct a poverty threshold that addresses both consistency and specificity in the context of the Philippines.
7. We believe that these two values adequately capture the poor and ultra poor.
8. Family sustenance income is the imputed value of family-produced goods for home consumption.
9. Crops produced by other households are the imputed values of share of crops, fruits, and vegetables produced, or livestock and poultry raised by other households.
10. Pensions in the Philippines are given only to the government's employees. Thus, the poor do not benefit from the pensions.

References

Atkinson, Anthony. B. 1970. "On the Measurement of Inequality." *Journal of Economic Theory* 2: 244–63.

Kakwani, Nanak. 1977. "Application of Lorenz Curves in Economic Analysis." *Econometrica* 45: 719–27.

———. 1980. *Income Inequality and Poverty: Methods of Estimation and Policy Application.* New York: Oxford University Press.

———. 2000. "Poverty, Inequality and Well-Being in the Philippines." Unpublished paper, Asian Development Bank, Manila.

National Statistical Office. 1998. *The Annual Poverty Indicator Survey.* Manila: Government of the Philippines.

Rodlauer, Markus, Prakash Loungani, V. Arora, and C. Christofides. 2000. "Philippines: Toward Sustainable and Rapid Growth." IMF Occasional Paper 187, International Monetary Fund, Washington, DC.

Evaluating Public Pensions

ROBIN BOADWAY AND KATHERINE CUFF

The Imperative for Public Pension Reform and Development

Virtually all countries of the Organisation for Economic Co-operation and Development (OECD) and an increasing number of developing countries have some form of public pension system. In a substantial proportion of them, reform has been or still is on the policy agenda. A good deal of thought has gone into public pension reform in the context of both OECD countries (Ahmad, Drèze, and Stern 1991; Disney and Johnson 2001) and developing countries (World Bank 1994). The purpose of this chapter is to provide a concise summary of lessons learned and the economic reasoning behind them. This will assist in evaluating reforms being contemplated in developing countries, as well as inform those countries wishing to establish such systems about the choices for public pension design.

To set out what might be called *best practices* in public pension design, it is useful to put the issue of public pensions into context. Why is public pension reform and development a timely issue? We can characterize the reasons for the urgency of public pension reform into three categories—demographic, economic, and political and institutional.

Demographic Patterns

Public pensions involve payments to the elderly as well as ancillary benefits such as public services, in-kind transfers, and social insurance. The design and viability of a given system is contingent on the relative number of elderly people in the population. A surprisingly common demographic characteristic facing many economies is the aging of the population, both in the recent past and in future projections. In 1990, old individuals (over the age of 60) constituted 9 percent of the world's population. By 2030, they will make up 16 percent of the world's population. Currently, the OECD and the transitional socialist countries have the highest proportions of old individuals. However, most of the projected growth in the world's proportion of old individuals will occur in developing countries (particularly those in Asia).

From the point of view of public pension policy, what is relevant is not just the raw age structure of the population, but more generally the ratio of the retired to the working (taxpaying) population, called the *dependency ratio*. The dependency ratio reflects a number of factors. Declining fertility rates, which often accompany development, reduce the number of young people relative to old people and put a greater burden on young taxpayers to provide a given amount of support. Increased longevity will increase the length of retirement during which public pensions may be received. For both these reasons, high-income countries with lower fertility rates and higher life expectancies have higher dependency ratios. In other words, the dependency ratio increases with per capita income.[1] In Asia, it ranges from 5.9 percent (Philippines) to 12.7 percent (Hong Kong, China), while the average in the OECD countries is 20 percent (Heller 2003; World Bank 1994).

In the face of these demographic changes, policies need to adapt. Tax or contribution rates supporting a given level of retirement benefit will no longer be adequate. Some policy changes are thus inevitable.

Economic Factors

A series of economic factors have conspired to compound the problem of sustaining public pension systems. In many countries, the 1980s and early 1990s were periods of fiscal deficits and rapidly accumulating public debts. This situation reflected in part relatively high inflation rates accompanied by high nominal interest rates, and in part higher than normal unemployment rates. Although these high rates had their primary effect on fiscal deficits, programs such as public pensions that typically were financed by earmarked payroll taxes suffered a decline in revenues. More generally, the decline in the rate of growth of productivity, and hence of real wages, reduced the rate at which contributions to public pension systems grew. The parameters of many pension systems had been set in the heady days of the 1960s and 1970s, when per capita income growth was high. Such systems cannot be sustained in the longer run without major changes to the benefit or contribution structures.

Along with the reduced ability of economies to finance existing public pension benefits at existing tax rates, the demand for economic security has increased. Those households becoming better off demand higher levels of social security. At the same time, inflation has eroded households' savings for retirement and thereby increased their dependency on public pensions. As well, the costs of social security in the broad sense are increasing. Household members are living longer, and as a result governments are incurring higher costs for services that accompany old age, especially health insurance. Indeed, technological advances in health care and pharmaceuticals are making the costs of catastrophic illness prohibitive.

As a result of this increased demand for and dependency on public pensions, some governments have become more responsive and responsible. Other governments' responses have only increased the pressure on their public pension systems.

Political and Institutional Factors

Public pensions have come under some pressure because of the actions, inadvertent or otherwise, of the governments or bureaucracies that administer the systems. Public pension systems are necessarily long-run in their nature because they are meant to provide support for persons who will not retire for a number of years, including those who are not yet born. However, governments may be shortsighted with respect to the needs of those who will be served by the pension fund in the distant future. Thus, public pension funds may be squandered by governments in various ways.

Governments may allow benefit levels to become dangerously high relative to contribution levels and thereby run down the pension funds, leaving large implicit liabilities for future generations. There is evidence in some countries that the level of unfunded liabilities in public pension schemes is of the same order of magnitude as the public debt, which has grown rapidly in many countries. Existing funds are often misused by the public sector. They may be made available for loans to the public sector, thereby relieving the government of pressure that might otherwise bring its deficits under control. They may also be used for investment projects that might not otherwise pass the usual tests of market efficiency or social benefit-cost analysis.

Public pensions may face other institutional constraints that hamper their viability. Coverage may be limited to the formal sector, and the ready movement of workers between the formal and informal sectors might reduce compliance with making contributions. Capital markets in some developing countries might be underdeveloped, making it difficult both for persons to save profitably and with relative certainty for their own retirement, and for institutions or employers to save on their behalves. There may be other difficulties with the pension administration that hamper the achievement of societal objectives. For example, take-up rates may be relatively low for some categories of the retired. Social insurance may be difficult to target: too many persons may be made eligible for disability benefits or for other needs-related benefits.

Finally, societies themselves may be changing in ways that affect the need for government-provided support. Urbanization, the increased mobility of labor, and sociological changes in society's norms and attitudes may cause a decline in traditional forms of support, including those based on family and voluntary organizations. All these factors have played crucial roles in increasing the demand for reform and expansion of public pensions.

The Rationale for Government Intervention

As a prelude to evaluating pension policy, it is useful to consider the economic arguments for (and against) government intervention. At the most abstract level, the case for government intervention is based on the standard efficiency and equity arguments of public economics, and arguments against are founded in government failure. We begin with a brief account of both, before turning to their application to pension systems.

Efficiency and Market Failure

Government intervention might be based on the inability of markets to provide efficient allocations of resources. There are several standard sources of market failure, each of which might call for a different form of market intervention.

- *Free-rider problems:* The fact that some goods or services yield benefits or costs to several agents simultaneously implies that, in the absence of exclusion, there is a free-rider problem. Public goods, such as defense, the conduct of foreign affairs, and environmental cleanup, are typically candidates for public provision. Another important externality is that associated with the fruits of new knowledge arising from research and development, learning by doing, investment, and the like. These types of externalities can be addressed by Pigouvian tax or subsidy schemes, or by more quantity-oriented policies such as regulations or mandates.

- *Other externalities:* Some markets are characterized by economies of scale or network externalities that make competition imperfect or nonexistent. Governments may respond through competition legislation, regulation, or public enterprise.
- *Information asymmetries:* One side of a market may be systematically better informed than the other side. Governments face a disadvantage here because they are not likely to have any better information than the least informed side of the market. Nonetheless, they may be able to pass rules, such as those related to honesty in advertising, professional certification, or conflict of interest, that help curb some of the excesses. Markets for risk and uncertainty are particularly prone to information asymmetries. Insurers may not know the riskiness of individuals seeking insurance (adverse selection). And they might not be able to monitor the actions of those who are insured—actions that can affect the chances of losses being claimed (moral hazard). Adverse selection leads to bad risks crowding out good risks in insurance markets and can forestall market equilibrium. In this case, governments might be able to improve things by making insurance compulsory. It is more difficult to devise policies to cope with moral hazard problems, because the government is not likely to be able to monitor behavior so as to enforce the policies.
- *Market frictions:* Some markets may not function well because of price or quantity rigidities, or other frictions in the market. For example, labor markets may not respond quickly to shocks and, as a result, unemployment will persist. Similarly, housing markets may be slow to adjust to economic changes simply because it takes a long time to change the quantity of housing. Other markets, especially those for assets, may be very unstable because their prices respond very quickly to relatively small changes in expectations. It is not clear what governments can do to correct for these market failures.
- *Underdeveloped markets:* Some markets may be very underdeveloped or may simply not exist for some types of transactions. For example, some types of risk cannot be well insured against because the potential market is very thin. Capital markets, which are fairly complicated institutions, may not exist in some areas of the economy or may be difficult to access for some households or firms.

Equity

In principle, government policy to address market failure caused by inefficiencies should be relatively uncontroversial. The intent of such policies is to increase the gains from trade, so that improvements for everyone should be possible. Problems of equity are necessarily more contentious because they involve value judgments. The welfare of one group of persons must be traded off against that of another group. Economists are presumably no better placed to make these judgments than anyone else. Nonetheless, governments do intervene to pursue equity issues and policies intended to correct market failures also have redistributive effects, so policy evaluations must address them. Economists are certainly equipped to evaluate the equity consequences of alternative public policies, using as a norm value judgments that might be widely accepted or explicitly cited as one of the aims of the policy.

The application of equity in practice involves redistribution toward the deserving members of the economy. That might call for three types of intervention, all of which are commonly found to some degree in most societies. First, there is intervention ex ante to improve the equality of opportunity among households. Education is obviously an important policy instrument for this purpose. Related to this notion of equality of opportunities is the idea that persons should be given the same capabilities to be fruitful participants in society (Sen 1985). Second, intervention might involve the ex post redistribution from those who have done well out of the market economy to those who have not been so successful. This might be done to achieve a societal objective that is welfarist in that individual preferences are paramount—individuals, rather than some paternalistic policy maker, are assumed to be in the best position to judge their own well-being—or nonwelfarist in that other nonutility objectives are used to determine the amount and direction of redistribution. Third, and clearly related to the first two, the government may provide various forms of social insurance to reflect the fact that some individuals have been more fortunate in life than others.

The pursuit of equity necessarily involves some trade-off with efficiency. Redistributive instruments typically blunt incentives. This means that the size of the pie declines as the pie is divided more equally. The choice of policies along the range of this efficiency-equity trade-off will inevitably involve a value judgment, and one that will be made differently by different societies. The best the evaluator can do is to indicate the options among which the policy maker can choose.

Government Failure

A constraining influence on government intervention for either efficiency or equity reasons is that the government itself may not be completely benevolent. Although the government is the vehicle for collective decision making on behalf of the population, that decision making may itself lead to inefficiencies. We have already alluded to the fact that governments may not be perfectly well informed. That fact will hamper both the ability to correct for market failures (caused by, for example, adverse selection and moral hazard problems) and the ability to implement redistributive policies (for example, because of the inability to distinguish perfectly who is needy from who is not).

Governments may also be unduly shortsighted. In democracies, they are responsible to the electorate but have mandates for only a fixed period of time, much shorter than the time horizon of many of the policies they enact. Moreover, even farsighted and benevolent governments may face problems of time consistency: policies announced at one point that can have an influence on the long-term decisions of households and firms are often reneged upon or revised after such decisions have been made. Time consistency problems have been alleged to lead to the excessive taxation of capital income, the confiscation of foreign firms, and other problems. Governments may not, however, be benevolent. Their decisions may be unduly influenced by self-seeking bureaucrats, pressure groups, or rent-seekers. These instances of government failure offer an antidote to the view that the government can correct all the problems faced by the private sector.

These various general arguments for (and against) government intervention also apply to intervention in the pension system. In principle, many of the components of the public pension system—especially those involving savings and insurance—could be left to the private sector. The question is whether there is a justification for public intervention in pensions. In the following subsections, we classify the reasons for public intervention and the form of intervention into three general areas: redistributive arguments, insurance arguments related to market failure, and arguments based on enhancing the savings rate.

Redistribution

In some societies most redistribution takes place without the coercive powers of the government. This is achieved through institutions such as extended families, communities, religious organizations, and other charitable organizations. These institutions may be quite cost-effective and successful at redistribution: they have good knowledge of those being served and are able to target their assistance effectively. However, given the voluntary nature of such institutions, a free-rider problem exists—implying that the level of redistribution is inefficiently low. Although government provision can enhance the extent of redistribution, it can also crowd out these voluntary but effective forms of redistribution.

The idea that governments should redistribute to the less well-off is widely accepted. Obviously, there are needy people all along the age distribution. The question is why redistribution to the elderly should be treated separately from redistribution more generally. There are two major sets of arguments that can be made, one related to intragenerational inequality and the other to intergenerational inequality.

TRANSFERS TO THE POOR ELDERLY TO REDRESS INTRA-GENERATIONAL INEQUALITY. There are a number of reasons why transfers are devised specifically for the poor elderly: The incidence of poverty among the elderly may be much higher than among other age groups. The elderly may have little or no earning power with which to support themselves. They may not have provided for their own retirement by saving during their working lives, especially if their wage incomes were low. And their expenditure needs may have increased in retirement because of health care costs or the need for pharmaceuticals or home care. These needs will vary according to circumstances and luck: some elderly poor will be healthier than others, and some will have access to family or community support. Finally, since they are not in the labor force, the incentive effects of work effort no longer exist, which implies that the ideal structure of the transfers system for the elderly poor may differ from that for the working poor. At the same time, transfers to the elderly will not be without incentive effects: high tax-back rates based on income can discourage saving for retirement, to the extent that household members are farsighted and able to anticipate the form of public pension program that will be in effect during their retirement. For all these reasons, transfer programs directed specifically to the poor elderly are not uncommon, especially in OECD countries.

Redistributive transfers to the poor must be financed, and the mode of finance raises its own issues of efficiency and equity. Transfers to the elderly poor, like other transfers, are generally financed out of general revenues. One issue here is that raising revenues for any purpose entails an efficiency cost. Transfers to the elderly will induce inefficiencies for this reason. The extent of inefficiency will be lessened by more targeted transfers, so less revenue will be required. This improved efficiency and lowered cost must be set against the disadvantages of targeting. The other issue is that general revenue financing will fall disproportionately on the working population, implying that there is an intergenerational transfer component in the system. That is, redistribution goes from one age cohort to another. This could be avoided in principle by financing transfers to the poor elderly through taxes on the better-off elderly—in other words, through the use of purely intragenerational transfers. But that would be impractical since it would require age-specific taxation.

TRANSFERS TO THE ELDERLY TO REDRESS INTERGEN-ERATIONAL INEQUALITY. Public pension transfer programs, even contributory ones, are often explicitly intergenerational in nature. Payments to the elderly are financed at least partly by taxes or contributions made by those working. As long as such a system is in place, it represents an ongoing transfer from younger to older cohorts. That can be avoided only by making the public pension system a fully funded one,[2] or by making compensating changes in other fiscal policies. In considering the case for intergenerational transfers, a distinction should be made between temporary and permanent intergenerational transfers.

Temporary intergenerational transfers are those that might be made to selected cohorts. The argument is that some cohorts, by reason of their date of birth alone, are systematically unluckier than others. They may have had to fight or finance a major war, or they may have faced relatively more natural disasters (floods, earthquakes, disease, adverse weather, and so forth). They may have lived through a major depression that curbed their earning power during working years. Or they may have been demographically unlucky. Persons born into a relatively large cohort will be at an economic disadvantage. The work force will be relatively large during their working years, making it more difficult to find a job and depressing wages. They will then be in retirement when the workforce is smaller. This will depress the return to their savings and will leave fewer taxpayers to finance the services they will rely on when retired. Temporary intergenerational transfers can serve as a form of social insurance against such adverse shocks suffered by particular age cohorts.

In abstract terms, if individuals had the opportunity to take out insurance against the risk of being born into an unlucky cohort, then presumably they would do so. But they cannot place themselves in that position—hence, the case for temporary intergenerational transfers. Such transfers can take the form of public pensions with funding suitably designed to assist those who are unlucky. Or they can take other forms, such as debt financing, which is commonly used to finance wars. In this manner, debt is equivalent to a postponement of tax liabilities to finance current expenditure. Because they are temporary, these intergenerational transfers for social insurance purposes should be self-financing over a series of cohorts. Such a system would put significant strains on governments, which must both be farsighted and have suitably long time horizons. Thus, instances in which intergenerational transfers might have been engineered to address the difficulties faced by particular cohorts (for example, public pension systems introduced in the wake of the Great Depression) have often lasted well beyond the anticipated length of time.

The case for ongoing or permanent intergenerational transfers is perhaps even more difficult to argue, even though the normative line of argument might be compelling. The argument is that productivity growth will make each succeeding future generation better off than its predecessor. If there were an overarching planner, it might want to reallocate resources systematically from future generations to present ones. One way to do this might be by a permanent, ongoing system of intergenerational transfers, such as a public pension system.

The problem is that implementing such a system is bound to be prohibitively difficult and fraught with problems. Even for an overarching planner, the system is likely to be extremely complicated and demanding. The planner must be able to foresee into the very distant future to implement a scheme that smoothes out lifetime utility across an indefinitely large number of future cohorts. This requirement is further complicated by the fact that continual increases in per capita gross domestic product (GDP) are by no means assured. Natural resources and the capacity of the environment are finite, so it is conceivable that their scarcity or degradation will eventually outpace productivity growth, implying that at some point future generations will start to become worse off. Moreover, the planner's calculation will have to account for the fact that intergenerational transfers might crowd out private savings and investment. To the extent that these are the engines of productivity growth, as proposed by the new growth theories, there will be a trade-off between equality among generations and growth in output.

But the most telling argument against a system of permanent intergenerational transfers to even out unequal lifetime utilities is the lack of capacity of even responsible governments to define and carry out such policies. Defining the appropriate amount of intergenerational transfers is in the end a value judgment, one that governments representing current electors have no mandate to make. Moreover, given that governments have limited electoral mandates, their time horizons are far too short to span the time needed to implement optimal intergenerational transfers. It is therefore inconceivable that governments can be relied on to abide by the intergenerational contracts necessary to implement optimal intergenerational transfers. What is more likely is that the shortsightedness of governments will lead to an excess of intergenerational transfers. That being the case, prudent policy may be needed to constrain them from doing so.

Economists have also stressed that redistributive transfers can to some extent be efficiency-enhancing. In particular, if preferences are altruistic, transfers from the better-off to the less well-off can make all households better off (that is, be Pareto improving). In an intergenerational context, this can occur through the mechanism of bequests. That being the case, some such intergenerational transfers will be undertaken voluntarily. This has some potential implications that have been stressed in the literature. Some have argued that the presence of voluntary intergenerational transfers can vitiate the effectiveness of public transfers (Barro 1974). The argument is that, if each cohort cares about the well-being of its immediate heirs, then indirectly cohort members will care about the well-being of all their descendents into the indefinite future: The sequence of cohorts will act as if their consumption-savings decisions had been taken by the existing cohort, maximizing an intertemporal utility function covering the entire future family dynasty, subject to the resources available to the family dynasty. Attempts to redistribute among generations will simply be offset by equal and opposite changes in bequests, rendering intergenerational transfers ineffective.

The extent to which intergenerational transfers such as public pensions and debt crowd out private saving for bequests is an empirical matter. Such evidence as exists does not suggest overwhelming support for the crowding-out, or Ricardian equivalence, hypothesis.[3] There are also serious theoretical concerns with the usual form of the Ricardian equivalence hypothesis. As Bernheim and Bagwell (1988) have pointed out, the construction of a dynastic utility function linking the family line of heirs is simply untenable once one takes account of the fact that marriage occurs between members of different family lines. In such a context, taking the Barro argument to its logical limits implies that each altruistic member of the current generation cares indirectly about the heirs of all his or her contemporaries. This implies that saving for future generations takes the form of a voluntary public good, with all its attendant free-rider problems. The implication, as stressed long ago by Sen (1967) and Marglin (1963), is that there will be significant undersaving for bequests. This provides an efficiency argument for public intergenerational transfers. But these intergenerational transfers would be such as to increase saving for future generations. That is, they would be transfers from the present to future generations—precisely the opposite of unfunded public pensions. Thus, this constitutes a further argument against unfunded public pensions.

IMPLICATIONS FOR GOVERNMENT INTERVENTION. The redistribution argument suggests that a case can be made for a program that transfers income to those elderly in need. The more general case for systematic intergenerational transfers to one age cohort from another is more difficult to sustain, although particular cohorts might be faced with extreme economic need because of major wars or depressions. But in this case, it is not obvious that pensions are the appropriate instrument. Public debt is a somewhat more flexible instrument in terms of providing finance when it is needed and not encumbering the economy with a public pension program that might prove difficult to dismantle.

Ideally, transfers to the elderly should be targeted to those in need. But there may be reasons why this cannot be fully accomplished. The needy may be difficult to identify, and it may be costly to screen them. Targeting by, say, income may result in adverse savings or labor supply incentives for potential recipients. Targeting by need may lead to low take-up rates, stigma, and administrative errors. As well, the use of targeting may reduce political support for redistributive transfers by reducing the size of the constituency that is entitled to receive them. These issues of design will be taken up again in the next section.

Insurance arguments

The second main argument for public pensions relies on market failure, especially the failure of insurance markets. The elderly face a number of risks which, if not unique to them, are at least particularly onerous for them. These risks include the following:

- *Risk of ill health:* The incidence of major health problems among the elderly is high.
- *Disability risk:* Injuries or accidents, even if they occur during working years, can increase expenses (and reduce pleasure) in retirement.
- *Longevity risk:* Uninsured uncertainty about the length of one's own life entails the accumulation of precautionary wealth to finance consumption in the event of a long life.
- *Investment risk:* Even if individuals save seemingly adequate amounts for retirement, unforeseen circumstances or bad luck may cause the returns to their investment to be unexpectedly low.
- *Inflation risk:* This is related to investment risk. One reason why investment returns may be inadequate is because of unexpectedly high inflation that was not reflected in indexed returns.

In principle, these risks should be in large part insurable because they are largely idiosyncratic with respect to the individual concerned. (An exception might be inflation risk, which may be common to an entire cohort.)

Moreover, unlike social insurance, the risks are not resolved at birth. Nonetheless, market failure can occur for various reasons. A catalog of reasons why markets may fail to provide adequate insurance coverage follows.

ADVERSE SELECTION. In a world in which risks are idiosyncratic and sellers and buyers of insurance both know the risks, competitive insurance companies will be induced to offer actuarially fair insurance policies and can pool the risks associated with each insured household.[4] Households can purchase enough insurance to offload all risk. But suppose that households differ in their riskiness (probability of having an accident), and that insurance companies do not know which households belong to which risk class. Then, various outcomes are possible, each of which is inefficient compared with the case in which full information is available. If insurance companies cannot observe the total amount of insurance each household purchases (because they can buy from more than one company), high-risk types cannot be distinguished from low-risk types. This means an equilibrium will be a pooling one: at the common premium, high-risk households will overinsure and low-risk households will underinsure. If the government has no better information than households do, policy cannot achieve the outcome expected when full information is available. But compulsory uniform public provision of insurance can be instituted so that the low-risk households are better off, while the high-risk ones might be better or worse off (Johnson 1977).

The more likely case is that in which insurance companies can monitor the amount of insurance bought by households. Then, insurance contracts can specify both a price and a quantity. In this case, as Rothschild and Stiglitz (1976) showed, a pooling equilibrium cannot exist: starting at a pooling equilibrium, some insurance company can always increase profits by offering a policy that skims off only the low-risk persons. Moreover, a separating equilibrium—one in which the high- and low-risk households self-select into an insurance policy intended for them—may or may not exist. If it does, low-risk households will be fully insured while high-risk ones will be underinsured. If such an equilibrium does not exist (for example, because there are relatively few low-risk types), a Pareto improvement can be achieved by a uniform compulsory scheme covering all persons. If a separating equilibrium does exist, then it will not be efficient. A Pareto-improving scheme of compulsory insurance may be possible, but only if households can supplement the scheme with their own voluntary supplements (Dahlby 1981).

From the point of view of pensions for the elderly, it is conceivable that annuity markets are plagued by adverse selection problems of this sort, although it is perhaps not likely. After all, life insurance markets seem to work reasonably well, and they too require information on the risk of death. Perhaps a more likely candidate for public insurance is health or disability insurance, because it might be more likely that households have more (private) information on the state of their health than do insurance companies. However, this is the sort of information that is likely to be readily available from a physician's examination, which insurance companies could require. Thus, by itself, adverse selection might not be a compelling argument for public insurance to the elderly.

MORAL HAZARD. Another form of insurance market failure that relies on asymmetric information involves moral hazard. This is the name given to the situation in which the probability of an accident occurring or the magnitude of its damage depends partly on the actions of the person being insured—the care exercised, the preventive measures taken, and so on. In the presence of moral hazard, insurance companies can at best offer partial insurance or coinsurance, perhaps with some deductibility to discourage small claims. Those who are insured end up bearing at least part of the risk, so the full efficiency of the market provision fails.

The relevance of this point for public intervention in pensions is mixed. It is not clear that governments can do any better than the private sector in overcoming this market failure: as with adverse selection, governments are unlikely to have any better information than private insurers, and they may well have poorer information. For another, it is not clear that moral hazard is a problem for many of the risks addressed by the pension system. For example, although persons can affect their longevity by private behavior, it is unreasonable to think that they would do so simply to exploit public pensions.

There are, however, two instances in which moral hazard may be relevant. First, households may be induced to expose their savings for retirement to excessive risk, if they anticipate that governments will come to their assistance in the event that they are unlucky enough to have inadequate income in retirement. This is an instance of the so-called Samaritan's dilemma, whereby prospective retirees exploit the fact that the government—as the Good Samaritan—will not allow them to suffer deprivation in retirement.[5] In theory, the Samaritan's dilemma can be avoided if the government commits in advance not to bail out those who have come on bad times merely through their own recklessness earlier in life. But in practice, governments would find it difficult to exercise such a commitment with credibility. The Samaritan's dilemma turns out to be important not only for influencing the riskiness of saving for retirement—the topic of the current discussion—but also for the amount of saving for retirement, discussed below.

Moral hazard may also be important in health insurance, which may be a component of retirement savings packages, either private or public. Here the argument is that households in which members become ill will demand too many health services, such as too many trips to the doctor, too many prescription drugs, too many x-rays, and so on. The problem is that if insurance covers these services at less than their cost, there will be an incentive to overuse them. The public sector may thus have a role in regulating the use of health services.

OVERUSE BY SUPPLIERS OF AN INSURED SERVICE. A related form of moral hazard occurs when the expenditures being insured are provided to those being insured by a third-party supplier. Thus, health services and prescription drugs may be prescribed by health professionals. These suppliers are likely to be better informed than either the persons being served or the insurers, and that is also likely to lead to overuse. In the context of pensions, this hazard may be a concern for health insurance and insurance of pharmaceuticals. It would affect the cost of private health insurance for the elderly, those who are subject to the greatest chance of health problems. Presumably it would make health insurance prohibitively costly for low-income retirees. Again, it is not clear that the public sector would have any informational advantage over private insurers in terms of controlling excessive use induced by suppliers. The ability of the public sector to regulate might curb the worst of the excesses.

ADMINISTRATIVE COSTS. It has been argued that the costs of administering insurance systems constitute a relatively high proportion of premiums or contributions under private insurance. Insurance companies must advertise and market, they must have extensive individual record-keeping systems, and they must devote considerable resources to substantiating claims. It has been argued that these administrative costs are substantial both in health insurance and in the provision of retirement savings annuities. In the latter case, the costs include management fees for investing funds. A single-payer system, by eliminating duplication and exploiting economies of scale, may be able to reduce these administrative costs considerably; however, that reduction may come at the expense of cost-effectiveness. Without the spur of competition, there is less incentive to provide services at least cost.

INVESTMENT AND INFLATION RISK. Private insurance markets may find it difficult to insure for the risks that investors face in saving for retirement, especially inflation risk and the risk of a major downturn in asset returns. The availability of indexed annuities seems to be relatively limited. It may be simply that these risks are difficult to insure against; for example, because the probability distributions are simply not well known, or the risks are just too great. Alternatively, it might be the case that the public sector has an advantage in insuring retirees against inflation and major downturns. The possibility of these events occurring is partly under the control of governments, not randomly determined. Insurance companies might find it difficult to provide insurance against adverse government policies. As well, risks faced by retirees may be intergenerational risks, and private insurance companies may have difficulty brokering risk-sharing contracts between generations. Whether governments are able to provide insurance against intergenerational risk is an issue already discussed. More generally, insurance fund managers may also be subject to the sort of moral hazard risks mentioned above. They may be induced to invest in risky portfolios if they expect that they will be bailed out in the event of financial failure.

IMPLICATIONS FOR GOVERNMENT INTERVENTION. The upshot of this discussion is that there may be many reasons why private insurance may be inefficient. Some arise from asymmetric information among insurees, households, and suppliers of services being insured. Others arise from the uninsurability of certain types of risks, partly because the government itself influences the outcome of the risky event. And others arise because of the supposed high administrative costs associated with competitive insurance markets. The implications for government intervention are not clear-cut. In many cases, the government will be no better informed than private insurers, so it can do no better at avoiding adverse selection and asymmetric information problems. The Samaritan's dilemma is endemic to retirement insurance schemes, and it is hard to know how to avoid it: governments cannot be prevented from helping those who, even owing to their own actions, find themselves destitute in retirement because of bad luck or bad judgment.

The worst contraventions of market efficiency may be avoided by prudent regulation, for example, to ensure that pensions are not held in an excessively risky form. But it is difficult to make a general case for government provision of insurance to retirees on the grounds of insurance market failure alone. Compulsory provision can in theory address problems of a lack of equilibrium in the face of adverse selection, but it is not clear that this is a particular problem for retirement insurance. An exception may be health and disability insurance, in which the main problem with private provision may not be market failure per se but the social insurance arguments mentioned above: some people are systematically uninsurable because of health characteristics they are born with.

Inadequacy of savings

The final argument for public intervention in pension systems involves another potential source of market failure—the possibility that private savings might be too low. There are two conceptually separate issues here. First, people might not save enough for their own retirement. Second, the aggregate savings rate, of which saving for retirement is an important component, may be inefficiently low.

UNDERSAVING FOR RETIREMENT. It has been well documented in some countries that a significant proportion of the population fails to save adequately to provide for retirement, at least according to what one might regard as reasonable lifetime preferences. A variety of reasons might be put forward to explain this, including the following:

- *Myopia:* As stressed by the World Bank (1994), some households might simply be myopic, living for the present and making decisions with relatively short time horizons.
- *Naïveté:* Household members, especially those with less education, might be unfamiliar with capital markets, including their role and how to use them. Even if household members set aside some of their current incomes, they may not invest those funds wisely.
- *Few saving vehicles:* There may be an absence of assets in which retirement savings might be held, especially for persons in isolated areas. Capital markets may be thin, rural banks scarce, or assets not portable.
- *Traditional forms of support breaking down:* People who had relied on extended families or communities to provide for them in retirement may find themselves deserted as mobility increases and community institutions undergo change.
- *Incomes inadequate:* A segment of the population may simply have incomes that are too low to allow for savings. For these persons, redistributive motives for public pensions presumably play a role.
- *Loss of income:* Perhaps the most serious deterrent to saving adequately for retirement is that households may face a temporary loss of income caused by unemployment, which requires them to use up their savings. This may be a particularly important problem in developing countries, where unemployment rates in the formal sector are high and unemployment insurance is limited.

▪ *Samaritan's dilemma:* We have already mentioned this problem in the context of inducing unduly risky activities, but a similar argument can apply to the incentive to save: if persons anticipate that governments will provide assistance to those in retirement based on need, they will have an incentive to exploit that possibility by undersaving for their retirement. In contrast to myopia, this reason assumes superrationality and presumably applies mainly to relatively low-income persons (because government support is likely to be at a low level).

The relative weight of these various explanations in terms of explaining why people underprovide for their own retirement is not clear.

LOW SAVINGS RATE. National savings consist of the aggregate of private savings (both household and corporate) and public savings (or dissavings, in the case of deficit financing). National savings, along with capital inflows from abroad, provide the financing for investment. Although there is some dispute in the literature over the exact relationship between national savings and domestic investment in an open economy, the presumption is that an increase in national savings will lead to at least some increase in domestic investment: the open economy does not segment the savings and investment sides of domestic capital markets completely. The adequacy of savings is therefore very much related to the overall impact of savings on domestic investment. There are a number of possible sources of inefficiently low national savings rates:

▪ *Underdeveloped capital markets:* The same sorts of problems with capital markets that prevent people from adequately providing for their own retirement also give rise to low savings rates: myopia, imperfect capital markets, and the existence of traditional forms of support.
▪ *Capital taxes:* Taxes on capital income and on capital itself can be relatively high and can discourage both savings and investment. An obvious remedy might be to reduce capital income tax rates, and indeed in OECD countries this is often done selectively for retirement savings. But governments seem intent on having relatively high tax rates on capital income, much higher than most economists would regard as efficient. One cogent explanation for this (the time inconsistency or holdup problem) is that the stock of previously accumulated capital is very high relative to new investment. Because previously accumulated capital is fixed, it is irresistible for governments to tax it. The fact that it might discourage some new investment in the future is outweighed by the large stock of old capital.

- *Public dissaving:* The tendencies of governments to finance expenditure by debt rather than by current taxes and to maintain unfunded liabilities in public pension schemes represent a large drag on national savings. Again, the obvious remedy would be to increase public sector savings, but this may be difficult for short-lived governments to do.
- *Investment externalities:* The "new growth theory" emphasizes the idea that investment is the engine of growth: it embodies new technologies and products, it provides training for managers and workers, it leads to learning by doing, and it creates jobs for the growing labor force. But many of these benefits are not appropriated by the firms undertaking the investing, so there is too little investment. Inducing more savings can increase the amount of investment that occurs and can act as a spur to growth.
- *Savings externalities:* We have mentioned earlier the idea that saving for bequests can be in the nature of a public good: others benefit from the altruism involved, besides the person doing the savings. If this is so, there is a classic free-rider problem, which leads to an inefficiently low amount of savings being done for future generations.

To the extent that any of these arguments are true, there will be inadequate savings. A case can therefore be made for introducing policies that increase the amount of savings persons do in their income-earning years.

IMPLICATIONS FOR GOVERNMENT INTERVENTION. A wide variety of instruments could be used for enhancing lifetime savings. The inadequacy of savings for one's own retirement can be addressed directly through mandatory savings schemes. However, such schemes can be viewed as paternalistic if they simply override individual preferences. Apart from addressing the adequacy problem, such schemes might also help develop capital market institutions that themselves can contribute to higher savings.

The role of the public sector, apart from the mandating itself, can be varied. The scheme can be operated by the public sector entirely, as in the case of provident funds. But even if the schemes are mandatory contributory public pensions, the funds themselves could be privately managed. Alternatively, the pensions may be privately operated, subject only to regulations that are needed to ensure the safety of the investments, portability and vesting, and rules about the size of required contributions and the manner in which pension payments can be received. These issues are all addressed below. Over and above the argument for mandating savings for retirement, additional measures may enhance the amount of voluntary saving for retirement or bequest. The various forms these incentives can take are discussed later.

We have now outlined the three main rationales for government involvement in pension systems: redistribution, insurance, and savings. These rationales lead to the three main forms of government intervention: transfers to the elderly (which deal with redistributive and social insurance aspects), contributory pension schemes (which encompass both insurance and savings issues), and the encouragement of voluntary savings (which addresses the problem of low savings rates).

We next turn to a consideration of the design and economic issues involved in each of these three forms of government intervention. The design issues include such aspects as the choice of policy instruments, the administrative structure, the delivery mechanisms for the pensions, and the type of financing. The economic effects include those on work and saving incentives, on risk faced by retirees, on traditional support mechanisms such as the extended family, and on the economy as a whole, such as the development of capital markets and the aggregate savings rate.

Transfers to the Elderly

A system of public transfers to the elderly is intended to address redistributive concerns, particularly those that are unique to the elderly. These concerns can result from inefficiencies or market failures in the market economy, or they can be a result of nature. We begin with a discussion of some of the design issues and alternatives that policy makers must consider, and then turn to the economic effects of alternative design strategies. The presumption here is that redistributive objectives will involve a public system of transfers. Nonetheless, the way in which public transfers interact with voluntary ones, especially whether they crowd them out, is a relevant consideration.

Design Issues

The design of transfer systems involves a number of different dimensions, from the objective to the scope, targeting method, form, formula, administration, and financing.

The objective function

A prerequisite to designing a system of redistributive transfers to the elderly is specifying the objective of the transfers. In the redistribution literature, three main forms of objective function have been prominent:

- *Welfarism:* In conventional welfare economics, the government is assumed to care about the distribution of well-being, or utility, across the population. Its objective function is summarized in a social welfare function whose arguments are the welfare levels of the households, referred to as welfarist. Two key properties of the welfarist objective function are relevant. The first is that it is an increasing function of individuals' utility levels and not their levels of consumption or income. The second is that welfarist objective functions can exhibit differing degrees of aversion to inequality in utilities.[6] The degree of aversion to inequality involves a fairly strong form of value judgment, requiring interpersonal comparisons of welfare. At one extreme, the objective function may be of the maxi-min form, seeking to maximize the well-being of the least well-off. At the other, it may encompass simply mild forms of altruism conforming to what the better-off households would voluntarily but collectively agree to transfer to the poor.

- *Poverty alleviation:* Rather than caring about the utility level of the poor, the government might aim to reduce some index of inequality, in terms of either the income or the consumption of the poor. Thus, it could aim to minimize some measure of poverty, such as a poverty headcount index (the number of persons below some defined poverty line of income or consumption) or a poverty gap index (the aggregate amount by which incomes or consumption of the poor fall below the poverty line). These measures are somewhat easier to implement than welfarist objectives because they involve only deciding upon a poverty line and measuring it. They are not welfarist because they do not take into account the nonincome components of welfare, such as leisure time.

- *Capabilities:* The government could care about the inequality of individual capabilities in the economy, where *capability* refers to the individual's ability to function in the economy. This capability is the product of the individual's personal characteristics and his or her environment. Features of individual environments that affect capability include physical surroundings, nourishment, health care, and educational opportunities. Under this objective, the government attempts to reduce the inadequacies in some individuals' environments. Whatever the objective of the government, it must decide which redistributive policy to pursue. In doing so, it must weigh both the potential benefits of the policy, in terms of achieving its goal, and the potential costs of the policy, including the policy's fiscal, administrative, and economic costs.

Scope of coverage of redistributive instruments

Redistributive schemes can take two distinct forms: universal and targeted. Universal redistributive programs are those in which eligibility for the program does not depend on the establishment of individual need. Targeted redistributive programs involve a set of criteria an individual must meet to become eligible for the transfer. The criteria can include means testing in which both eligibility and the level of transfer are conditioned on measures of need, such as income, wealth, and extent of family support. The criteria can also condition transfers on observable characteristics of the individual, such as age, family circumstances, and health status. Generally, targeted programs seek to exclude individuals of means—that is, the nonpoor—by the use of either or both types of criteria. This is in stark contrast to universal programs, which do not attempt to exclude any individual who meets the minimum eligibility requirements. In the context of transfers to the elderly, the whole population is not eligible for universal transfers. Because these programs are intended to redistribute to the elderly, they will be restricted in the sense that a certain age requirement must be met to obtain the transfer. This type of universal transfer program is known as a *demogrant*.

Several considerations are involved in deciding between a targeted and a universal scheme. One involves political support. A targeted scheme might elicit greater political support as a result of the belief that only those individuals deserving of support will receive it. This may reduce the resentment felt by taxpayers who finance the programs and, thereby, gain their support for the program. Highly targeted programs may lose the support of the majority because the majority does not benefit, either directly or indirectly, from the program.

Another consideration is the extent of coverage. Targeted schemes can lead to undercoverage. Individuals who truly need the benefits might not be identified by the program, perhaps because of errors in administration (discussed further below), or because of low take-up rates (the ratio of program participants to potential eligible recipients).

There are several reasons for low take-up rates. One is the existence of a stigma associated with the targeted transfer program. If individuals are stigmatized for being poor, then having to prove they are poor will prevent some individuals in need from qualifying for benefits. The costs involved in being stigmatized must also be considered when evaluating the transfer scheme. One way to circumvent this problem is to introduce a universal scheme, such as a demogrant pension, in which all individuals of a given minimum age qualify. However, the stigma associated with acceptance of public transfers may still exist and continue to deter individuals in need from participating in the program. It is also possible that the more targeted a program is, the less stigma taxpayers attach to it and the more likely it is that those in need will apply.

Another reason for low take-up rates is that it can be costly in terms of time to apply and this cost deters eligible individuals from applying. This time cost may be unintentional or intentional. Alternatively, individuals who are technically eligible for the program may have alternative resources, such as family support, that the program does not screen for but that nevertheless deter the individuals from participating. Finally, individuals might not be informed about the program. This ignorance could result from language barriers, illiteracy on the part of potential participants, or inadequate advertising on the part of the program administrators.

Uneven coverage implies that some of the needy may be worse off with the targeted program than without it. A universal program has much more complete coverage and may thus be viewed as a more equitable scheme.

Methods of targeting

There are several methods of targeting a redistributive program. The most common is means testing implemented by self-reporting. Benefits are awarded on the basis of individuals' reported incomes and asset holdings. The obvious problem with such a scheme is the incentive on the part of individuals to understate their true financial situations in order to qualify. To counteract this incentive, there may exist some way to verify an individual's means. If the transfer is delivered through the income tax system, the machinery of tax auditing could be used. However, especially in a developing country, a program of transfers to the elderly is likely to be separate from the income tax system. In that case, a separate compliance mechanism is required.

The larger the potential benefits of the program are, the greater is the incentive to misrepresent and the greater the need for verification. Verifying an individual's means could entail documentation requirements, such as bank statements, and interviews with friends and family. If benefits are received over an extended length of time, it might be necessary to conduct such verification procedures throughout the period to ensure the individual's situation has not changed. This effort might require home visits, random audits, and the like.

It might also be the case that the means of the individual are difficult or costly to assess. For example, the income of an individual might include goods produced at home. In such situations, the program administrators might use additional characteristics to determine eligibility. Such characteristics might include the type of housing the individual lives in, whether the individual rents or owns, whether the individual owns an automobile, and where the individual lives.

In addition, programs may be targeted to categorical groups, for example, the disabled, the ill, or veterans. As in the case of means testing, some form of verification must be undertaken to ensure that those who really deserve benefits receive them. This verification is typically done by ex ante screening of applicants rather than by self-reporting. This can be a costly procedure, as well as one prone to errors.

Both means-tested targeted schemes and categorical schemes rely to some extent on the self-selection of individuals into the programs. One way self-selection is achieved is through the time cost of applying for and qualifying for benefits. This feature of targeted programs (which could also simply be a result of the administrative structure of the program) attempts to discourage those not necessarily in need from applying. Of course, there is no reason to think some individuals in need are not also discouraged from applying. For instance, some poor individuals may have a high cost of time because of their responsibilities in the home. Other programs require observable actions from individuals or nonincome tests to qualify. For example, workfare programs require individuals to participate in some form of community service in order to receive welfare benefits, after their need for benefits has been established. Once again, this is to deter those not truly in need from receiving benefits. The form of transfer given in the targeted program can also lead to self-selection on the part of individuals.

Universality does not run up against these verification issues, because all individuals of at least a given age (which is easy and inexpensive to verify) qualify for benefits. Fraud on the part of beneficiaries is reduced, although it might not be entirely eliminated: payments might continue to be made after a person has died. Of course, universal transfers are also more expensive for a given per person transfer.

The form of transfer

Redistributive transfers can take two broad forms. Individuals can receive either transfers of goods or services (*in-kind transfers*), or transfers of cash. In-kind transfers can include medical care, special needs care (such as a wheelchair or home care), housing, and food. The use of in-kind transfers is justified along three lines. First, it can serve as a form of targeting. If the needy systematically require certain types of goods and services that the better-off do not require, in-kind transfers can be a cost-effective way of getting resources to them.

Second, the quality of in-kind transfers can be used as a screening device to reduce the cost of ensuring that only those individuals without means receive the transfer. The idea is that if the government offers lower quality goods, such as public housing and basic foodstuffs, only those individuals who are truly in need of the goods will voluntarily accept them. Individuals who prefer higher quality goods and have the means to purchase them will self-select out of the transfer program. This can also occur with medical care: free, publicly provided medical care is typically of lower quality than private medical care and will be taken up by the less well-off. The problem with this approach is that the poor elderly might have a significantly lower quality of life as a result of the lower quality in-kind transfers. It might also be possible that a strong stigma attaches to using public in-kind transfers (although the stigma itself may be part of the mechanism of self-selection).

Third, governments may use in-kind transfers if they have paternalistic objectives, where the value they put on the use of transfers differs from the value the recipients put on them. For example, policy makers' preferences may reflect the altruistic preferences of the better-off taxpayers, who are in effect acting as donors for the transfers. The government may believe that individuals, if given a cash transfer, will not spend the money on the goods and services most valued by the donors. Although a cash transfer is more utility-enhancing from the point of view of the recipients because it leaves them to choose what to consume, it does not satisfy the paternalistic preferences of the donors.

The apparent paternalism may also arise from a form of the Samaritan's dilemma. The government may be unable to avoid helping the poor who have spent their money unwisely or without concern about the future. An individual might have gambled the cash transfer or spent it on fast food rather than tending to health care or housing needs. For example, if the individual did not purchase available health insurance with the cash transfer and then became ill, it is most likely that the government would step in and pay for the individual's medical services. More generally, if individuals know the government cannot avoid aiding them when in need, this knowledge will distort their choices of consumption if they are given cash transfers in a way that increases the fiscal burden of redistribution. One way to avoid this situation is to deliver transfers in kind.

The transfer formula

A formula for determining the amount of transfer must be chosen whether universal or targeted transfers are used. In the case of universal transfers the size of the transfer needs to be specified, while for targeted transfers the tax-back rate as well as the definitions of eligibility must be specified.

The level of the transfer depends on the objective function of the government. Governments that are more averse to inequality will choose a higher transfer than those that have minimal redistributive objectives. Governments may simply aim to guarantee a minimum level of support to poor individuals. Alternatively, they may want to ensure that these individuals are not living in poverty. Both goals require some standard in order to determine the level of benefits that will achieve them. The first requires some notion of what a minimum level of support is. The second requires some measure of poverty.

The minimum level may involve some cost-of-living indexes or the amount of money required to purchase some minimum necessities of life, including not only food, clothing, and shelter but the basic requirements of good health. Poverty measures may involve some well-defined poverty line, often a relative measure based on some proportion of the average income of all households in the economy. There is no agreed-on measure of the poverty line: taxpayers will have different ideas about it. The measure will ultimately be determined politically.

The policy objective may be to reduce the poverty index, measured by relating individual incomes to the poverty line. As mentioned earlier, the actual form of this comparison can vary: it can be based on a headcount or a poverty gap measure, or more generally on a Gini-based measure. If the government uses a welfarist objective, it will in principle be concerned with minimum utility levels rather than income levels. For persons in retirement, there may be little difference between these two objectives.

The way in which the level of transfers changes over time will also need to be specified. If the transfer is based on a poverty line that is calculated as a relative measure, it will typically rise with per capita incomes. Even if the transfer is based on an absolute measure of need, it will have to be indexed to the rate of inflation so that its real value does not erode.

For transfers that are targeted to income, a tax-back rate will have to be included. The choice of a tax-back rate involves a trade-off between the cost of the program and the incentive effects of targeting. The higher the tax-back rate is for a given minimum level of guaranteed support, the less tax revenues are required to finance the program. But higher tax-back rates give rise to adverse incentives: reductions in the incentive to work, save, and take risks—whether in retirement or in one's working life—and increases in the incentive to underreport income.

Benefit levels may also vary across different categorical programs for other reasons. Variations can result from political value judgments in which some groups are deemed more deserving or needy than others. They can also be due to the existence of interest groups who lobby for more generous benefits for certain groups.

A major problem in selecting the formula for transfers is the possibility of leakages, the fact that some transfers go to those not in need. Leakages can occur in both universal and targeted programs. Obviously, in universal cash transfer programs, the nonpoor will receive transfers. However, the use of in-kind transfers, even in otherwise universal programs, may result in some self-selection and therefore, reduction of program costs. But this can backfire. If the take-up of in-kind transfer programs requires some special information or application, the better-off may be more able to take advantage of it. For example, higher levels of schooling may be of more benefit to the rich than to the poor. Targeted schemes may not involve self-selection, but screening by administrators. If they are imperfectly informed about the need of individuals, leakages can result. It is often alleged, for example, that acceptance into disability programs is excessively lax in some countries, partly owing to administrators erring on the generous side so as to avoid screening out truly needy persons.

Administration

An overriding consideration, along with the economic effects of various transfer formulas, is the choice of administrative regime. There are a number of issues of concern here.

- *Delivery systems:* Cash transfers, including those to the elderly, can be delivered in two ways—through the tax system or through separate agencies. The use of the tax system takes advantage of existing administrative machinery, which may be more or less developed depending on the country. Income tax administration is characterized by self-reporting and ex post auditing. It therefore imposes compliance costs on both the transfer recipient and the government. Its disadvantage is the fact that it is better suited to targeting on the basis of income than other measures of need. As well, it might be slow in responding to changed circumstances of transfer recipients. Administrative agencies set up expressly for administering transfers, analogous to welfare or unemployment insurance systems, operate through more discretionary systems. Applicants are screened to determine eligibility and need, and continual monitoring ensures that changes in circumstances can be assessed in a timely way. Payments can be made immediately and frequently without waiting for filing. The choice between the two systems depends on the institutional capacity of the government, the degree of targeting desired in the transfer system, and the evaluation of the extra cost that is involved in using a separate agency.
- *Targeting issues:* In designing targeted transfer schemes, the choice of a screening rule is the first order of business. What are the criteria for eligibility? The criteria will affect the accuracy of targeting and its cost. Targeting can involve both Type I and Type II statistical errors: the denying of benefits to the truly deserving and the awarding of benefits to the nondeserving.

The accuracy of targeting depends on the resources available to administrators. The loss of privacy to the individuals applying for the transfer might be considered an additional cost of the program. The more targeted the program is, the greater is the intrusion by administrators into the individual's life, and the greater the loss in privacy. Type II errors increase the cost of programs and Type I errors reduce the cost, albeit at the expense of losing some benefits. It is possible that this fact biases the response to these two types of errors on the part of administrators. That is, they may care more about avoiding Type II errors than avoiding Type I errors. Arbitrary screening rules can lead to both types. Furthermore, in targeted programs, there can be a great deal of discretion on the part of the administrator. This can give rise to so-called *agency problems:* it is difficult to ensure that administrators are exerting adequate effort in screening applicants. In addition, this can lead to corruption. For both reasons, it is necessary to monitor the administrators, which gives rise to further costs. In universal programs, there is no need for such complex administration; however, corruption can still exist.

Role of voluntary forms of support: The role of voluntary, or traditional, forms of support for the elderly, such as through the extended family, communities, and nongovernmental organizations, should not be understated. These entities play an important role in both industrial and developing countries. They can provide benefits to individuals (typically in kind) and act as lobbyists for certain groups. It is also possible that these entities can obtain better information about local conditions than the government. They may also be less corrupt. The main issue concerns the possibility of crowding out these voluntary transfers as a result of government intervention. To the extent that such crowding-out occurs, government transfers are rendered less effective. Crowding out may also act in the opposite direction. For example, support received from voluntary entities, including those outside the country, can reduce the government's incentive to develop redistributive programs. The extent of crowding-out depends on the preferences of the entity relative to the preferences of the government, and perhaps also on the incentive structure of government programs.

Financing

Redistributive transfers to the elderly must be financed, typically from general government revenues. Given that tax revenues are generally costly to raise—more costly than the amount of money transferred, because of inevitable inefficiencies associated with tax systems—this also raises issues of program design. By targeting programs to alleviate poverty among the elderly, the government is able to reduce the number of beneficiaries and thereby reduce the fiscal cost of the program. This is one of the main reasons to target redistributive programs. The cost savings from targeted schemes can be used either to reduce the tax burden of those financing the program (that is, working individuals), or to increase the benefits that individuals receive in the program. Of course, one must set against this savings the administrative costs of a targeted program, which may outweigh any fiscal savings.

As an alternative to general revenue financing, earmarked revenue sources could be used. For example, payroll taxes could be earmarked for transfers to the elderly, even if the program is not funded. Earmarking may enhance the accountability of the program and provide some notion of permanency by protecting accumulated funds from diversion to other fiscal needs. Earmarked contributions could also be accumulated in a fund so as to reduce or eliminate the intergenerational component that would otherwise accompany transfers to the elderly that are financed out of general revenues.

If the transfer program were targeted by means testing this would amount to an intragenerational transfer. This transfer could potentially reduce the adverse incentive effects that otherwise arise from general revenue financing, to the extent that contributors to the fund view their contributions as a form of insurance premium against the possibility of requiring assistance in their retirement. However, some individuals might put zero weight on this possibility—that is, they know with certainty that they will not qualify for government assistance in their retirement—and this may led to contribution evasion. Using an earmarked fund for a universal transfer program would be equivalent to a mandatory contributory pension, discussed in more detail in the next section.

Economic Effects of Transfers to the Elderly

An important consideration in deciding on a targeted or a universal scheme concerns their economic effects in the labor and capital markets.

Labor market effects

By the elderly, we are implicitly assuming we mean individuals in their retirement years, which by definition implies they are not working. Therefore, a transfer program will have no effect on their current labor supply. The problem arises if individuals, while young, anticipate the transfer program. Presuming that individuals choose their labor supply to maximize their welfare, then the introduction of a universal program will not affect their optimal labor supply choice. Individuals will always receive the transfer, so the best they can do is work the amount that maximizes their welfare without the program.

Alternatively, if individuals must qualify for the transfer in a means-tested targeted program, then labor supply decisions made while they are young may be distorted to enable them to receive the transfer when they are old. For example, individuals with low incomes while young might increase their lifetime welfare by reducing their labor supply (earning even less income), so that their accumulated savings are such that they can qualify for the government transfer. Individuals earning higher incomes are less likely to have this incentive. The higher the tax-back rate in the targeted scheme is, the greater are the potential distortions. If the targeted transfer program was unanticipated by the current older population when those individuals were younger, then labor distortions will not arise. However, once established, the program will be anticipated by the current young generations and distortions may result.

The potential distortionary effects of targeted schemes (resulting from high tax-back rates) must be traded off against the lower revenue requirements needed to finance the program. If this revenue is taken from general tax revenues, then the less revenue is required, the less likely it is that individuals will attempt to avoid and evade taxes. Universal programs, alternatively, have much greater financial requirements and are more likely to induce evasion on the part of taxpayers. This will also be the case when funding for these schemes comes from earmarked taxes.

Capital market effects

The main concern with transfer programs is their effect on individual savings and on nongovernmental support systems. If individuals do not anticipate the transfer program, or if it is a universal program, then their individual savings decisions will be unaffected because their savings will already have accumulated by the time they retire. However, if a targeted program is anticipated, it may adversely affect savings while an individual is young. In addition, targeted programs might induce individuals to misrepresent their true needs when they are old. The higher the tax-back rate is for a given minimum level of guaranteed support, the greater the incentive is to decrease savings when young and to underreport income when old. To reduce this distortion, effective administration must be adopted. Of course, this additional cost of a targeted program must be taken into account when evaluating the program.

Another concern is that government programs to support the elderly may crowd out traditional forms of support, such as the family and the community. In developing countries, these traditional forms of transfers are the main source of support for the elderly. It is important that government intervention attempt to complement these support systems rather than substitute for them. This goal gives rise to another argument for the use of in-kind transfers. For example, provision of public medical care might prolong the life of an elderly individual who receives financial support from private transfers. Another example is the conditioning of in-kind transfers on family provision of support (such as public housing or housing allowances for families living with elderly parents), or care-giving support services for individuals (such as those caring for an elderly relative). Alternatively, transfers can be targeted to individuals who lack family support. One concern with this type of arrangement is the adverse effect it might have on traditional family structures. For example, the conditioning of welfare benefits on single parenthood might lead to marriage breakups.

In deciding to pursue targeted or universal transfer schemes and to use in-kind or cash benefits, governments must consider the effect that their design choices will have on both individual decisions and the decisions of individuals' family and community members.

Contributory Pension Schemes

Contributory pension schemes exist to allow, or ensure, that income earners save adequately out of their incomes. The presumption is that not all income earners choose to do so voluntarily so some coercion is necessary. It may also be the case in developing countries that suitable financial instruments for retirement savings, including those provided by employers, are not broadly available.

A wide spectrum of forms of public intervention can be used to address this issue, forms ranging from maximal to minimal reliance on the private sector. At one extreme, the government might simply mandate either savings by individuals or the provision of pensions by employers. Along with mandating, governments might regulate certain features of private pension plans, such as asset composition and portability. The government might also set down administrative parameters for these plans, such as whether they are defined-benefit or defined-contribution plans, and the form that pension payments might take (annuities, lump sum, and so forth). There may also be tax incentives available for pension savings. The government might be a more active participant. The pension scheme can be a public one, with contributions being made to a public fund (or paid out directly to pensioners if the plan is unfunded). The fund itself may be managed privately or publicly.

General Design Issues

Where the scheme lies along the private-public spectrum is clearly a policy decision. Whatever policy makers decide, a number of design issues must be addressed. We consider those next. Subsequently, we consider specific issues that arise in private pension schemes, public pension schemes, and mandated savings schemes and then turn to a discussion of their economic effects.

Coverage

In deciding on particular pension designs, the government must recognize the limitations its choice will place on the amount of coverage provided by the various types of pensions. The fact remains that not all income earners may be covered by contributory pensions. In the case of mandated employer-provided pensions, coverage is typically limited to larger firms in the formal sector: they are the ones that may be able to administer employee pension plans. Workers in small firms, the self-employed, and part-time, occasional, or seasonal workers and workers in the informal sector are typically excluded. Coverage could be extended by allowing financial institutions to provide pensions for at least some of these groups. With public contributory schemes, the extent of coverage can be decided on by the public sector. In principle, it could include all income earners, whether employees or self-employed, part-time or full-time, primary or secondary, and so on. There would still be some difficulty in reaching those in the informal sector. As well, there is the issue of whether to include persons outside the workforce, such as homemakers (or to prevent them from participating).

Funded versus unfunded

Pension benefits may be paid out of a fund that has been accumulated on the basis of past contributions, or they may be paid out of current contributions. Fully funded pensions are those that are actuarially fair: the size of the fund is maintained so that all future liabilities can be met. Fully funded pensions include no implicit intergenerational transfers and thus should provide no net incentive on aggregate savings. For unfunded, or pay-as-you-go, pensions, all current contributions represent an intergenerational transfer. Pensions may also be partly funded, whereby an accumulated fund from prior contributions finances a portion of current and future pension benefits. However, it can be partially funded only for a limited time, because ultimately the fund will run out and the plan will become unfunded. (Of course, pensions may be temporarily unfunded, or overfunded, as when the government wants to make temporary intergenerational transfers.)

Among fully funded pensions, there are two possibilities. They can be actuarially fair from the point of view of each individual contributor. Pensions that maintain individual accounts in the fund are often of this sort. In fact, the use of individual accounts establishes entitlements that might serve the political purpose of maintaining funding. Alternatively, pensions might be funded in the aggregate, but not for all persons. That is, there might be systematic cross-subsidization of some types of households (for example, those with families or nonworking spouses) by others. If so, there should be redistributive arguments for doing so.

Pension benefits: Defined-contribution versus defined-benefit

Even if pensions are funded, their payments to the retired can be calculated in one of two ways. They may be defined-contribution payments, in which case the level of contributions is predetermined as, say, a percentage of earnings each year. The pension benefits are then determined by the amount of accumulated contributions plus expected investment returns, taking into account the actuarial probability of the length of time over which the individual is expected to receive benefits. Defined-benefit plans predetermine the level of retirement benefit based on a specified ratio of pension benefits to some measure of income earned during the contribution period—perhaps the earnings in the last few years of employment, or the highest earning years—with perhaps a flat-rate component or even a means-tested one. Contributions are set to cover the predetermined levels of benefit. Benefits themselves can come in alternative forms, including annuities, lump-sum payments, fixed-length securities, or some combination of these.

The choice between defined-contribution and defined-benefit plans, as well as the form of benefits, affects the risk faced by households as well as by the government. Defined-contribution plans can expose individuals to rate of return risks, while in defined-benefit plans these risks are assumed by the provider, be it private or public. Either type of plan may involve inflation risk unless defined benefits are explicitly indexed. Private pensions may be less able to index defined-benefit plans if the source of inflation risk is future government actions. Defined-contribution plans, if accompanied by identifiable individual accounts, may increase the probability that politicians will not take actions that may erode their future value. Pensions that are paid out as annuities provide insurance against longevity risk. Those paid out as a lump sum allow for the possibility that they will be exhausted too quickly and the public sector may be faced with the prospect of providing further support.

Nature of contributions

Pensions can be financed by various forms of contributions. From a compliance point of view, the simplest form might be payroll taxes withheld by the firm on behalf of its employees. These can be calculated based on employer contributions, employee contributions, or some mix of the two. To an economist these should all be equivalent because their incidence should not depend on who pays them but on the demand and supply characteristics of labor markets. But it is sometimes argued that employers and employees view the two as different and react differently to them.

Contributions may also be levied directly on individuals. This is a somewhat more costly procedure than payroll tax deductions, and it can lead to more leakage. Yet it can also bring into the social safety net persons who are not employees of large firms. More generally, contributions can be funded from general revenues, although this tends to break the link between contributions and benefits to the detriment of the pension's political sustainability and its economic incentives.

Individual access to pension assets

Although compulsory pensions are intended to ensure that households have adequate savings to support themselves in retirement, there may also be a need for extraordinary expenditures before retirement. These might include education and training expenses, the acquisition of housing or other major consumer durables, and emergency health expenditures. Some countries allow individuals to draw down their retirement assets for these purposes.

A couple of important considerations are involved. First, such expenditures might contribute to individuals' abilities to take care of themselves in retirement. Education and training should increase current incomes, out of which savings can be made. Housing produces a necessary form of consumption services in retirement and could be viewed as a form of saving for retirement. However, financing human capital accumulation can be risky and may not lead to any significant increase in future income. It could be argued that encouraging and financing human capital accumulation should be a separate program. The second consideration, which applies particularly to emergency expenditures in health and other areas, is that allowing households to use pension assets amounts to requiring them to self-insure. This is a particularly inefficient and inequitable form of insurance.

Auxiliary insurance programs

As well as providing retirement income, pension schemes may provide various forms of insurance, including that for health, disability, injury on the job, maternity leave, and survivors' benefits. Many of these are of particular concern to persons at or near retirement. They can be an integral part of the pension scheme whose contributions are built in, or they can be offered in parallel. They can be voluntary or a compulsory adjunct to the pension system. And their coverage can extend beyond that of an employee-sponsored pension to include individuals who did not contribute to the pension plan. These auxiliary insurance plans may or may not be actuarially fair. That is, they may serve a social insurance purpose and involve some cross-subsidization. In this event, it is presumably better for the cross-subsidization to come from taxpayers in general than from other contributors.

The issues discussed above apply to contributory pension systems wherever they lie along the private-public spectrum. Further special design considerations apply to different institutional delivery forms. We next outline the design issues that arise in the three main forms of contributory pensions—occupational private pensions, public pensions, and mandated savings plans, and then discuss their associated economic issues.

Occupational Private Pension Design Issues

Occupational pension plans are those provided by employers on behalf of their employees. They may be mandatory for all firms, quasi-mandatory in the sense that employees must participate in the public plan if employers do not provide them voluntarily, or a result of collective bargaining. In all cases, coverage is likely to be limited to firms of a minimal size in the formal sector and to primary employees. Individuals who have uneven employment histories are unlikely to be covered (for example, some women). Some of the specific design issues that arise with occupational pensions are as follows.

Form of benefits

As mentioned above, benefits may be paid according to defined-benefit or defined-contribution schedules, or some combination of the two. Defined-benefit plans typically provide an annuity based on a specified rule, the two most common of which are unit benefit plans and flat benefit plans. Unit benefit plans are based on a formula that relates benefits to past earnings for each year of service. For example, an employee receives a unit of benefit (typically defined as a percentage of a specified earnings base or assessed income) for each year of employment. The earnings base can be specified as final earnings (the individual's earnings in the last year of employment before retirement), career-average earnings (the average of the individual's earnings over a specified number of years before retirement), or best-average earnings (the average of the individual's earnings over a given number of years for which the individual's earnings were the highest). Flat benefit plans are independent of earnings. They provide pensions of a fixed monetary amount for each year (or for each time interval less than a year) of employment. The generosity of the benefits may be determined by the firm perhaps being subject to collective bargaining, or it may be influenced by government policy. Mandated pensions may specify a minimum level of pension benefits, perhaps related to earnings. As well, the tax deductibility of pension contributions may be limited to some level of contributions.

Defined-contribution pensions are of two sorts, money purchase plans and profit-sharing plans. With money purchase pensions, contributions by each employee (or by employers on behalf of each employee) may be based on earnings and, as with defined-benefit plans, may be influenced by government decree. The stream of contributions is accumulated in a fund on behalf of the employee, the size of which then determines the level of benefits. With profit-sharing plans, the bulk of the contribution stream depends on the profit of the firm. As with defined-benefit plans, the benefits can be taken as an annuity in retirement. Alternatively, benefits can be given as a lump-sum payment, as a deferred annuity (purchased while still working), or as a fixed-term pension.

These different plans essentially impose different risks on individuals. Virtually all private plans have some inflation risk because the private sector is not able to insure asset holders entirely against inflation risk—some assets are not fully indexed for inflation. But some pension plans are more inflation-proof than others. Defined-benefit plan benefits are typically not indexed for inflation. Unit benefit plans tend to be more effective at insuring against inflation because wages on average tend to rise over time at the same rate as inflation (plus real productivity growth)—but this does not avoid the lack of indexation of benefits during retirement years. Under other defined-benefit plans, individuals will suffer a real wealth loss in the presence of unexpected or expected inflation during both their work and retirement years. The only way inflation risk can be avoided altogether is to induce employers to provide fully indexed funds, perhaps through regulation. But this would be difficult to enforce.

Another potential risk faced by pension participants is investment risk. Defined-benefit pensions might better shield beneficiaries from this risk, because their benefit levels are defined independently of the returns on the pension fund at any given point. However, contributors' benefits are based on some part of their earnings profiles, which may be uncertain. As well, employees may face certain risks arising from their place of employment.

The employer may have a right (subject to certain qualifications, such as unlawful dismissals) to fire a worker or to terminate or change the structure of the pension plans. Employees also may face the risk of employer insolvency and job mobility. This risk may be less under a defined-contribution plan, especially one that is financed primarily by employees. Finally, profit-sharing plans increase the risk to the employee, because the generosity of the plan depends on the fortunes of a single company.

Source of contributions

The share of funds contributed by employees versus employers can vary from one extreme to another. Each side may bear a fixed share or, in a defined-benefit system, employees may contribute given proportions of their earnings, with the employer making up the difference to ensure employees receive the promised pension benefits. As mentioned earlier, the sharing rule should not matter in principle. But in practice it might matter if the employees' rights to the pension fund are more secure when the contributions are made by the employees themselves. There might also be tax benefits from using employer contributions when a company's tax rates are higher than those of its employees, and the contributions are tax-deductible. The pension plan may also be sponsored by multiple employers; that is, it can be an occupational (industrywide) pension, rather than a firm-specific pension.

Vesting and portability

Vesting refers to an employee's rights to all or part of the contributions made by the employer on his or her behalf if employment with the firm is terminated before he or she reaches retirement age. If benefits are not vested, then the terminated employee is entitled only to his or her own contributions, plus any accumulated interest. Governments typically impose some vesting rules on occupational pensions. These rules might include minimum lengths of service and possibly an age requirement on the part of an employee beyond which total vesting is required. The purpose of vesting requirements is to protect employees from loss of pension benefits if they change or lose their jobs: firms might prefer not to have vesting requirements so as to reduce their employee turnover.

Vested pension benefits are said to be *locked in* if they can be taken only as a deferred pension rather than as an immediate cash settlement. Some firms set up vested pension benefits such that individuals can choose to accept the cash value of their own contributions immediately or take the deferred pension including the firm's portion of contributions. By taking the cash settlement, individuals lose some of their pension benefits and the firm gains the cost savings from the forfeited benefits. It is possible that individuals are not aware of the benefits they are losing by this decision. Thus, locking in benefits can prevent firms from exploiting former employees' ignorance. At the same time, locking in ensures that individuals use contributions for retirement income rather than for increasing their current consumption by accepting a cash settlement.

Portability refers to the right of employees to transfer the value of a pension to another plan, perhaps that of a new employer. If a defined-benefit pension is an industrywide pension plan sponsored by multiple firms, then portability is straightforward. The pension can readily be transferred between firms within the industry. Transfers will not be as straightforward if the pension is firm-specific. On the whole, defined-contribution plans tend to be more portable—even the portion that has been financed by employer contributions. As with vesting, the government can require total or partial pension portability.

Funding requirements

Ideally, pension funds should be fully funded so that the accumulated value of past contributions at any point equals the present value of expected future accumulated obligations. By definition, defined-contribution pension plans are fully funded, because the payouts are strictly determined by the amount that has been accumulated. This structure insures against the risk of employer default. A partially funded scheme will require an injection of additional funds in the future to cover benefits. Governments typically mandate that occupational pensions be fully funded at all times. Of course, even pensions that are fully funded in actuarial terms are not immune from investment risk. As mentioned, employers bear that risk in defined-benefit plans because they promise the pension benefits.

In defined-contribution plans, workers face the investment risks. But they might have some choice about how to invest their pension assets so as to express their preferences about risk. They may be offered a menu of bond, equity, and money market assets chosen by the employer. Alternatively, the employer might make the investment decisions on behalf of the pension participants. It is possible that the fund manager will have preferences that differ from those of the individuals contributing to the fund. Agency problems might arise in this situation.

Administrative costs

Occupational pension plans have relatively low administrative costs. Contributions are collected by payroll deduction, taking advantage of administrative machinery that already exists. Marketing costs by investment firms are typically low as well, because rather than dealing with individual employees they deal with firms who represent many employees. Firms can also use life insurance companies or other financial institutions to administer fully funded pensions.

Government regulation

As the discussion above implies, virtually all occupational pensions are subject to some government regulation. This is a virtual necessity to ensure that firms act responsibly on behalf of employees, many of whom have no understanding of the complexity of the pension plan and may have no close or permanent attachment to the firm. The government also has an interest in ensuring that pension plans are solvent, efficient, and equitable. Participants in pension plans that fail will ultimately become burdens on the taxpayer. A challenge thus exists for developing countries that may not have the institutional ability or experience to monitor and regulate pensions effectively.

Although we have mentioned many forms of government regulation already, it is worth summarizing their main forms here:

- *Reporting requirements:* Pension administrators may have formal reporting requirements both to the government and to fund participants. As well, there may be recurrent monitoring by regulators for compliance. The purpose is to enhance accountability.
- *Funding requirements:* Programs may have to comply with actuarial valuation principles to ensure that the level of funds is sufficient to meet future liabilities.
- *Fund management:* Pension administrators may require minimum professional qualifications, and fees and commissions charged by fund managers may be regulated.
- *Portfolio restrictions:* There may be portfolio diversification rules (equity versus private debt versus public debt), as well as rules about maximum foreign asset holdings. The purpose should be to ensure prudent fund management, but such regulations might also be used to achieve political objectives.
- *Vesting and portability:* Minimum vesting and portability rules might apply that cover both employer and employee contributions.
- *Government guarantees:* An important consideration is the government's role in guaranteeing private pensions in the event that pension funds or firms go bankrupt. Problems of moral hazard arise that must be traded off against the security provided to employees: government guarantees to

meet pension obligations in the event of bankruptcy may induce firms or pension funds to take greater risks than are efficient.

- *Tax treatment of contributions and benefits:* In countries where income taxes are well developed, tax treatment is relevant. The standard practice in OECD countries is for contributions (both employers' and employees') to be tax-deductible, but benefits to be taxable. This is based on the notion that the contributions are not available for household consumption until retirement. The full amount of the contribution is available for investment, investment returns accumulate tax-free, and tax rates applicable in retirement may be lower because of progressive marginal tax rate systems. As discussed later, this also parallels the treatment that is often offered for additional voluntary savings for retirement (to provide some incentive for such savings). Benefits received in retirement may also be partly tax-deductible, although this amounts to a double deduction. In developing countries, the issue of tax treatment may be less relevant at the household level because the coverage of income taxes is limited, especially for investment income.

Public Pension Design Issues

Unlike private pensions, a public pension is a single-provider system: all participants contribute to the same system and there is a single fund (although in principle workers might be able to opt out if they had suitable private pensions). A single publicly administered pension system may have possible cost savings owing to economies of scale and lower advertising, marketing, and coordination costs. However, the absence of competition reduces the incentive for cost-effectiveness, and the public nature of the plan leaves it open to politically motivated policy changes that might effectively be shortsighted.

Coverage of public pensions is typically very broad, including all income earners in the economy (at least in the formal sector), whether they are in small or large firms, and employed or self-employed. Contributions are compulsory, but eligibility for pensions is based on a minimum contribution period. Pension payments begin at a statutory retirement age, but there are usually provisions for early retirement. For example, those who retire before the statutory age may be eligible if they have reached some minimum age and have paid contributions for some minimum time period. The benefits that an individual receives are reduced in proportion to the difference between his or her age and the statutory retirement age. Benefit levels typically rise over time, often with the growth rate of average wages; sometimes they rise with the rate of inflation, as measured by the consumer price index (CPI).

There are a number of specific features of public plans that the government must determine. The following are some of the more important ones.

Defined-benefit versus defined-contribution

Although public pensions could be defined-contribution plans, they are typically defined-benefit plans. That reduces the investment risk that would otherwise be faced by retirees. Of course, investment risk must be borne by someone, either the taxpayers or future contributors: if investment returns are lower than expected, funds must be found to meet future liabilities. In a fully funded plan, this need is likely to be passed on to future contributors. In defined-contribution plans, each contributor bears the cost of investment shortfalls on his or her past contributions. As mentioned earlier, defined-contribution plans may enable the application of more discipline by the government to keep the fund viable and healthy.

Defined-benefit levels are usually based on target wage replacement rates. The right replacement rate depends on household preferences (the desired consumption pattern over a lifetime, taking into account uncertainties about health, the cost of living, and so forth), the growth rate of the economy, and the choice of wage base. If the rate is too low, some persons will not have enough to live on when retired. As well, the rate may not be adequate to address the failure of insurance markets to provide efficient levels of annuities to pool longevity uncertainty. But a low rate will minimize evasion and distortions in capital and labor markets. High replacement rates may also induce financing problems. An option is to keep the replacement rate relatively low but to have a lower bound that covers basic needs. Defined-benefit schemes also often impose a ceiling on contributions and benefits (a maximum replacement rate).

Defined-benefit schemes often contain elements of cross-subsidization to address redistributive concerns, even though their primary purpose is to ensure adequate savings for retirement. As mentioned, guaranteed minimum pensions may be available for low-wage persons. Survivor benefits may favor married over single persons. And there may be elements of social insurance built into the pension system, such as disability benefits or health benefits.

Source of funds

Public pensions may be financed in a number of ways. The most common form is an earmarked payroll tax paid by income earners—employees or employers, and the self-employed—as a proportion of earnings. This is a transparent form of financing, and one that is easy to administer for countries that have well-developed income tax systems. An alternative is for individuals to contribute directly to the public pension scheme. This method entails greater compliance (and enforcement) costs but allows for potentially broader coverage than payroll tax deductions. This method also establishes clearer entitlement to pension benefits for contributors, so it might provide pressure to maintain the funding of the pension system. General revenues might also be used to fund public pensions, but doing so would undoubtedly turn the scheme into a more redistributive one. It would break the link between contributions and benefits and increase the adverse incentive effects of the scheme.

The extent of funding

Public pensions may be funded, unfunded (pay as you go), or partially funded. As mentioned earlier, the absence of funding implies that there is an intergenerational transfer component implicit in the pension scheme. This has obvious redistributive effects, which can be viewed as unfair to certain generations. It can also crowd out private savings and therefore be detrimental to economic growth.

Under a pay-as-you-go system, current expenditures equal current revenues in each year; there is said to be financial balance. More formally, assume there are P pensioners and N workers or contributors. Average pensions and average contributions are given as proportions of the applicable average wage base. Suppose average wages for the current pensioner when he or she was working were W_P, and the average wage of current workers is W_N. Let t be the average contribution rate and b be the average wage-replacement rate. For financial balance, revenue must equal expenditure in any time period, implying $tW_N N = bW_p P$. The equilibrium contribution rate is then $t = b(P/N)(W_P/W_N)$, where P/N is the system's dependency ratio (sometimes referred to by its inverse, the support ratio, $S = N/P$), and W_P/W_N reflects the growth in average wages.

This expression for the equilibrium contribution rate has two important implications. First, there is a weak link between contributions and benefits received: it depends on the dependency or support ratio and the rate of wage growth. The fewer workers there are relative to the number of retirees, the lower the support rate is, and the higher must be the equilibrium contribution rate t relative to the level of benefits b. The support rate is determined by demographic factors (the birth rate and average longevity), employment conditions, and the statutory retirement age. The key point is that because an unfunded public pension is an intergenerational transfer, it is vulnerable to demographic and economic change. This raises the issue of sustainability. Future generations will be less willing to pay into the fund if the dependency ratio becomes high or there is an economic depression; alternatively, it may be unfair to expect them to pay in. Preexisting parameters may simply become financially nonviable, and something must give—contribution rates, benefits rates, or eligibility.

The second implication of the relationship between t and b concerns the implicit rate of return in the pay-as-you-go system. If the contributions t had been invested in the capital market, as in the case of a funded system, they would have yielded a benefit in retirement of $B = t(1 + r)$, where r is the compound market rate of return between the time of contribution and the receipt of benefits in retirement. Instead, the pay-as-you-go system yields $b = t(N/P)(W_N/W_P) \approx (1 + g)$, where g is the rate of growth of the economy.[7] If the rate of growth of the economy is less than the rate of interest ($g < r$), which is typically the case over the longer term, the implicit rate of return to the system will be less than that in a funded system. Thus, the pay-as-you-go system will, in the long run, make contributors worse off than a funded system would. Of course, when the pay-as-you-go system is introduced, those who are retired or sufficiently close to retirement will get a windfall gain: they will receive pensions without having paid contributions. Thus, the effect of the pension will be to make older generations better off, and younger and future generations worse off, at least as long as the system remains in effect. In this sense, the pay-as-you-go system has very similar effects to deficit financing by the government. Moreover, one can calculate the implicit value of pay-as-you-go debt as the present value of future unfunded liabilities of the public pension.

Funded pensions are significantly different. They maintain actuarial balance, such that the size of the existing pension fund plus the projected contribution revenues equals projected expenditures within a given period of time. There are no unfunded liabilities. Full funding can be achieved indefinitely by calculating the value of the fixed premium actuarially on the basis of future liability requirements. Of course, if benefits change, so must contribution levels. Changes in circumstances (life expectancies, investment returns, and so forth) will also affect the fund's projected liabilities. As a result, the plan requires continual monitoring. Planned revenues must be received on time and in full; there needs to be an efficient administration of reserve funds; and periodic actuarial valuations need to be carried out. In practice, funded programs run the risk not only of inefficient administration but also of being subject to political manipulation.

Pensions may be partially funded, either by design or because the fund is allowed to fall below its actuarial level. Such a system induces some implicit intergenerational transfers. If left unchanged, the fund would eventually run out (unless demographics or economic factors change fortuitously) and the plan would lapse into a pay-as-you-go one. To re-fund the plan may be difficult politically, because it requires either benefits to fall or contributions to rise.

Fund management

Even if a pension is public, so that contributions and benefits are administered by the public sector, the management of the fund may be private. The public sector could contract out the role of investment management to financial specialists. The advantage of doing so is twofold. First, public sector managers might not have the expertise to invest wisely. Second, public management may be subject to political interference. Funds might be used for public debt or to finance public sector projects of low return. Private managers still must be monitored to ensure that investments are within acceptable wealth parameters and that administrative costs are not excessive.

Regardless of who manages the fund, asset composition is an issue. Broadly speaking, there is a choice among three options—government securities, private debt, and private equity. These all vary in their risk-return characteristics, and presumably any portfolio will maintain a mix of all three. The exact mix depends on how the government, acting on behalf of its citizens, trades off risk against return. In practice, a public pension fund may be relatively large compared with the local capital market as a whole, and this can have unexpected consequences on market prices and yield returns, depending on the investment choice.

Mandatory Retirement Saving Schemes or Provident Fund Design Issues

A variant of a fully funded pension scheme is to require individuals to participate in an individualized retirement savings scheme, rather than one organized by their employers. Versions of these have been referred to as *provident funds,* for example, in Malaysia and Singapore. These types of funds, unlike public pensions, are typically defined-contribution funds and fully portable. They have virtually no redistributional element, either intergenerational or intragenerational. Each household has its own account, based on its past contributions.

Participants' pensions are financed from their savings accounts, which accumulate until retirement. The size of the benefit depends on the contribution rate, the growth of earnings, the interest rate, the number of years of employment, and the age at retirement. To maintain pension benefits at a given level of support, the contribution rate must be higher (a) the lower the pension fund's rate of return is relative to the growth of earnings, (b) the longer the length of retirement period is relative to the working period, and (c) the higher the administrative costs of the plan are. Because pensions are based on earnings, the plans do not apply to nonparticipants in the labor force and are of limited use for persons who have interrupted careers, such as women who stop work to raise children or persons who are persistently unemployed. For these persons, there is no assurance that adequate savings will be accumulated to support themselves in old age.

Benefits can be paid out in various ways. In some countries, they are paid out simply as a lump sum on retirement, leaving it to beneficiaries to use the funds as they see fit. Ideally, beneficiaries would acquire annuities to avoid longevity risk and ensure that funds are available to support them throughout their retirement. But annuity markets may not be well developed, especially for indexed annuities, or households may simply choose not to purchase annuities either because they are not fully informed or knowledgeable about annuities or because they are myopic. In this case, part of the purpose of the mandatory savings scheme is forfeited. Alternatively, pension plans could pay benefits in the form of annuities. In addition, some schemes permit accumulated balances to be withdrawn before retirement for other purposes, such as housing, health care, and education.

As with other compulsory pension schemes, savings in provident funds are usually tax favored, sometimes very generously. Contributions are usually deductible, and investment income in the fund accumulates tax-free. Lump-sum payments on retirement may also be tax-free (although early withdrawals may be taxed). This amounts to very favorable tax treatment, much more generous than a consumption tax system. This may be justified to encourage compliance, and to ensure that participants have adequate income in their retirement at low contribution rates. However, the deduction system especially favors higher-income persons who are in higher tax brackets. This regressive situation could be partially avoided by offering a tax credit rather than a deduction from income. Some OECD countries offer much less generous tax regimes for retirement savings schemes, for example, by subjecting pension funds to a tax as they are accumulating.

As with public pensions, the management of the pension system, especially the fund, is critical. The system could be managed centrally, with the government administering the contributions as well as determining the use of funds. This allows economies of scale to be achieved and possibly enhances compliance, but it can result in both unproductive investments and inefficient administration, as has been alleged in the government-managed schemes in Malaysia and Singapore. Alternatively, private companies can be allowed to administer the system and manage their own funds, as in Chile. In this case, individuals have a choice as to which private company to use.

Competition encourages efficient operation and maximum investment returns, partially insulated from political pressures. But a complex regulatory structure is needed to ensure financial soundness and solvency and the integrity of financial managers. Regulation would encompass such items as entry criteria and minimum capital margins, protection against fraudulent behavior, disclosure of information rules, and investment rules concerning approved assets and diversification. Private pension administration can also result in higher transaction, marketing, and operating costs, and these higher costs will be reflected in higher management fees and commissions. Further regulation may be required to restrict the type and size of fees that can be set. An alternative that may avoid some of these problems is to have a mixed public-private system in which a public body collects contributions and disburses pensions but allows the pension fund to be managed by the private sector on a competitive basis.

Economic Effects of Contributory Pension Schemes

The choice of the form of contributory pension system to ensure that income earners have adequate savings for retirement and the choice of its parameters will be influenced by the way in which the system affects economic behavior. Induced changes in behavior can both increase the cost of the system and induce inefficiencies in the market economy. There may also be redistributional effects, either intentional or unintentional, to consider. Contributory pensions involve setting aside a portion of one's earnings, largely from labor income, to be used to finance a system of savings for retirement. As such, the largest impact will be on labor and capital markets.

Labor market effects

The system of contributions to the pension system, as well as its institutional features, can affect both the supply and the demand sides of the labor market.

LABOR SUPPLY. There are a myriad of labor supply decisions, ranging from hours of work to participation to occupational choice. These decisions can be influenced by the structure of both contributions and benefits. The following summarizes the ways in which the pension system can affect labor supply decisions.

- *Earnings:* Required contributions are like payroll taxes, so it might be expected that they would affect the incentive to supply labor. But this effect will be mitigated by two factors. First, to the extent that benefits in retirement are directly tied to contributions, there should be no incentive effect. Second, if there is an upper limit on contributions, persons with earnings above the limit will have no marginal tax rate effect. This suggests that provident funds and occupational pensions that are strictly funded at the individual level should not have a major effect on labor supply. Public pensions, however, even if funded in the aggregate, will discourage earnings to the extent that benefits in retirement are independent of earnings. That will be true for most defined-benefit public pensions. Earnings might also be discouraged if pensions are subject to tax-back in retirement.

- *Retirement age:* As above, a pension that is actuarially fair at the individual level should not affect the decision to retire. Otherwise, retirement can be encouraged, especially if pension benefits are available on early retirement. The additional opportunity cost of staying on the job will include additional contributions that must be made when working, plus any forgone pension benefits that are available on early retirement. Pension systems that allow retirement after a given length of service are open to these incentives.

- *Participation:* The effect on participation is ambiguous. In a provident-type fund, individuals might be induced into the labor market in order to be able to participate if the fund offers services that might be less readily available on an individual basis: pooled investments, disability, and health insurance. In a public pension system, in which the implicit returns might be low and benefits are not closely tied to contributions, individuals may choose not to participate, at least for part of their working lives. An obvious and important alternative in developing countries is to work in the informal sector or in the underground economy, where contributions cannot be enforced. This might be encouraged to the extent that benefits are not tied to contributions: if a minimum pension is available after a given number of years of contribution, workers might be induced to move to the informal sector after accumulating the required years. Yet another alternative is to underreport incomes, a possibility that is open to the self-employed and perhaps to employees in smaller firms. Employers themselves may connive in effectively evading the tax, for example, by using fringe benefits as a form of compensation rather than wages.

- *Human capital accumulation:* Investment in education and training is not likely to be affected by payroll tax systems, at least if increased earnings are subject to a common rate of tax. However, human capital investment might be encouraged if individuals can draw on their provident funds for financing, given that borrowing from the private sector to finance education is typically very imperfect.

- *Labor mobility:* Workers will be discouraged from changing jobs if pensions are not fully vested and portable. This will be an issue for the employer's contribution to occupational pensions only. Public pensions and provident schemes that are provided at the individual level will be independent of employment by design, and the employee's own contributions are typically fully vested. The loss due to the absence of vesting depends on the type of pension. For defined-contribution plans, it is the accumulated value of employer contributions. For defined-benefit plans, it is the amount needed to purchase the pension benefits to which the employment history of the individual would have entitled him or her—that is, the actuarial value of the deferred pension less the accumulated value of the individual's contributions. For some types of defined-benefit plans, the employee may pay most of the cost of the accrued pension during his or her early working years; hence, the benefits of vesting may be close to zero. For example, in a contributory unit benefit plan, the employer's contributions increase with the employee's age because the younger the employee is, the longer their contributions will accumulate and the more likely it is that they will leave the plan before they qualify for full pension benefits. It is possible that the present value of pension benefits will be higher as an employee approaches retirement and therefore impedes labor mobility. This is known as *backloading*.

LABOR DEMAND. The behavior of employers can also be influenced by contributory pension systems. In some cases, this might be a consequence of an agreement between the employer and its employees, either explicit or implicit. Some of the most important ways are as follows.

- *Turnover:* Firms have an incentive to use pension plans as a means of lowering turnover (which is costly to them). A preferred means of doing this might be to set wage schedules that increase with time, so that firms can recoup the costs of training and hiring costs, as well as increases in labor productivity. But collective bargaining agreements might prevent this escalation, forcing firms to fall back on limited vesting of their contributions to employee pension plans. If firms are forced to vest pensions, turnover can increase. This can be good or bad. On the one hand, increased turnover enables workers to move to better job matches and increases the flexibility of the labor market. On the other, it reduces the incentive for firms to engage in training, unless they can find a substitute way to hold workers. Thus, the argument for vesting can cut both ways, even if one views pension benefits as deferred wages. Vesting might also reduce the incentives for individuals to evade, since they should view their contributions less as taxes than as savings for their retirement.

- *Hiring:* If firms are mandated to provide pension plans for their employees, and especially if they must make contributions, the cost of hiring can increase. This will be especially true if pensions are vested by regulation, because then firms can no longer use pensions to keep workers with the firm, so as to spread fixed hiring costs into the future. They may prefer to hire short-term or contract workers, for whom pension benefits may not be required. Obviously, this reduces the number of workers covered by the mandatory pension.

- *Matching of workers to jobs:* Occupational pensions that are sponsored by employers can influence the allocation of workers to jobs. Different firms may have different qualities of pension plans; for example, plans may differ systematically between small, new firms and large, established firms. Firms with more attractive pensions can attract workers more readily. Provident funds and pension funds provided by the public sector avoid this problem. With provident funds, even if the pension is privately provided, individuals can select the investment fund that is best suited to their needs, independent of their employers.

- *Employment effects:* In a fully flexible labor market, payroll taxes levied to finance pensions will be absorbed by employers and employees according to the elasticities of demand and supply for labor, and no involuntary unemployment should be induced. But if there are wage rigidities in the labor market, including those imposed by unions or government policies, employers will not be able to shift the payroll tax to workers, so unemployment can be induced.

Capital market effects

A pension system's effects on the labor market are transmitted primarily through its contribution structure. Its effects on the capital market, however, depend on its benefit structure. In particular, the funding provisions of the benefits, how benefits are financed, and how any existing funds are managed and invested are all relevant. These funding requirements and the institutional features of the system will affect the supply of capital in the economy through their effect on individual savings, public and private investment, and capital market development.

INDIVIDUAL SAVINGS. Analyzing the effects of a pension scheme or a mandated savings scheme on individual savings decisions requires some theory about individuals' savings behavior. Why do individuals save? The most common explanation is that individuals want to smooth their consumption over their lifetimes and, given their lifetime earnings profile, some savings is required. Assuming individuals expect to be retired for some period of time, they will save in their earning years and dissave when they retire. This is known as the *life-cycle hypothesis.* It predicts that the shape of the consumption profile can be determined separately from the earnings profile, but its level depends on lifetime wealth, which includes both the value of the household's initial asset wealth (both financial and real) and the present value of the household's current and future earnings income. An increase in lifetime wealth will increase the entire profile of consumption. Savings in each period is the residual between income and consumption, and thus depends on the profile of each.

If this prediction is correct, then any pension scheme can affect individual savings for two reasons. It might change the household's lifetime wealth. And it might affect the profile of (after-tax and transfer) income of the household. The effect of pensions on aggregate saving also depends on the distribution of savings between the private and the public sectors, especially the extent to which pension schemes or mandated savings schemes crowd out individual savings. We return to this issue later.

To see the effect of pension policies on individual savings, assume a simple life-cycle model in which capital markets are perfect and there are no taxes and no uncertainty. Assume for the sake of simplicity that the interest rate is zero and that earnings are fixed, so that there are no labor market effects. Suppose individuals live for N economic periods, that is, those starting from the time they enter the labor market. They work from period 1 until they retire at age R. Each year that they work they earn W in labor income, and they have no initial wealth. Therefore, their lifetime income Y is simple to calculate: $Y = WR$, undiscounted because of the zero interest rate assumption. Suppose they fully smooth their consumption over their lifetime, that is, they have no pure time preference. Their consumption each year (C) is calculated as $C = Y/N$. To achieve this, they must save while they work. Their annual savings while they work (S) are calculated as $S = W - C = (N - R)W/N$.

Now suppose a pension scheme is introduced that promises an aggregate benefit equal to B for each year the individual works or, equivalently, a mandated savings scheme that requires an annual contribution of B. The total pension benefit that the individual receives on retirement is equal to BR. (Again, this would have to be augmented by accumulated interest if the interest rate was positive.) If the employee is the contributor, his or her annual net income is reduced by the amount he or she must contribute to the pension account. Alternatively, to the extent that the employer is a contributor, the employees' wage earnings are reduced by the amount of the employer contribution because productivity has not changed. In either case, the individuals' net earnings are $W - B$ for each year worked, and they receive BR on retirement. Total lifetime income is unchanged, and therefore annual consumption over the lifetime will be the same. What does change is the income profile over the life cycle, and this affects the savings made while working. Given that individuals are going to receive an aggregate benefit of BR when they retire (either as a lump sum or as an annuity), they reduce their savings while working accordingly, so $S = W - B - C = (N - R)W/N - B$ each year. The pension promise of B completely crowds out private savings.

However, the net effect on aggregate savings might be zero. In a fully funded system, the contribution B goes into the pension fund, so it is a component of savings. This is true whether the funded pension is private or public, and whether contributions come from the employee or from the employer. However, if the pension is unfunded, contributions that crowd out private savings that would otherwise have gone into capital markets are now used to finance the consumption of the currently retired. Thus, not only are private savings crowded out, but so are aggregate ones. We return to this point later.

This prediction that a pension scheme or mandated savings scheme will completely crowd out individuals' savings depends crucially on the assumptions of the simple model. Real-world observations indicate that these assumptions may not hold, and as a result individual savings may be affected by the introduction of a funded or unfunded pension scheme. There are several possible effects:

- Individuals might be myopic and save too little, for the reasons outlined above. In this case, compulsory pension plans have relatively little crowding-out effect on private savings.
- Wages may not be flexible enough to fall to offset employer contributions. Private savings by employees will not be entirely crowded out, but unemployment may ensue. As well, because profits of firms decline, corporate savings may well fall.
- Individuals might be unsure about the value of pension benefits because of uncertainty about pension fund investment returns, the credibility of the firm, future costs of living, and inflation. Alternatively, investment returns might be expected to be lower if pension funds are expected to be poorly managed. Again, this may reduce the extent of crowding out.

- Individuals might save for reasons other than to smooth consumption. For example, individuals may be altruistic and save for bequests, or they might save for precautionary reasons. The need for precautionary savings might be affected if the pension scheme is accompanied by insurance, or if annuities are provided that the market would not otherwise provide.
- Not all working households are savers. Younger ones will typically be borrowers, to finance education, housing, and other durable goods. They may face capital market imperfections or borrowing constraints that would force them to save more than they would like to (that is, to dissave less than they would like). In these circumstances, pension contributions might come largely from reduced consumption rather than crowded-out personal savings.
- Pension schemes might affect the decision to retire, which in turn has implications for savings. If individuals are induced to retire early, they must save more during their shorter working lives to finance their consumption over their longer retirements. Again, crowding-out of savings will be far from complete.

AGGREGATE SAVINGS AND INVESTMENT. Aggregate savings is the sum of private (individuals and firms) and public (government) savings. Capital market equilibrium requires that investment equals savings plus capital inflows from abroad. Increases in long-term savings will boost investments in productive capital formation and increase economic growth, unless domestic and foreign savings are perfect substitutes. Whether or not a pension or mandated savings scheme increases aggregate savings depends on its effects on both private and public savings. The indeterminacy of the effects on individual savings of the various pension and savings schemes means that the effect on aggregate savings will also be difficult to assess. For example, tax provisions to encourage retirement savings might increase individual savings, but aggregate savings might decrease if the cost to the government of the tax provision is great and it must borrow to finance it.

There are three ways in which the choice of financing of a public pension can affect the savings rate:

- by affecting the average wealth of individuals in the pension plan, which was discussed earlier
- by redistributing wealth among individuals in the same age group (intragenerational transfers), which can affect savings to the extent that the propensity to save out of wealth increases with wealth
- by redistributing between different age groups (intergenerational transfers)

To discuss this last effect, we need to add a dynamic aspect to the simple life-cycle model used earlier. This dynamic version is called an *overlapping generations model*. The prediction of the simplest form of this model is that a fully funded scheme will not influence aggregate savings unless the contribution rate is extremely high, whereas an unfunded pay-as-you-go scheme will decrease aggregate savings. This is the main economic argument against the use of pay-as-you-go public pension schemes.

In the simplest overlapping generations setting, individuals are identical and live for two periods, and in each time period a new generation of individuals is born. Thus, the only thing that differentiates households is date of birth. It is assumed the population grows at rate n. At time t, there are N_t young individuals. In the first period of an individual's life, he or she supplies a given amount of labor, earns wage income W, and consumes the amount C_1. An individual is in retirement in the second period of his or her life and consumes C_2. Lifetime utility is given by $u(C_1) + \beta u(C_2)$, where β is a positive discount factor and utility is assumed to be increasing with diminishing marginal utility. In order to consume in the second period, individuals must save while working. There is assumed to be a positive interest rate r. Individuals maximize their utility subject to the budget constraints of their life period.

Consider first the case in which no pension scheme is imposed by the government. In the first period, consumption and savings must be equal to wage income, and in the second period consumption must be less than or equal to savings (principal and interest earned). The amount an individual optimally saves will depend on the wage earned and the interest rate. Savings depends positively on wage income, but the effect of a change in the interest rate is ambiguous. An increase in interest rate will have an income effect (the level of second period consumption that can be financed from existing savings will be higher and this will tend to decrease savings) and a substitution effect (the returns to savings is higher and therefore the amount of savings will increase).

The savings of the young generation is used to finance the capital stock, which produces capital income for the members of that generation when they are old. (We neglect foreign capital inflows for simplicity.) The economy is assumed to comprise many competitive firms, each with a constant returns-to-scale production function $Y = F(K, N)$, where K is the amount of capital stock. Output per worker is calculated as $y = f(k)$, where k is the capital-labor ratio. Firms will maximize profits and choose a level of k such that the marginal product of capital is equal to the interest rate and the marginal product of labor is equal to the wage rate. The goods market must be in equilibrium, which requires that savings equals investment, or the savings of the young equals the stock of capital. Together the firms' and individuals' behavior, with the goods market in equilibrium, determine the interest rate and wage rate. In the long run, the economy will approach a steady state in which the capital-labor ratio is fixed, as are C_1, C_2, and the level of lifetime utility.

Suppose now that a fully funded public pension scheme is introduced. The government collects contributions T_t from the young generation at time t and creates a pension fund that is invested in the capital stock. It also pays benefits to the old equal to the amount of contributions it collected in the last period when the contributors were young plus interest, so $b_t = (1 + r_t)T_{t-1}$. Equilibrium in the goods market now requires that the capital stock equals the savings of the young plus pension contributions. Individuals' savings choices will be the same as without the fully funded pension scheme. The reason is that they earn the same return on their pension savings as on their own savings; thus they reduce the amount of their voluntary savings by the amount of mandatory savings. In other words, the pension scheme does not affect individual savings. However, this is contingent on the required contribution rate being less than the level of voluntary savings that occurs without the pension scheme. If this were not the case, the pension scheme would result in higher aggregate savings as individuals are forced to save more than they would do voluntarily. In summary, individuals' lifetime wealth is not affected by the introduction of the pension scheme. In other words, no social security wealth is created, because the present value of expected benefits is equal to the present value of contributions at the market rate of interest. There are no intergenerational wealth effects, and the same steady state equilibrium is achieved.

Next, suppose an unfunded public pension is introduced. In this scheme, the government collects contributions from the young of T_t per worker, and uses them to finance the benefits b_t for each old person. By budget balance, $b_t = (1+n)T_t$. When the scheme is introduced, the first retirees receive a windfall because they paid no contributions: their consumption will increase. For subsequent generations, savings will fall: if the implicit rate of return on their contributions n is less than the market rate of interest r_t, then their wealth is decreased, and their savings will fall by less than T_t. Moreover, they will be worse off because of the adverse wealth effect. The new steady state will involve a smaller capital stock, and a lower level of per capita utility. The effect of introducing the unfunded pension will be to transfer income from younger to older generations, and aggregate savings will fall. If $n > r_t$, the savings of future generations will still fall but by more than b_t, and they too will be better off. But this is an unlikely scenario: empirically, the rate of return on capital is typically greater than the rate of growth of the economy.

This simple overlapping generations model is based on the life-cycle savings model with perfect capital markets. The predictions of the model will not apply exactly to the real world to the extent that the assumptions are violated. The possibility of altruistic bequests can, in theory, offset the intergenerational transfer that the pay-as-you-go pension imposes. The old may change their bequest behavior to prevent the intergenerational transfer—and thus prevent the effect on savings from occurring—thus neutralizing the effect of the pension, in the so-called Ricardian equivalence hypothesis. Empirical evidence does not support the extreme form of this hypothesis. Borrowing constraints and myopia will also prevent unfunded pensions from crowding out personal savings completely. However, public pensions may reduce the need for precautionary savings to ensure against longevity.

We can conclude that the stronger the link is between contributions and benefits, the more likely it is that individuals will view contributions as another form of saving and the more likely it is that they will substitute their pension savings for their voluntary savings—and the smaller will be the possible negative effect on aggregate savings. These links depend both on how the pension scheme is financed, as illustrated above, and on the particular benefit structure of the scheme. For example, pensions with flat rate benefits imply that any increase in wages will result in an increase in the amount of contributions but will not necessarily result in an increase in benefits. However, a defined-contribution plan implies that any increase in the level of contributions necessarily implies an increase in the amount of benefits received.

CAPITAL MARKET DEVELOPMENT. Whether or not a private or public pension stimulates the development of capital markets depends on how the pension funds are managed. A prerequisite is the existence of a fund in which to invest. Thus, pay-as-you-go schemes with no existing long-term funds will not induce the development of investment instruments; indeed, by reducing the funds going to the capital market, they might well have the opposite effect. There is a tendency for publicly managed funds to be invested in low-return assets, such as government bonds and public enterprises. In addition, public management might encourage the government to overspend and increase government deficits. Competitive, privately managed funds are more likely to help modernize the capital markets through the development of banking systems, legal institutions, and risk classifications. Public regulation of private investment companies can also induce capital market development, as well as increase investors' confidence in the capital market.

Transitional effects

Currently, pension systems in most developed countries are administered as pay-as-you-go schemes and are relatively mature systems; that is, they have reached their targets of coverage and benefit levels. Immature plans are ones in which benefit levels have not reached their full size, so low contribution rates can cover the benefits of the small number of beneficiaries. As those systems mature the benefit requirements will increase, and to maintain them there will be a need to increase payroll taxes or finance the increase out of general revenues. This fiscal burden will certainly affect the domestic economy, but if the country is a large, industrial one, then it will also affect the world economy. As illustrated in the introduction, pressure on such systems and their apparent unsustainability have resulted in calls for pension reform.

There are four main ways to address the possible unsustainability of current pay-as-you-go schemes:

1. Change the parameters of the existing scheme (contribution rates, retirement ages, pension benefit formulas, insurance components).
2. Implement a transition to a fully funded scheme.
3. Make other fiscal adjustments (change other tax rates and expenditure on other government services).
4. Undertake policies to change the size of the labor force—that is, policies to encourage increased participation in the labor force and immigration.

Parameter changes to existing schemes can be made on the revenue side or on the expenditure side. On the revenue side, the government can increase the contribution rate. However, given the existing high rates in most countries, it is likely that such policy reform will be met with opposition. On the expenditure side, the government can increase the statutory retirement age, tighten the eligibility requirements for early retirement, and lower the level of benefits by changing the benefit determination and indexation formulas—that is, lower the imposed maximum replacement rate. It is imperative that a government considering changes in these structural parameters take into account the economywide effects of such changes—for example, how labor supply, labor demand, and private savings will respond to the changes. For example, if the parameter reform—either a reduction of average expected pension benefits or an increase in contributions—is unanticipated, then it is possible that private and public savings will both increase.

Alternatively, the government could build up a financial reserve so as to reduce the need for these parameter changes. At the extreme, the government could switch from a pay-as-you-go scheme to a fully funded scheme. Macroeconomic simulations have been used to illustrate the effects of this switch on aggregate savings, and societal welfare. The results depend on what type of transition is assumed (or how pension rights already accrued are treated). There are two types of transitions: a sudden transition, in which all individuals must participate in the new scheme (and current pensioners are cashed out), and a gradual transition, in which only new entrants to the labor force are required to participate in the fully funded scheme. In a sudden transition, the government must continue to pay current retirees from finances borrowed from the young. But individuals now earn a rate of return on their savings of r_{t+1} rather than n. Assuming $r > n$, this will generate an income effect and individuals will reduce their private savings. How the government finances the costs of transition will also have implications for the effect of the switch on individual and aggregate savings.

Encouragement of Voluntary Provision for Retirement

Mandatory pension schemes backed by public transfers to the elderly should provide adequate resources to as many retired persons as possible. Arguably, however, pension policy should go much further, providing households with an incentive to save amounts over and above what is mandated or even encouraging the family or the community to voluntarily assist those in retirement. Individuals save for a variety of reasons: life-cycle saving for retirement, saving for bequests, and precautionary saving to meet unanticipated needs for high expenditures (health reasons, home repairs, and so forth). Each type of savings has advantages, all of which have been addressed earlier. Higher savings rates provide much-needed financing for investment, which can contribute to growth and employment. Higher precautionary savings can reduce the potential for retired individuals to rely on government transfers in the event of adversity. Saving for future generations can have a public good aspect to it, as can the care of the destitute elderly. All these arguments call for measures to encourage savings.

Such encouragement can result from broader economic policies. Household confidence can be inspired by macroeconomic policies that ensure a relatively low rate of inflation, fiscal policies that contain tax rate levels, or policies that encourage the development of stable financial institutions. More active measures such as tax incentives for retirement savings or for the acquisition of personal forms of capital, such as housing, personal businesses, and human capital, all contribute. Fiscal incentives can also be used to assist voluntary organizations that provide for the elderly. These institutions complement public programs by identifying and reaching individuals overlooked by the public sector.

Policy makers should be mindful of the special circumstances that exist in developing countries—the state of capital markets, the availability of financial assets, individuals' reliance on land investments, the importance of traditional forms of support in retirement, and the immature income tax systems. With that in mind, we next summarize the design issues and economic effects of measures that encourage voluntary provision of retirement income.

Design Issues

There are a number of ways to encourage additional voluntary savings, without precluding continued voluntary assistance to the elderly.

- *Stable economic environment:* Savings are long-run decisions, heavily influenced by confidence in the future. Individuals will be more reluctant to entrust their life savings to the capital markets in an unstable political and economic environment. The value of sound government policies cannot be underestimated. These policies include proper monetary policies that achieve a noninflationary environment with a stable currency, and sound fiscal policies that ensure good government finances and a reliable, nonpunitive tax system. Prudent regulation also ensures reliable, and therefore credible, banks and financial institutions.
- *Increasing awareness:* Individuals are often preoccupied with their current problems and content to live for the day. They may neglect to save more than the minimum required for their retirement. There is a limit to the extent to which the government can mandate that individuals save. By educating working individuals about the need for retirement savings and precautionary savings for unexpected emergencies, especially those occurring later in life, governments can encourage individuals to save of their own volition.
- *Tax incentives:* The government can design the tax system to encourage voluntary savings. As mentioned earlier, tax incentives can encourage private occupational pensions and family support for the elderly. In addition, the government can allow for special tax treatment of personal savings that are earmarked for individuals' retirement. This is commonly done in OECD countries. These savings are deducted from individuals' taxable earnings and the interest earned is not taxed until retirement, when the benefits are withdrawn and most individuals are in a lower income tax

bracket. This policy encourages individuals who are not covered by private plans (such as the self-employed) to save for their retirement. However, this policy requires a developed income tax system.

- *Use of provident funds for voluntary savings:* The ability of individuals to save for their retirement can be hampered by thin capital markets or because assets are not readily available in their communities. One benefit of provident-type retirement savings funds is that they allow the collective mobilization of savings by a single institution. Provided these funds are sound and immune from political interference, they can provide an ideal vehicle for individuals to save voluntarily over and above what is mandated.

- *Encouraging traditional forms of support:* Although traditional forms of support may have uneven coverage, they are an indispensable complement to public or mandatory schemes. Government policies, at the very least, should attempt not to crowd out traditional forms of support. For example, tax-back rates applied to recipients of public transfers should be low enough not to displace voluntary transfers. Moreover, positive incentives, such as subsidies, might encourage an expansion of traditional forms of support and take advantage of the special expertise such forms can have.

Economic Effects

Being voluntary and private rather than mandatory and public, additional individual provision for retirement avoids many of the economic disincentive effects of other schemes. Indeed, encouraging voluntary savings for retirement can improve efficiency if capital tax rates are excessive, and there are positive externalities associated with savings. Voluntary savings allow individuals to choose their investment instruments. Policies that encourage savings enhance efficiency. Sound macroeconomic policies that ensure stability encourage growth. Regulation of financial institutions encourages capital market development. These policies may also increase aggregate savings and, if the economy is currently below the optimal level of savings, could enhance economic growth and societal welfare. As well, additional retirement savings, even though they constitute a relatively small proportion of most individuals' retirement income, reduce potential reliance on the public sector in retirement.

However, adverse economic effects may occur. In particular, tax incentives may have perverse distributional consequences. Higher-income individuals tend to benefit more from tax-advantaged savings—especially in developing countries, where the income tax applies especially to them. A system of retirement savings deductibility is more beneficial the higher the individual's income tax bracket is, because the individual's potential tax savings are greater. Limiting the amount of savings that are eligible for tax advantages or using a tax credit rather than a deduction can be more equitable. In addition, these tax policies might induce high-income individuals to shift their savings to tax-advantaged saving instruments rather than increasing their total savings. The revenue loss from these tax incentives might require increases in other taxes or reductions in government spending to reduce the resulting budget deficit.

Conclusion: Issues for Evaluation

Public policies to ensure that the retired have secure and adequate incomes are among the most important policies that governments undertake. In most OECD countries, public pensions and transfers to the elderly constitute a significant proportion of total government spending. They are bound to become increasingly important in developing countries for political, economic, and demographic reasons. Higher incomes increase the demand for income security and social insurance programs. The development of the market economy, especially the increase in flexibility and mobility in the labor market, tends to weaken traditional ties and reduce the traditional support mechanisms on which the retired used to rely. The predicted increase in the elderly dependency ratio makes the delivery of an adequate level of care both more urgent and more costly. Thus, tending to pension systems is an important item on the policy agenda.

In this chapter, we have summarized the main issues in the development and reform of pension systems. As a prerequisite to formulating good policies, it is necessary first to identify the objective of such policies—in particular, the reason why the public sector needs to become involved in what was an economic issue. Thus, we began with a careful look at the rationale for government intervention in the pension area and identified three main purposes: to redistribute wealth toward less well-off retired persons, whose needs are often uniquely associated with their age; to facilitate savings for retirement, both to compensate for the tendency of persons not to save adequately for their retirement and to increase the aggregate savings rate itself; and to insure elderly individuals against various risks that the private sector is unable to cover. This threefold set of purposes allowed us to focus on the sets of policies that were appropriate to address each of the three broad issues, recognizing that there is necessarily overlap among policies and objectives. For each of the roles of the public sector, we identified the various economic costs and potential benefits of alternative pension plan design and reform options available to the government.

The benefits of pension reform included the following:

- *Reduction in inequality:* Public pensions and transfers to the elderly improve the well-being of the neediest among the elderly, whatever the objective of the government might be: to increase the well-being of the least well-off for welfaristic reasons, to reduce the poverty index by increasing the consumption or income of the poor, or to increase the capability of the elderly to function in society. These objectives can be met by various forms of transfers, including cash transfers, in-kind transfers, and the provision of public services and social insurance. Moreover, public intervention can widen the coverage of assistance to the elderly beyond what is available through traditional forms of support.
- *Increase self-sufficiency of the elderly:* By inducing households to provide more for their retirement, individual reliance on the public sector in the future is reduced.
- *Encourage economic growth:* Inducing persons to save for their retirement will also increase savings rates, thereby contributing to the financing of investment, which increases employment opportunities and productivity growth. As well, increased savings can offset an externality that might prevent households from saving enough for future generations, thus enhancing the efficiency of capital markets.
- *Reduce individual risks:* Public pension schemes can provide forms of insurance that capital and insurance markets may find it difficult to provide. Examples include insurance against longevity risk, inflation risk, the risk of disability or injury, and the risk of bad health.
- *Induce the development of capital markets:* Savings for retirement can constitute a substantial portion of savings flowing into capital markets. The existence of such savings will encourage the development of assets in domestic capital markets, and this will improve the capacity of capital markets to intermediate between savers and investors.

These benefits do not come easily. Against them must be set the costs and constraints associated with public intervention. They include the following:

- *Fiscal burdens:* To the extent that pensions and transfers to the elderly are provided by the public sector, financing is required. Given the difficulty of raising revenues, this can be costly and motivates choices of policy designs that deliver a given objective in the least costly way.

- *Incentive effects:* Related to this is that fact that contributions, benefits, and regulations that are imposed on the system by the public sector will inevitably have incentive effects, which may induce inefficiencies in the market economy. These incentive effects will apply especially in the markets for labor and capital. Labor market effects include effects on both labor supply and labor demand, as well as effects on human capital investment, the choice between working in the informal or formal sectors, and evasion. In capital markets, individual and aggregate savings can both be affected by funding provisions. Finally, there may be negative (crowding-out) effects on traditional support systems.

- *Administrative costs:* The effort to identify the target population, classify the elderly by need, and provide the required transfers or services can be very costly. These costs will be an important determinant of the division of responsibilities between the private and public sectors. Administrative costs will differ between the two sectors, and the institutional capacity of both sectors may be important constraints on program design, coverage, and cost-effectiveness.

- *Public sector inefficiency:* The private-public balance is also affected by the efficiency with which the public sector operates, including the efficiency of the bureaucracy, the accountability of the political decision makers, and the farsightedness of policy makers. The public sector does not operate under the discipline of the market, so it may not have the incentive to deliver programs efficiently. Many components of the public pension scheme can be delivered by the private sector and overseen by the public sector.

- *Unintended redistributional effects:* Large public programs inevitably have unintended consequences. Public pension programs are especially prone to intergenerational redistribution, unless they are fully funded. Partially funded or unfunded programs will have transitional benefits to older persons when they are introduced, and they can impose especially large burdens on smaller cohorts. Social insurance programs typically cross-subsidize some groups at the expense of others.

Public intervention in the pension area, as in other policy areas, inevitably involves weighing the benefits against the costs and correctly balancing the trade-offs. This balance is one that must be decided upon by the policy makers; economists can do no more than clarify the elements of the trade-off.

In the context of developing countries, three special general considerations apply. First, pension systems must be feasible. Institutions must be capable of delivering them, and the resources of the nation must be adequate to finance them. Governments might be able to undertake actions to expand the set of feasible options. Second, the system must be sustainable. It must be politically acceptable; it must be capable of adapting to changing demographic circumstances; and it must be on a sound financial footing both now and in the future. If it is not sustainable in any of these aspects, reform is required. Third, it should be transparent, so that the population understands it. This will ensure that the take-up rate is satisfactory, and that bureaucrats and politicians cannot take advantage of it for their own or short-run purposes.

To conclude, it is worth reiterating what we have argued are the most important policy or design issues to be addressed in selecting a suitable pension system:

- *Public versus private role:* Some functions, such as delivering transfers to the needy elderly, can be provided only by the public sector. But for many aspects of pension policy, there is a choice between public and private provision. Pension and retirement savings schemes can be provided by employers or private financial institutions, or they can be administered by the public sector. In either case, there can also be a role for the other sector. Accumulated public pension funds can be managed by private investment firms, and occupational pension schemes can be mandated by the public sector. The extent of the government's role as regulator of private pension schemes, capital markets, and financial institutions must also be decided upon.

- *Universality versus targeting:* Within the redistributive component of the public pension scheme, transfers to the elderly can be universal demogrants or they can be targeted to varying degrees, and the targeting can take a wide variety of forms, including the use of in-kind transfers. A large number of considerations go into this decision, including institutional delivery capacity and administrative costs, economic incentive effects, individual take-up rates, and political economy considerations.

- *Funded versus unfunded:* Public components of the pension system, including social insurance components, can be funded or unfunded. If funded, the funding can be at the aggregate level or the individual level. The extent of funding affects the sustainability of the program, its effect on saving, and the extent to which it redistributes intergenerationally. The funding arrangements can also influence the extent to which the program is immune to political and bureaucratic manipulation.

- *Mandatory versus voluntary:* Pension policy can involve varying degrees of mandating as opposed to inducing voluntary compliance. The mandating can be at the individual level or the firm level.

■ *The structure of pensions:* The level of pension or transfer payments must be decided on, as well as the form of contributions and the rate structure applying to both. These decisions will involve the classic trade-off between efficiency and equity effects.

All these design issues involve political decision making. The responsibility now rests with policy makers, in both developed and developing countries, to choose among the wide variety of alternatives to ensure the stability of their economies and the well-being of their populations.

Notes

1. See World Bank (1994), figure 1.4, page 32.
2. A funded pension system is one in which payments to the retired come entirely from a fund that has been accumulated using the prior contributions of those to whom the pensions are paid. Note that funding can be at the individual level—so each person has his or her own pension account—which determines what they receive in retirement, or funding could be done in aggregate in the sense that payments made to all households of a given cohort come from the aggregate contributions made by that cohort.
3. See the summary of the U.S. evidence in the symposium in Yellen (1989).
4. Actuarial fairness implies that the premium equals the expected payout, so that in the aggregate total premiums equal total payouts. Of course, the administrative costs of running the insurance companies would have to be factored into this in reality.
5. This term was coined by Buchanan (1975).
6. Technically, the aversion to inequalities can be illustrated using the following commonly used social welfare function: $W = \sum_{i=1}^{N} u_i^{1-\alpha} / (1 - \alpha)$, where u_i is the welfare of household i and $i = 1, \cdots, N$. The parameter α is the degree of aversion to inequality. Its value is assumed to range from zero to infinity. See Boadway and Bruce (1984), chapters 5 and 9 for a detailed discussion.
7. The support ratio is approximately equal to $(1 + n)$, where n is the rate of population growth. Changes in the retirement age affect the support ratio but do not necessarily affect the rate of population growth. The ratio of wages is equal to $(1 + p)$, where p is the rate of productivity growth in the economy. The multiple of these two terms is given by $(1 + n)(1 + p) = (1 + g)$, where g is the rate of growth in the economy.

References

Ahmad, Ehtisham, Jean Drèze, and Nicholas Stern, eds. 1991. *Social Security in Developing Countries.* Oxford, U.K.: Clarendon Press.

Barro, Robert J. 1974. "Are Government Bonds Net Wealth?" *Journal of Political Economy* 81: 1095–17.

Bernheim, B. Douglas, and Kevin Bagwell. 1988. "Is Everything Neutral?" *Journal of Political Economy* 96: 308–38.

Boadway, Robin, and Neil Bruce. 1984. *Welfare Economics.* Oxford, U.K.: Basil Blackwell.

Buchanan, James 1975. "The Samaritan's Dilemma." In *Altruism, Morality, and Economic Theory,* ed. Edmund Phelps, 71–85. New York: Russell Sage Foundation.

Dahlby, Bev G. 1981. "Adverse Selection and Pareto Improvement through Compulsory Insurance." *Public Choice* 37: 547–58.

Disney, Richard, and Paul Johnson. 2001. *Pension Reform in OECD Countries.* Aldershot, U.K.: Edward Elgar.

Heller, Peter S. 2003. *Who Will Pay: Coping with Aging Societies, Climate Change, and Other Long-Term Fiscal Challenges.* Washington, DC: International Monetary Fund.

Johnson, William R. 1977. "Choice of Compulsory Insurance Schemes under Adverse Selection." *Public Choice* 31: 23–35.

Marglin, Stephen A. 1963. "The Social Rate of Discount and the Optimal Rate of Investment." *Quarterly Journal of Economics* 77: 95–112.

Rothschild, Michael, and Joseph E. Stiglitz. 1976. "Equilibrium in Competitive Insurance Markets." *Quarterly Journal of Economics* 90: 629–50.

Sen, Amartya K. 1967. "Isolation, Assurance, and the Social Rate of Discount." *Quarterly Journal of Economics* 81: 112–24.

———. 1985. *Commodities and Capabilities.* Amsterdam: North-Holland.

World Bank. 1994. *Averting the Old Age Crisis.* Oxford, U.K.: Oxford University Press.

Yellen, Janet L. 1989. "Symposium on the Budget Deficit." *Journal of Economic Perspectives* 3 (2): 17–93.

5

Gender in Public Expenditure Reviews

BARBARA BERGMANN

There are strong reasons to believe that a lessening of gender inequality is important in the promotion of economic growth and in the reduction of poverty (Murphy 1997; Blackden and Bhanu 1999; Presser and Sen 2000). A reduction in gender inequality, especially in its more extreme forms, is also desirable from a human rights prospective. The World Bank's Public Expenditure Reviews (PERs) offer potentially important opportunities to further the reduction of gender inequality. The PER process might be used to advocate the desirability of making more room in a country's budget for programs that would promote women's employment, health, education, safety, and productivity in the home and in the formal and informal economy. It might also promote a greater devotion of the country's revenues to ostensibly gender-neutral infrastructure, such as piped clean water, that would make household operation—and therefore women's lives—easier.

The easiest way to convey what a useful gender analysis under the PER process might look like would be to point to a good model. In a number of countries, both developed and developing, and in a number of international organizations, the idea of gender-sensitive budget analysis has been taking shape. The country documents that have been produced under this rubric (called *gender budgets,* and in some cases, *women's budgets*) are not fully fledged alternative versions of the countries' budgets. Rather they typically discuss a selected set of current government programs or departments from a gender perspective. One might have expected that the purpose of such exercises was the promotion of significant changes in the actual budgets or expenditure patterns, but very seldom do specific suggestions for changes in appropriations appear in these documents.

It is not clear that the Bank's work on gender in the PER process should take any of the existing gender budgets as a model, although the shorter version of the South African study, reviewed later, seems to come the closest to an acceptable model. Given the differing viewpoints, institutional interests, time constraints, and professional training of the authors, one would expect that a women's budget assembled by a women's organization within a country would be likely to differ from a document concerning gender generated in the course of the Bank's PER process for that country. However, the two kinds of gender-sensitive evaluations of the budget address the same underlying problems, and some of the same considerations apply. Therefore, the literature that has been generated by the gender budget movement is of relevance in considering the approach to be taken in the PER process, and so it is worthwhile to review them. At a minimum one can extract from them a handy list of relevant issues.

Those who have written on gender-sensitive budget analysis consider it to be a tool for achieving effective policy implementation (Esim 2000). Presumably, the result to be hoped for from such an effort is more than just educational. It should ideally lead to or accelerate changes in the budget, and in the government programs financed by that budget that further gender equality and women's well-being and that improve the country's health, productivity, and economic growth. We may take that to be the desired result of attention to gender issues in the course of the World Bank's PER process as well.

If it is accepted that the aim of the gender-sensitive budget exercise is to promote actual changes in policy, then questions arise as to what those changes should be and how best to use the PER process to promote their implementation. The answers will be different for each country for which the exercise is performed, depending on the degree of development, the traditions, the types and extent of gender inequalities that exist, the availability of data, the presence or absence of a substantial women's movement, the receptivity of public officials, and the ability to make room in the budget for any new spending that such changes in policy might require. For each country, there are questions of

- the appropriate choice and range of topics on which to focus
- the nature of the description of the current situation that is to be included

■ whether remedies and changes in policy and budget are to be suggested and how detailed and specific the policy suggestions, if any, are to be

After a discussion of issues under these three headings, a review of gender budgets for four countries—Israel, Sri Lanka, Barbados, and South Africa— is presented, including for each a list of topics considered.

Choice and Range of Topics

A number of documents giving advice on how to do gender-sensitive budget analyses have been written (Elson 1997, 1999; Budlender and Sharp 1998; Taylor 1999; Çağatay and others 2000; Esim 2000; Commonwealth Secretariat 1999a, 2000). All of them make the important point that gender analysis should by no means be restricted to programs that are directed specifically to women, such as banks set up to lend to women, training programs aimed at women, prenatal care services, and the like. Other programs are related to subjects such as infrastructure investment and agricultural development, which have effects on the lives of women and need to be considered from a gender point of view. In such programs, a previous failure to consider the distribution of benefits or clients by gender may have resulted in policies that perpetuate gender inequality. In some cases, the staff that administers such programs is skewed genderwise, and in others, underspending or overspending may be involved.

However, these authors appear to go beyond the advice to include all highly relevant issues, seeming to favor what might be called an all-sectors approach. In that approach, all aspects of budgeting and policy are considered relevant and an attempt is made to get gender considerations introduced and considered under every topic, or at least as many as possible.

An alternative to the all-sectors approach is one that concentrates closely on areas of government functioning where program changes have the obvious potential for reducing gender inequality, raising the productivity of women's work, having favorable effects on the birth rate, improving women's and children's health, and improving women's lives. While some of the programs to be considered under a more selective approach would be those aimed specifically at women, others would be programs that affect women importantly but in which those effects have been ignored, to the detriment of gender equality.

Only one of the four country studies examined below attempts to follow the all-sectors approach, and there is a good reason for that. The all-sectors approach is a highly demanding one, and there have to be serious questions as to its feasibility in most contexts, even in the case of countries for which a considerable body of data has been collected and is available. Where time, energy, resources, patience, and even good will are severely limited, it makes sense to concentrate on the most urgent issues, and what these issues are is usually no mystery.

In following a selective approach, the questions that arise concern the criteria for choosing which gender issues to raise in the PER process, and the number of issues that might be raised. One obvious method of choosing issues is to seek the advice of the country's ministry of women's affairs, where one exists, and of nongovernmental organizations (NGOs) concerned with gender issues, where they exist. Further, one can list some obvious criteria that would apply everywhere: the importance of the issue (to the economy, to public health, to the reduction of poverty, to women's well-being), the availability of information about the issue, and the likelihood of support within the country's government and population for progress on this front— or, conversely, the strength of the resistance likely to be encountered in any moves for change. If changes that are important to gender equality can be made at a relatively small budgetary cost (as might be the case, for example, with the judicial punishment of domestic violence), then that would argue for those changes to be included in a short list of issues to be taken up.

Women constitute about half of the population in most countries. Their productive activity, both paid and unpaid, is an important part of any national economy and is highly dependent on the presence or absence of expensive infrastructure that is not universally provided in many countries. So we would have to expect that some programs that are potentially most important for promoting gender equality and greater productivity for women could not be implemented without considerable expenditure. At this writing, proposals have been made that the Bank identify critical gender issues in each of the countries to which it lends. Such lists of issues would provide a ready-made agenda for the PER work in each country.

An examination of the gender analyses of budgets that have been done yields the following list of major headings:

- public utilities that assist in household operation activities usually performed by women (piped water, electricity, trash collection)
- health care
- education (see Leo-Rynie and Institute of Development and Labour Law 1999)
- government employment of women (by grade) (see Commonwealth Secretariat 1999b)

- the needs of single parents (cash benefits, child care, child support from absent parent)
- personal safety (domestic violence, rape, sexual harassment)
- access to credit
- agricultural issues (legal and traditional barriers to women's ownership of land, government assistance to farmers by gender)

Those who favor the all-sectors approach have expressed particular concern that macroeconomic issues, such as taxation and trade policy, be analyzed for gender effects (Zuckerman 2000). There may be cases where women are particularly affected by such issues, and it would be a mistake to say that they should never be considered in a gender-sensitive budget analysis. Nevertheless, one would anticipate that such cases are likely to be rare, judging by the paucity of actual work. Inevitably, the budget issues that most affect women are in the areas of public provision of infrastructure, training, health services, social services, transfer payments, and protection. None of these are usually considered the province of macroeconomics. Moreover, staff attention to macroeconomic issues is not in short supply at the Bank (even leaving aside the International Monetary Fund), while attention to gender issues arguably is. So the allocation of time to macroeconomics by those who have been commissioned to give attention to gender issues may represent an uneconomic shift of resources from an underserved area to one already well served.

Methodology of Analysis

The authors of the how-to manuals endorse the recommendations of Elson (1997), who proposes a number of more or less formal measurement tools that might be used in a gender-sensitive analysis of the budget. The following description of them is based on material in a kit prepared by Hewitt and Raju (1999).

- *Gender-disaggregated beneficiary assessments.* These assessments involve asking beneficiaries, using opinion polls, attitude surveys, focus groups, whether current programs match their priorities.
- *Gender-disaggregated public expenditure incidence analysis:* This analysis looks at the allocation of benefits from government programs between men and women. The benefit of a government service to each gender is taken to be the unit cost of the service multiplied by the number of units used by persons of that gender. For an example of such an analysis in the case of Ghana, see Demery and others (1995).

▓ *Gender-aware policy appraisal:* This appraisal is an analysis of how policies and resource allocations affect women and men, and how they are
likely to affect gender inequalities. An expected causal chain leading from
the planned public expenditure to the impact on men and women is to
be specified. For example, an assessment might be made of whether social
and cultural factors might prevent an increased school enrollment of girls
despite an increase in public expenditure on primary education. (Hewitt
and Raju 1999).

▓ *Gender-aware budget statement:* This statement is a breakout of expenditure according to the following classifications:

— *Gender equality–targeted expenditure:* the share of expenditure targeted to women to help redress past inequality; includes expenditures
on education, health, equal opportunity initiatives in employment,
and programs to support women's businesses

— *Women's priority public services:* expenditure share devoted to public
services of highest priority in reducing the burdens on poor women
especially; for example, household water supply and sanitation, and
rural electrification

— *Gender management system in government:* share of expenditure devoted
to government offices that attend to women's issues

— *Women's priority income transfers:* transfers having highest priority in
reducing women's income inequality and dependency; for example,
child benefit, women's pensions

— *Gender balance in public sector employment:* share of women and men
employed at each grade, earnings by gender at each grade, by ministry

— *Gender balance in business support:* shares directed to each gender
(training loans, subsidies) in agriculture, manufacturing, and services

— *Gender balance in public sector contracts:* shares going to male- and
female-headed firms

Elson also recommends a gender-disaggregated tax incidence analysis
(breaking down taxes paid by gender) and gender-disaggregated impact of
the budget on time use (an analysis of the effect of the budget on women's
unpaid work).

In the matter of incidence analysis, the substantial country studies that
have been done again go in a different direction from the how-to literature.
Where breakdowns of operations or clients or beneficiaries or employment
or enrollment or expenditure are available by gender, they are given. However, the formal apparatus of incidence analysis is conspicuous by its absence.
This is not surprising. Such analyses would be highly demanding of data,
time, and effort, and would not be focused efficiently on those areas where

the payoff to policy change might be most effective. (The one exception is the gender-aware budget statement. However, it could be assembled only by a country's ministry of finance, in cooperation with all the other ministries.) These measures suffer from being elaborate descriptions of the status quo, rather than being oriented toward high-priority changes in policies and expenditure patterns. They may be considered as diagnostic tools, but unless accompanied by suggestions for change, they are unlikely to be productive.

It could be argued that there is a flaw in the suggestion for gender-disaggregated public expenditure incidence analysis, since no mention is made of the differing needs of women and men. If the same amount is spent on both genders (say in the health field), that is not to say that the allocation between them is fair. If one or the other has greater needs (maternity in the case of women, heart problems and alcoholism in the case of men), then equal spending would not always produce fair results. As the Barbados budget analysts (St. Hill 2000, 5) wisely remark, "Resources disproportionately allocated to women to fulfill functions such as child-care responsibilities or prenatal health will rarely reflect discrimination against men." Nor, it might be added, would such a finding indicate that enough has been spent on such functions.

In the case of expenditures for such sectors as the military budget, some sort of accounting of the benefits by gender would certainly be interesting, if it could be done in a way that would strike most people as valid. However, the result would be based on subjective assessments and would inevitably be subject to contention and dissent, rather than to agreement on policy changes. *The Third Women's Budget* (Budlender 1998) for South Africa does deal with defense issues, but no incidence analysis is attempted.

Under the selective approach, the only problems dealt with are those where the need for a change in policy is obvious to anyone who favors greater gender equality, or who sees attention to women's needs as encouraging healthier growth. So a formal incidence analysis of current policy, even assuming it could be done, is unnecessary, because the harm from the present situation and the benefit from action to ameliorate it can be conveyed without such analysis. Obviously, any data that are available on the distribution of benefits by gender (children enrolled in educational institutions, medical treatments received, benefits to owners of agricultural plots) are clearly useful, where they are available.

Provision of Data

An attempt to make a gender analysis of all or a large number of budget sectors may not be possible or optimal. However, there will be some sectors for which there would be considerable benefits from such an analysis, but for which analysis cannot be performed because of the lack of data on beneficiaries by gender. The PER process might be an appropriate occasion to urge the collection and publication of such data. However, the postponement of any policy initiatives against the day when more data are available should be avoided, because some desirable directions for policy are usually quite obvious even when data are lacking. Some of the country documents reviewed below consist largely of statements that more data are needed, and thus they pass up a chance to affect policy in the near term.

A frequent suggestion (Waring 1988) is that the national income accounts be enlarged to include the value of unpaid work, most of which is performed by women. The benefits from this exercise are said to be a rescue of women's work from invisibility and from low or zero valuation, a greater appreciation of the extent to which the operation of the country and the economy depends on this work, and the possible emergence of some ideas about how to raise the productivity of the labor involved and make it easier to perform.

The national income accounts of many countries do include the value of some of the goods and services not traded for money, such as the value of food grown and eaten on farms and the value of the housing services of owner-occupied dwellings. The exclusion of the value of women's unpaid work from these accounts is certainly not justified, given that it involves half the population and constitutes a major proportion of any nation's productive activity. That omission originally occurred because of the low status and low valuation of women and the work they do.

However, the omission of women's unpaid work in a country's gross domestic product (GDP) accounts, while regrettable, is not a cause of gender inequality—it is merely a minor and relatively harmless symptom of that inequality. Removing that symptom is not going to further gender equality; only an attack on the causes of gender inequality through specific policy measures will do that. Thus, specific policies likely to change the degree of gender inequality should be given higher priority in the PER process than efforts to make the national income accounts more inclusive—satisfying though the latter might be for some advocates.

Remedies and Changes in Policy and Budget

One might have expected that the purpose of such exercises in gender-sensitive budget analysis is the promotion of significant changes in actual budgets or expenditure patterns or policies. The manuals on gender-sensitive budgeting are notably silent on this important matter. And the examples of gender budgets that have been produced for particular countries contain little or nothing in the way of specific suggestions, apart from rather vague statements that more needs to be done. Statements such as "An appropriate goal would be an increase in the budget for the installation of piped clean water by 20 percent, using funds saved by an equivalent reduction in the defense budget," are not to be found.

The extent to which the pursuit of actual policy changes in the service of gender equality are addressed and the nature of suggestions for such change are likely to depend in practice on the specificity with which policy changes in other parts of the budget are being advocated in the PER process. If detailed policy changes are being urged in the course of the PER, then detailed policy suggestions related to gender should certainly be included. Where policy advice is given, numerical goals as well as timetables for achieving those goals (for example, for increasing female educational enrollment or female representation in the upper levels of the civil service by a certain percentage by a certain date) may be useful.

If the PER document were to suggest significant changes because of a gender-sensitive analysis of the budget, it is likely that it would call for an increase in expenditure under certain budgetary headings. Some important changes can be achieved with little or no expansion of expenditure (say, reducing gender discrimination in government employment, or reorienting the police and the justice system to deal with domestic violence). However, others can call for big changes in suggested spending on infrastructure, health, and education. Such changes would require a reduction in expenditure under other headings, an increase in government revenues, or deficit financing.

In most countries, the most likely source of funds for significant increases in investment in infrastructure that a gender-aware budgetary process would suggest (apart from increased taxation and a reduction in corruption) is the military budget. *The Third Women's Budget* for South Africa deals with overspending for defense and is notably outspoken and derisory about it:

> Is the proposed force design appropriate in the changing political climate [in the region] and in the light of South Africa's commitment to meeting the socioeconomic needs of its people? . . . The Defence Review acknowledges that poverty, rather than an external military threat, is one of the major threats facing vulnerable groups in our society. Yet the DoD seems determined to equip the national defence force in readiness for fulfilling its *fictitious* primary function. (Budlender 1998, 209, emphasis added)

We would not expect a document issued by the World Bank to take such a tone, but the same truth might be conveyed more gently.

Examples of Gender-Sensitive Budgetary Analysis

Although details of gender relations differ from one country to another, many of the problems and conditions that underlie gender inequality do not. It is remarkable that topics such as discrimination against women in employment, the kinds and degree of help given to single-mother families, and domestic violence are live issues—as important in highly developed countries such as the United States and Israel as they are in India or the countries of Sub-Saharan Africa. The topics that are given high priority in one country's gender-sensitive budget exercise will deserve high priority in many others.

Of the four country studies reviewed here, perhaps the shorter version of the South African study is closest to being a reasonable model of what a gender-sensitive PER study might look like. However, like the others (with the exception of the Israeli document), it fails to offer strong and specific suggestions for policy changes.

Israel

One interesting example of gender-sensitive budget analysis comes from a women's advocacy group in Israel (Adva Center 1997). It does not attempt to cover all items in the budget. It is short (a mere 11 pages), highly selective, and to the point. It presents a list of items in the 1998 budget bill that would particularly affect Israeli women, some of which it opposes and some of which it favors. The analysis was produced at a time when the budget on which it commented was before the legislature and was being considered. The document is essentially a list of talking points for lobbyists.

- *Health services:* The budget proposals would allow health funds to exclude coverage of contraceptives, set up a fee-and-service structure that would be unfavorable to single women and sole mothers, and privatize mother-and-child clinics. (opposes)
- *Education:* The proposed budget cuts funds devoted to lengthening the school day, which hurts job-holding mothers. (opposes)
- *Child allowances:* The proposed budget switches the payment from the mother to the father. (opposes)
- *Vocational training:* Current practice segregates vocational courses by gender; those for men last considerably longer. (opposes)
- *Social affairs:* The proposed budget increases government funds for battered women's centers. (favors) It decreases day-care fees paid by parents. (favors)

South Africa

The work that has been done on gender budgets for South Africa takes an approach that is unique in terms of coverage and length. The Gender and Economic Policy Group of South Africa has so far issued four annual *Women's Budget* books (Budlender 1996, 1997, 1998, 1999), which together run to more than 1,200 pages. This is the one country study that does attempt to deal with gender issues in all sectors and aspects of government, including issues such as taxation and trade policy. These publications would make an excellent textbook for a high school or college course on government. If they were actually used in this way, they would be likely to spread in the younger population a lively understanding of important aspects of government operations, and while doing so, would spread an appreciation of gender issues from a point of view favoring gender equality. (However, if they were intended for such a use, they probably should have been issued under a more gender-neutral title.)

Unlike the Israeli document, which addressed current budget issues and attempted directly to influence legislators' votes on particular issues, the four *Women's Budget* volumes, despite their length, are most likely not specific enough to affect the legislative process. In these volumes specific recommendations for changes in policy are few and far between, and those chapters that discuss areas lacking obvious gender relevance are the ones most lacking in that respect. They do make clear the general direction that the authors would advocate for policy on many issues, but they do not provide any specific proposals and provide no specific quantitative suggestions for raising spending.

These volumes represent a huge amount of skilled labor, time, dedication, and effort. Yet one has to question whether the result represents an efficient use of the time and energy of the country's advocates for gender equality. Less attention to trade and taxation and more to describing and advocating detailed policies crucial to women's advancement might have had a better payoff. In the Bank's PER process, an all-sectors approach, at least as exemplified by the four Budlender volumes, is clearly out of the question.

Perhaps to move in the direction of greater brevity and more specificity in policy proposals, the Group has issued two volumes that provide a more popular summary of issues and proposals (Hurt and Budlender 1998, 2000). It is from the latter two volumes that the list of topics summarized in table 5.1 has been compiled. As the table makes clear, the South African document is strong on description of current problems but very weak on proposals for explicit remedies via the budgetary process.

TABLE 5.1   Summary of South African Gender Budget Document

Problem	Suggested Policy Change
Public utilities	(No specific changes suggested.)
water and sanitation (only 45% of households have an inside tap; only half have flush toilets), electricity, rubbish collection	
Work	
small enterprises	Improve women's access to finance, information, and markets; target women for training, stop the treatment of street trading as illegal.
wages and hours regulation	Enforce labor laws on farms and private homes.
unemployment insurance	Extend coverage to domestic workers.
government contracting	Make it easier for people to put in tenders, divide large contracts into smaller ones, increase the representation of women on tender boards.
Land affairs and agriculture	
land ownership	Land and housing should not be registered only in the names of men.
"Chiefs, husbands, brothers and sons . . . do not want to give up their male power, privilege and status. These patriarchal attitudes stop women from having their own right to land." (Hurt and Budlender 1998, p. 29)	Make sure women benefit from land reform; establish special ways to help women get loans, and special ways to give women security of tenure, gender training for all officials involved. Grants should not go to male migrants who will use them in urban areas.
Education	
gender stereotyping	Policies are needed to work toward getting rid of it.
technical colleges	Increase women's registration
adult education	Help women attendees with transport, safety measures, childcare.
early childhood development	Increase appropriations.
gender bias in schools	Train teachers in nonsexist ways, to stop giving boys more attention and encouragement than girls.

(*continued*)

TABLE 5.1 Summary of South African Gender Budget
Document (*Continued*)

Problem	Suggested Policy Change
sexual harassment and rape in schools	Educate students and staff about what sexual harassment is and how to put an end to it.
administrators principally male	Educational institutions should have policies against gender discrimination.

Health

fewer women than men have medical aid to help them pay for private health services	Increase public provision.
insufficient funding for Free Health Care program for pregnant women and children under 6	Increase funding.
gynecological services, HIV/AIDS and STD	Services need to be integrated. Improve physical infrastructure and equipment of clinics. Supply test equipment for cervical cancer.
domestic violence	Government should supply funding for shelters and counseling services, currently all funded by NGOs. Health workers should be trained to deal with domestic violence.

Social benefit programs

state maintenance grants for single mothers	Remarks that the budget covers only half of those eligible, but no specific change advocated.

Safety and security

domestic violence (also see above under *Health*.)	A survey is needed to document the extent of domestic violence.
	Police officers need training to offer proper help. There are many special police groups to deal with property crimes, but none to deal with domestic violence. The Prevention of Family Violence Act needs to be better publicized.
Rape	In a survey, 90 percent of police officers said they would not know what to do with a rape complaint. Training is needed.

(*continued*)

TABLE 5.1   Summary of South African Gender Budget
Document (*Continued*)

Problem	Suggested Policy Change
police criminality: police officers themselves commit many rapes and killings.	No recommendations.
police organization: there is a maldistribution of police stations, with comparatively few in areas where blacks live	No recommendations.
Public service	
high degree of sex segregation by occupation in public employment	Women should be trained for nontraditional public service jobs.
	Goals and timetables for remediation should be set up and kept.
very few women in top echelons of management	Goals and timetables for remediation should be set up and kept.

Sri Lanka

The authors profess to have the objective of assessing the country's budget so as "to use the knowledge gained to improve the gender impact of future budgets" (Department of National Planning, Sri Lanka 2000, iv). Yet the document contains few explicit suggestions for change; those that exist are rather vague. For example, it finds imbalances in the production sectors, but says they "cannot be dealt with merely by allocating more money, but require sociological investigation and program reorientation" (vii).

There are chapters on government employment, government programs in education, health, social welfare, agricultural services, and industrial services. In all sectors, the poor representation of women in management is noted. In agricultural services, the participation of women on the staff and in the programs is noted as low. The report takes the tack (presumably on gender equity grounds) that functions in which women predominate should be expanded. This is not necessarily the best course, because the expansion of programs should respond to the benefits that the expansion would bring, rather than a desire to create a distribution of benefits by gender that mechanically doles out equal amounts to each. Gender imbalances in benefits that are the result of segregation of occupations or functions by gender might best be dealt with by desegregation.

Barbados

The gender-sensitive budget analysis for Barbados (St. Hill 2000) looks at the operations of programs under four government ministries. As table 5.2, which summarizes this document shows, the authors are dedicated to increasing gender equality, and they appear to have been frustrated by the sexist responses received from some ministries. But like the other examples of gender-sensitive budget documents, this one is more descriptive than prescriptive. Very few specific suggestions for changes in policy are provided.

TABLE 5.2 Summary of Gender Budget Document for Barbados

Problem	Suggested Policy Change
Ministry of Agriculture and Rural Development	
Women farmers benefit little from government help in agriculture, in extension services, or training.	Use should be made of the Association of Women in Agriculture. More women farmers should be registered with the ministry, and more training should be given to women farmers.
In the ministry, women are disadvantaged in terms of the number of jobs and the types of jobs. There is a shortage of trained female executives and professionals.	Data on occupational training and mobility of agricultural specialists by sex should be gathered.
Ministry of Social Transformation	
Insufficient funds for operating a shelter for battered women and their children.	Long-term commitment to government finance of shelter needed, and a higher level of funding. Permanent low-cost housing for women made homeless by violence is needed.
Misunderstanding within the Ministry of Social Transformation "over the meaning of gender and how it is to be applied to Ministerial social and policy mandates. . . . The Ministry has identified the following as gender issues or problems to be addressed: Male marginalization as an outcome of excessive attention to women's issues." (p. 45)	Making the ministry's hiring and promotion gender-equitable. "The fact that [anti-female] sentiments are gaining acceptance and legitimacy at the same time as there has been an undeniable rise in violence against women and public hostility against further encroachments by females in most areas of public life, it is essential that the ministry, and its Bureau of Gender Affairs produce a strategy for gender analysis that will play a role in helping to shape the national discussion around issues of gender." (p. 45.)

(continued)

TABLE 5.2 Summary of Gender Budget Document for
Barbados (*Continued*)

Problem	Suggested Policy Change
Many sole mothers are poor because their family responsibilities interfere with their labor market roles. The failure to recognize them as "heads of household" adversely affects the benefits they can get.	Collection of more sex-disaggregated data requested.

Ministry of Education, Youth, and Culture

Two single-sex schools have disparate academic results, with students at the girls' school performing better than the those at the boys' school. In the latter, fewer trained teachers are on staff. The courses offered in each of these schools reflect gender stereotypes, with girls being prepared for "less technical, less scientific, lower skilled and lower paying sectors of the economy." (p. 54) Students at both single-sex schools perform below the national average for coeducational schools.	"Reform of these gender patterns in the educational curriculum is important. . . . As to whether single sex secondary schools are the solution to reversing trends of educational under-achievement among males, much more gender-focused research is required to assess this." (p. 54)
The teacher's college is turning out male and female teachers with gender-typical specialties.	It should "be vigilant" on that score.
In the Barbados Youth Service, a service for "difficult" youths, only males are given polytechnic training. Male trainees do not respect female counselors who are in the majority in the program, and who are thought of as soft and not street-wise.	"On the one hand the BYS must provide mentors whom the trainees will respect and at the same time try to change the young people's concept of what forms of social interaction should generate respect and are worth of modeling" (p. 60)

Summary

How useful is the work previously done on gender budgets for those working to include gender issues in the PER process? Grading the four gender budget documents summarized above on the criterion of their likely effectiveness in changing the country's budget in the direction of furthering gender equity, we might award the Israeli document a grade of B, give the South African document a C+, and give the other two grades of D. Perhaps they are most useful as examples of what tendencies to avoid.

The procedures put forth, principally by Elson, that are meant to guide the work of compiling gender budgets, and that are universally endorsed in the literature on this subject, seem to have provided very little real help, judging by the documents that have been produced. By being overly ambitious, they are impracticable, give little useful guidance, and perhaps have done more harm than good. These suggested procedures prescribe enormous research efforts on a broad swath of topics. The alternative, which might work best for those engaged in the PER process, would be to take a small number of clearly pertinent and important topics, to develop detailed proposals, and to provide numerical goals, timetables, and cost estimates.

References

Adva Center. 1997. "How the Proposed 1998 Israel State Budget Will Affect Women." Adva Center, Tel Aviv. http://www/adva.org/budwomen.html.

Blackden, C. Mark, and Chitra Bhanu. 1999. *Gender, Growth, and Poverty Reduction.* Washington, DC: World Bank.

Budlender, Debbie, ed. 1996. *The Women's Budget.* Cape Town: Idasa.

———. 1997. *The Second Women's Budget.* Cape Town: Idasa.

———. 1998. *The Third Women's Budget.* Cape Town: Idasa.

———. 1999. *The Fourth Women's Budget.* Cape Town: Idasa.

Budlender, Debbie, and Rhonda Sharp, with Kerri Allen. 1998. *How to Do a Gender-Sensitive Budget Analysis.* London: Commonwealth Secretariat.

Çağatay, Nilüfer, Mümtaz Keklik, Radhika Lal, and James Lang. 2000. *Budgets as If People Mattered: Democratizing Macroeconomic Policies.* New York: United Nations Development Programme.

Commonwealth Secretariat. 1999a. *Gender Management System Handbook: Gender Mainstreaming in Development Planning.* London: Commonwealth Secretariat.

———. 1999b. *Gender Mainstreaming in the Public Service.* London: Commonwealth Secretariat.

———. 2000. *Improving the Effectiveness of Applying a Gender Analysis to Government Budgets.* London: Commonwealth Secretariat.

Demery, Lionel, Shiyan Chao, Rene Bernier, and Kalpana Mehra. 1995. "The Incidence of Social Spending in Ghana." PSP Discussion Paper Series 82, Poverty and Social Policy Department, World Bank, Washington, DC.

Department of National Planning, Sri Lanka. 2000. *Engendering the National Budget of Sri Lanka.* Colombo: Centre for Women's Research.

Elson, Diane. 1997. "Gender-Neutral, Gender-Blind, or Gender-Sensitive Budgets?: Changing the Conceptual Framework to Include Women's Empowerment and the Economy of Care." *Preparatory Country Mission to Integrate Gender into National Budgetary Policies and Procedures.* London: Commonwealth Secretariat.

———. 1999. *Gender Budget Initiative: Background Papers.* London: Commonwealth Secretariat.

Esim, Simel. 2000. "Gender-Sensitive Budget Initiatives for Latin America and the Caribbean: A Tool for Improving Accountability and Achieving Effective Policy Implementation." Paper prepared for the Eighth Regional Conference on Women of Latin America and the Caribbean–Beijing +5, Lima, February 8–10, 2000.

Hewitt, Guy, and Sabhita Raju. 1999. *Gender Budget Initiative: A Commonwealth Initiative to Integrate Gender in National Budgetary Processes.* London: Commonwealth Secretariat.

Hurt, Karen, and Debbie Budlender, eds. 1998. *Money Matters: Women and the Government Budget.* Cape Town: Idasa.

———. 2000. *Money Matters Two: Women and the Local Government Budget.* Cape Town: Idasa.

Leo-Rhynie, Elsa, and Institute of Development and Labour Law, University of Cape Town, South Africa. 1999. *Gender Mainstreaming in Education.* London: Commonwealth Secretariat.

Murphy, Josette. 1997. *Mainstreaming Gender in World Bank Lending.* Washington, DC: World Bank.

Presser, Harriet B., and Gita Sen. 2000. *Women's Empowerment and Demographic Processes: Moving beyond Cairo.* New York: Oxford University Press.

St. Hill, Donna. 2000. "Gender Analysis of the National Budget: 1998– 1999: Barbados Pilot." Unpublished paper. Commonwealth Secretariat, London.

Taylor, Viviene. 1999. *Gender Mainstreaming in Development Planning.* London: Commonwealth Secretariat.

Waring, Marilyn. 1988. *If Women Counted: a New Feminist Economic.* San Francisco: Harper & Row.

Zuckerman, Elaine. 2000. "Macroeconomic Policies and Gender in the World Bank." Unpublished paper, World Bank, Washington, DC.

6

Citizen-Centered Governance

A New Approach to
Public Sector Reform

MATTHEW ANDREWS AND ANWAR SHAH

Public sector reforms are pervasive in the developing world. Unfortunately, the failure of public sector reform is equally pervasive. The literature increasingly shows that many of the traditional and new reform types have failed to make lasting and effective impressions on recipient countries. Unresponsive, unaccountable, inefficient, and ineffective bureaucracies seem impossible to change with the current tools—requiring a new approach to the reform question. This chapter tackles this issue by presenting a new approach, the citizen-centered governance framework, to frame reform agendas. This model combines participatory decentralization with results-oriented management and evaluation to create a framework for reform that we expect will counter some of the most glaring problems with governments in developing countries.

The first section outlines the common problems in developing country governments: low capacity, organizational centralization, service monopolies, social insulation, and poor evaluation. The second section identifies reform elements typically adopted in response to these problems and then discusses their weaknesses. It shows that macroeconomic stabilization reforms, capacity-building initiatives, results-oriented management, decentralization, and participation reforms have all suffered from conceptual and practical weaknesses.

These weaknesses have limited the influence that reforms have had on the problems they were designed to solve, requiring a new approach for development and reform—especially at the local level, where governments have increased in number and complexity over the last decade. The third section presents the citizen-centered framework as this new approach. It shows how a new bottom-up reform can introduce real change into public organizations by countering commonly problematic incentives and focal points. The conclusion shows how this approach constitutes a holistic answer to the pressing problems of governance in developing countries.

The Public Sector Reform Challenge in Developing Countries

It is easy to identify public sector weaknesses in the developing world. Observers tell stories of governments with governance structures that have degenerated completely or are in the process of doing so. Peterson (1998) synthesizes the situation by saying (of Africa specifically), "The catalogue of organizational ills one finds in public bureaucracies . . . is daunting" (39). Table 6.1 lists some ills or weaknesses typically evident in such governments. Each is discussed thereafter.

TABLE 6.1 Common Governance and Administrative Weaknesses in Developing Countries

Low capacity	▪ Low personnel capacity ▪ Low systems capacity
Organizational centralization and top-down governance	▪ Process orientation ▪ Permanence and noninnovation
Service monopolies	▪ Uncompetitive and unaccountable public production processes ▪ Weak incentives for production efficiency
Social insulation, low transparency, and poor participation	▪ Social exclusion based on process and normal professionalism ▪ Internally biased, nonresponsive incentive structures
Poor organizational evaluation and accountability mechanisms	▪ Weak internal evaluation mechanisms ▪ Few external (social) evaluation mechanisms

Low Capacity

Weak operational capacity is often presented as a reason why governments fail to serve constituents, with abilities often being inconsistent "with the (governance) task at hand" (Shah 1998, 7). Coston says that "governance problems" in general "may derive from a lack of capacity" (1998, 480). Governments are typically shown to suffer from weak personnel and systems capacities, both entrenched by insufficient skill bases, low compensation, and poor human resource and organizational policies.

Organizational Centralization and Top-Down Governance

Developing country governments are often portrayed as hierarchical, centralized, and top-down. Such structures emphasize control in the governance process and require role players to adhere to process above all else. This process orientation yields administrative entities that are unresponsive, with top-down structures seen as devices for insulating bureaucratic heads from political masters and constituencies (Desai and Imrie 1998). An allied problem relates to the common status quo bias, whereby governments organized according to the classic bureaucratic model emphasize permanence (of process and position) and noninnovation, entrenching unproductive and unresponsive production processes and limiting potential for change (Peters 1996).

Service Monopolies

Public entities in the developing world are often monopolistic and are criticized for producing services using inefficient production processes, having no incentive to do otherwise.[1] This problem is argued to manifest itself in the tendency of the public budget to grow.[2] Uncompetitive production processes are also argued to hinder accountability, particularly when production and information barriers provide opportunities for corruption and self-maximization (Egeberg 1995). Such situations facilitate rent-seeking because barriers provide buffers to external scrutiny and because corrupt gains can easily be passed off as waste related to the poor production method.[3]

Social Insulation, Low Transparency, and Poor Participation

Governments are typically portrayed as insular, nontransparent, and nonparticipatory (Blair 2000; Brinkerhoff 2000). This is largely because of their dominant bureaucratic structures, in which organizational survival requires a protective shield against external influences that might unbalance the balanced bureaucracy, described by Stillman (1991) as "stateless" and destructive to human and democratic values (see Peters 1996). The centralizing nature of public organizations encourages a rule-based internal focus that buffers decision-making processes or information from citizen access (Kraan 1996; DISHA 2000).[4] Participation threatens established interests and the incentives that structure behavior. Neither political representatives nor administrators have an incentive to open governance processes to citizen involvement, because doing so would threaten established lines of relationship, decision making, and influence.

Poor Organizational Evaluation and Accountability Mechanisms

Effective evaluation underscores institutional arrangements and incentives.[5] Evaluations in developing countries, often undertaken by the public protector's office or auditor general's office, tend to have limited influence and are often open to criticism of political interference (see Schick 1998).[6] Another criticism of these evaluations relates to their irregularity and inconsistent quality (Feinstein and Picciotto 2000).[7] Furthermore, evaluations tend to be one-dimensional, concentrating only on fiscal probity and rule adherence. This institutionalizes the centralizing structures discussed earlier and reinforces process-oriented incentives (at the expense of social responsiveness and efficiency) (Andrews 2001). Furthermore, most developing countries lack evaluation entities in civil society that ensure citizens can make a direct comment on government performance.

Conventional Reform Approaches, the Legacy They Leave, and Their Problems

Many attempts have been made to develop governance interventions (reforms) that deal with the areas of administrative weakness discussed. Coston (1998) identifies waves of reform, which tie closely to the chronological adoption of ideas regarding government improvement. Peters (1996) presents similar models of governance in a more theoretical explanation of recent reform thinking. Major reform elements and themes are shown in table 6.2.

What Legacy Do Conventional Reforms Leave Behind?

The list of reform elements in table 6.2 shows that there are many varying ideas about how governments should be improved. Crucial questions asked in the broad reform literature center on the degree to which reform elements

TABLE 6.2 Major Themes and Elements of Reform
in the Developing World

Themes	Elements
Administrative reforms	▨ Focus on internal controls ▨ Privatization ▨ Downsizing
Capacity building	▨ Pay restructuring ▨ Skills development (usually centralized) ▨ Formal process development (usually centralizing)
Results-oriented management	▨ Outputs (or outcomes) focus: customers matter ▨ Subsidiarity principle in management (intragovernmental) ▨ Government as a business needs business tools
Decentralization	▨ Subsidiarity principle ▨ Competitive service delivery ▨ Customer orientation
Participation	▨ Government responsive to citizens (as more than customers) ▨ Citizen involvement in decisions (direct democracy) ▨ Devolution (local accountability)

have been successful in tackling the problems with which they are most directly associated. In many instances, evidence suggests that reforms have a legacy of limited success. Consider the following examples:

n A 1997 World Bank report of public expenditure reforms under adjustment lending examined the degree to which reforms between 1979 and 1994 shaped spending policies in developing nations (Huther, Roberts, and Shah 1997). The paper concludes that reforms based on adjustment had "small positive effects on expenditure patterns" and points out a number of reform shortcomings, particularly suggesting that reforms failed to change government incentives and mind-set.

▨ Observers question the effectiveness of reforms focused on improving public performance through civil service adjustments. de Merode and

Thomas (1994, 481) state, "No conclusive evidence was found of better pay and leaner staffing . . . leading to major productivity gains."

▨ The Medium-Term Expenditure Framework (MTEF) is a promising reform in the developing world, designed to bring direction and control to public budgeting processes. The South African MTEF, with its fiscal discipline and development focus, is seen as a better application of the reform and is argued to have facilitated reduced deficits since 1993 (Walker and Mengistu 1999).[8] Unfortunately, the MTEF reform tenure has also seen decreases in key expenditure types, particularly capital spending.[9] These results raise questions about the MTEF's success: While fiscal discipline in South Africa's particular case appears to have improved, other fiscal outcomes have not, potentially thwarting the development effort.[10]

▨ Desai and Imrie (1998) suggest that the New Public Management reform in India has produced more rhetoric than results. They report that, contrary to reform promises, governments remain insular and bureaucratic, with "much of the new managerialism" proving "contradictory and flawed, characterized by de-democratizing tendencies and a fixation with procedural and technical processes" (645).

▨ A number of results-oriented, New Public Management reforms were introduced to Malawi in the 1990s (Adamolekun, Kulemeka, and Laleye 1997). They included budget reform and a privatization program which, although implemented, appear to have had little impact on behavior in the governance process. Reform elements have actually proved to contradict each other (decentralization of government and centralized financial planning are not complementary, for example), further hampering any positive effects.

Why Have Reforms Had Limited Effects and What Can We Learn from Them?

There is no one reason why reforms fail to meet expectations or counter public sector problems. This is especially evident when comparing failures over a variety of settings. Experience suggests various problems that seem commonly prevalent, however, relating to the elements themselves, the way they are arranged, and the degree to which they facilitate culture or incentive changes through active evaluation. These issues combine to raise questions about the kind of framework within which reforms are being conceptualized.

Problems with the reform elements themselves

The literature outlines various weaknesses, conceptual and practical, with all the prominent reform elements:

⬚ Administrative reforms aim to make government more stable, disciplined, and competitive, and less socially burdensome. The reforms are, however, widely criticized for one-size-fits-all approaches. Observers also question national readiness for these reforms, or indeed the appropriateness of the reforms in the development context.[11]

⬚ Capacity building aims to enhance capacity and make governments more competitive. De Merode and Thomas (1994) question the influence of such programs that concentrate on government size and pay restructuring initiatives: "No conclusive evidence was found of better pay and leaner staffing alone leading to major productivity gains . . . This suggests that pay and employment reforms, although important determinants of performance, need to be supplemented with other measures." Grindle (1997) and Coston (1998) also comment that many capacity-building reforms have limited effect because of their one-dimensional, supply-side focus. Supply-side initiatives ignore demand and incentive-related capacity constraints. Dia (1996) and Qualman and Bolger (1996) note this as a reason why, even with capacity-building reforms in place, areas such as Africa still suffer significant capacity problems.

⬚ Results-oriented reforms aim to replace top-down, monopolistic, unresponsive public organizations with flat, performance-oriented, productive, and responsive public organizations. Evidence from industrialized countries suggests, however, that the reforms are not always having these effects. Where such reforms have been implemented, public organizations have not appeared to change much (Melkers and Willoughby 1998; Andrews 2002). Reforms are implemented in a centralizing way, limiting the ability of line agencies to develop results-based competencies and reinforcing process-based organizational incentives and insularity (goals are set internally, procedures are audited internally, and results are evaluated internally). In the developing world, these reforms generally show themselves as a loose collection of ideas, which countries are encouraged to implement in a copycat fashion, often to mimic best practice in the private sector. Polidano (1998) and Desai and Imrie (1998, 645) describe such reforms as "contradictory and flawed." This description is apt in many cases, where results-oriented reform tools have been introduced as add-ons to existing process-oriented organizational structures and actually reduce civic access and government responsiveness.

⬚ Decentralization is intended to encourage local-level, competitive, bottom-up, participatory governance, but evidence suggests that such effects are slow in coming and limited. Many such reforms are limited to intergovernmental delegation (with central entities making decisions about provision but local entities contracted to produce services) instead of decentralization (with local entities enjoying authority over decisions about provision and production). The central argument in favor of such delegation is that local governments lack governance capacity. The downside of such delegation is that it prohibits demand-led capacity development in localities and undermines the central goal of decentralization.

Provincial governments or municipalities with tight mandates from central governments have no reason or incentive to create personnel or process abilities related to decision making, prioritization, planning, and allocation. This is evident in cases of South African municipalities, where central influence over municipal entities retards spontaneous local-level capacity-building incentives.[12] Given this argument, although in most cases decentralized governments can indeed be seen to have poor capacity, delegation or deconcentration exacerbates the problem. Tight accountability lines between central and subnational governments also have an effect of entrenching top-down governance (a problem discussed earlier). Organizational hierarchies are maintained, simply running over formal intergovernmental boundaries, with subnational governments responding to the demands of higher-level governments (rather than their own citizens). In most instances the nature of central-subnational interaction is through top-down controls, which bind provincial and local level entities to specific processes—limiting any chance of citizen-based, results-oriented governance. This has resulted in numerous observers questioning the structure of decentralization initiatives (Prud'homme 1995; Litvack, Ahmad, and Bird 1998; Shah 1998). Studies by Shah (1998, 1999), Shah and Schacter (2004), Shah and Thompson (2004), Gurgur and Shah (2002), and Huther and Shah (1998) find that decentralized governments do appear to have positive effects on public governance,[13] but that the structure of decentralization bears significant influence on that effect. Devolved governments (where decision-making responsibilities are decentralized) tend to be more effective than deconcentrated governments (where minimal decision-making authority is devolved) (Shah 1994).

Participatory reforms are intended to bring citizens into the governance process, leading to bottom-up governance, greater public sector competitiveness, and capacity through community partnership. These initiatives typically bypass local governments and thereby weaken the formal system of local governance. (Brinkerhoff and Kulibaba 1996; Turner and Hulme 1997; Schneider 1999; Blair 2000; Brinkerhoff 2000). Many examples of participatory reform in the developing world—from Nigeria (Wunsch and Olowu 1996), to India (Dhesi 2000), to Bolivia (Blair 2000), and Brazil (Atkinson and others 2000)—tell a tale in which citizens largely remain disempowered and excluded from the governance process after interventions take place. Tauxe's study of U.S. local government (1995) shows that reforms tend to be centrally driven from within insular structures, rather than bottom-up initiatives aimed at opening such structures. In such instances, technical administrators enjoy a powerful influence over the nature of participation, limiting it significantly. Such limitations are also prevalent in situations where political processes are undemocratic, centralized, or unrepresentative.

Problems with reform arrangements

Reform combinations in the developing world are commonly seen to reinforce problems associated with the public sector problems of process orientation and centralization.

Earlier discussion held that most governments in the developing world, structured in the mold of the Weberian bureaucracy, are overly focused on process and hard controls emphasizing input management (Shah 1999, 399). Citizens, however, are understood to have an interest in government performance and service. The disjoint between what government organizations focus on (inputs) and what citizens look for from governments (outputs, outcomes, and impacts) is evident in figure 6.1, Shah's results-oriented management and evaluation chain for the public sector (Shah 1999). The chain presents different phases of public production and distribution, from program and project identification through social impact. The government focal point remain or inputs, while citizens are concerned with service delivery performance.

Instead of introducing mechanisms and changing incentives to focus government attention on the entire results chain, reforms are typically arranged to consolidate hard input controls. This is evident in the dominance of macroeconomic stabilization reforms (focused on stabilizing processes and improving input management, typically related to personnel and cash management) and capacity-building initiatives (typically concerned with improving personnel and process inputs). Reforms tend to concentrate

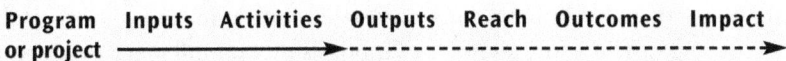

| Program | Inputs | Activities | Outputs | Reach | Outcomes | Impact |
| or project | | | | | | |

FIGURE 6.1 Results-Based Chain and the Process Bias of Common Reform Combinations

on introducing controls and ensuring probity and central capacity before they move into managing for results, decentralizing and devolving service provision, and enhancing participation. In those instances where reforms have progressed to include results-oriented management, the focus is still limited to intermediate outputs and governments are still not given any motivation to consider their more important social effects. This is evident in Desai and Imrie's (1998, 645) comment that the new managerialism is "characterized by de-democratizing tendencies and a fixation with procedural and technical processes." There are two explanations for this process concentration in reform arrangements:

1. Reforms are sometimes viewed as cumulative. Complicated elements such as results-oriented management, participation, and decentralization are seen to build on other elements—most importantly, capacity building. Capacity-building initiatives usually dominate the organizational reforms in developing countries. Poor capacity is considered the most serious impediment to good governance and is countered through initiatives focused on administrators: teaching administrators how to plan and manage resources and providing administrative entities with necessary processes.
2. What could be called the *bureaucratic stage argument* holds that administrative entities mature through specific stages. The argument, offered by authors such as Schick (1998), is that bureaucracies have to learn about the importance of hard controls (focused on inputs) before they can successfully implement soft controls (focused on results). The argument is used to legitimize interventions in the developing world that continue to concentrate on the introduction of basic budgeting and civil service controls. The idea is that, once governance processes are strengthened, reforms can refocus on other sections of the results and evaluations chain, steadily moving from left to right. The argument makes two critical assumptions: (a) that reforms will be successful in establishing such controls, and (b) that administrators conditioned to focus on process will be able to shift their views to focus on results and performance.

Reforms also commonly combine in a centralizing fashion. Figure 6.2 shows participants in the results and evaluation chain, and reforms at different stages. The figure shows the emphasis on and influence of administrators and executive office holders in the reform process.

The view that reform combinations centralize governance processes arises from the observation that dominant reforms related to macroeconomic stabilization and capacity building are almost wholly devised and run by the central government and central agencies within central government. Even reform elements that are designed to redress the centralized character of governance processes are driven centrally. Hence, results-oriented programs, decentralization initiatives, and participation programs are generally shaped and manipulated by central agencies. Andrews (forthcoming) argues, for example, that participation programs often fail because they are conceived by high-level government agents that have no knowledge of participation needs and no interests in ensuring that participation programs actually work. Citizens and their direct representatives in legislatures are often either co-opted to support centrally devised programs or kept out of the reform design stages completely. The result is that top-down reform influences dominate bottom-up influences of citizens and their representatives.

There are two plausible explanations of the centralizing effect in reform combinations:

- Reform elements fall into a hierarchy, which yields some elements that are more important than others. The reform hierarchy is dependent on a number of factors, including the normative values ascribed to different reform elements, reform incentives created by external reform participants (such as international organizations) and economic pressure groups (notably business), and the chronological order of reform introduction. In many instances these factors yield macroeconomic stabilization, the most important reform element. This reform element is usually charted, implemented, and driven by central agencies. All other reforms, such as results-oriented reform, decentralization, and participation, are nested in this reform. Reforms that counter centralization are thus hidden within reforms that reinforce centralization.

- Another explanation, given by Shah (1999), relates to the direct influence that external reform partners have on the kinds of reform adopted and the location (within governance structures) of reform initiatives. Shah argues that external reform partners favor centralizing reform structures and initiatives because "a centralized hierarchical system lowers transactions costs for external assistance and enlarges the comfort zone for external participants in terms of monitoring the utilization of their funds for intended purposes" (416). The lending-based incentives that international organizations create for reforming governments encourage them to adopt top-down, control-oriented reforms.

Evaluation weaknesses in reforms

Reforms can also be faulted for paying insufficient attention to the evaluation problems of developing country governments. Interventions to develop evaluation capacity in developing countries are relatively new and have yet

Program or project	Inputs	Activities	Outputs	Reach	Outcomes	Impact

Administration and Executive
(assisted by development partners)

- Craft macroeconomic reforms, requiring policy decisions about where to cut spending, how to cut spending, and so on.
- Introduce capacity building in internal processes and organization, focusing on strengthening internal abilities (and increasing their own importance in the governance process).
- Incorporate results-oriented management tools into extant programs, alongside capacity-building initiatives (once again focusing tools on their internal operations and goals).
- Fashion decentralization reform to suit internal interests, with process-oriented ties facilitating control over deconcentrated agents.
- Promote limited participatory programs involving politically passable mechanisms based on principles of normal professionalism and controlled participation.

Strong Top-Down Reform Influences

Weak Bottom-Up Reform Influences

Legislature and Citizens
- Have very little influence over macroeconomic stabilization issues.
- Are seldom consulted about capacity building.
- Have no say on results management.
- Are either encouraged to support limited decentralization (legislature) or have little say in decentralized structures, which are answerable to higher-level government authorities.
- Are uninvolved in determining what participation programs look like. Participation programs shaped by other reform interests.

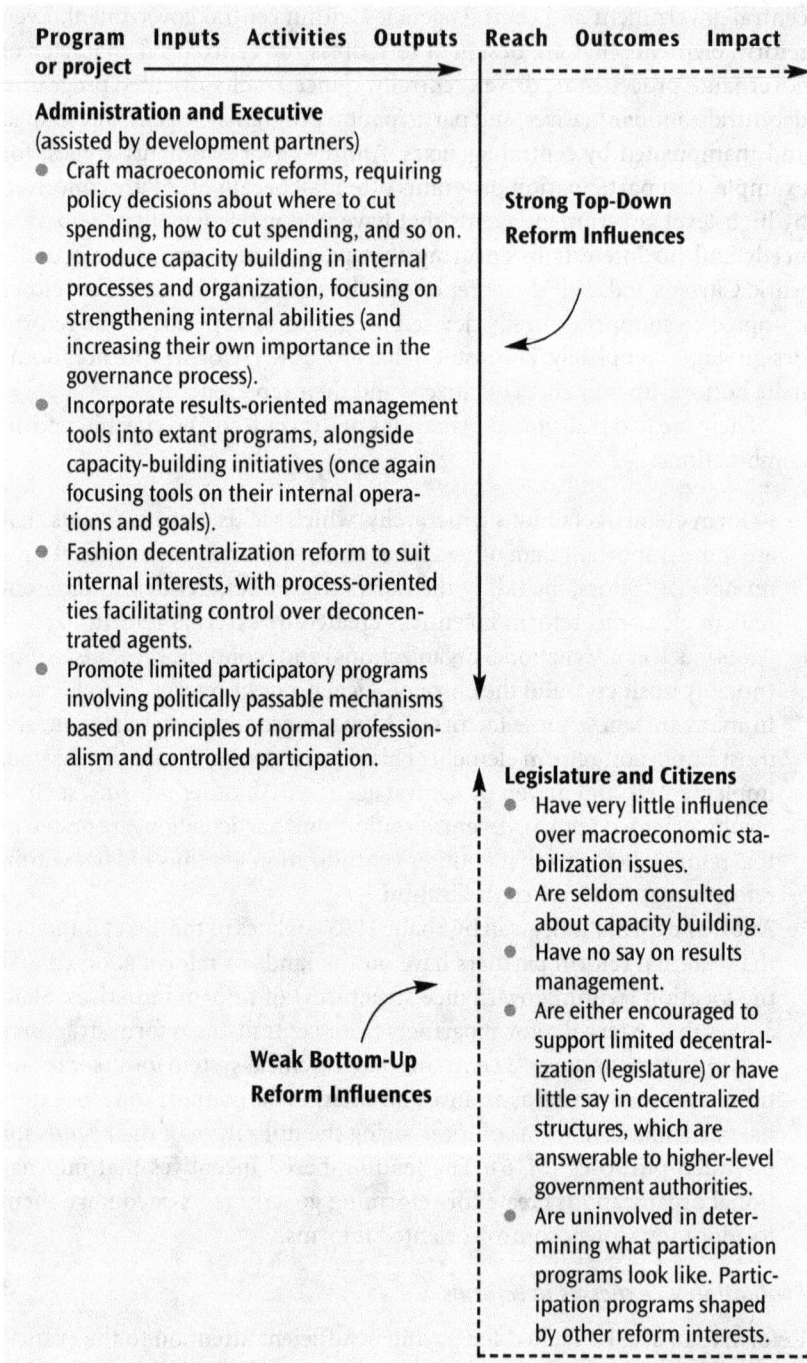

FIGURE 6.2 The Top-Down, Centralizing Nature of Common Reform Combinations

to be reflected in mainline reform elements (Feinstein and Picciotto 2000). Evaluations are important for a number of reasons, the chief one being that they shape and enforce behavioral incentives in social settings. It is important to promote evaluations that facilitate the institutional and incentive changes that are necessary for effective reform. Without such evaluations, incentives do not change from those associated with traditionally flawed public organizations, and behavior cannot be expected to change either.

Examples of the evaluation problem abound. Dia (1996) talks of African countries with the personnel, skills, and process abilities to govern well, yet with records of poor governance (perhaps because of poor governance evaluations?). Andrews (2001) speaks of inconsistencies in results-oriented reforms related to the lack of attention given to changing the nature of process-based audit evaluations facing results-oriented managers. Andrews comments that, "In such situations, managers are receiving a conflicting message: 'Manage for results . . . but remember that you will be audited on your adherence to process (not on the results)' " (10).

A New Citizen-Centered Framework to Guide Reform

There is obviously a need to rethink the framework in which public sector reform is being conceptualized in the developing world, so that reforms effectively counter the weaknesses and ills evident in governments. To this end, we present a citizen-centered governance framework, developed as a response to the problems experienced with individual reform elements, the process and centralizing tendencies of reform arrangements, and the lack of an evaluation aspect to reforms. This citizen-centered government framework is different from those preceding it, not so much because of the kinds of elements in the model, but rather because of the way the model is organized and because of the elements that are emphasized.

Citizen-centered governance focuses on creating the right institutional environment for results-oriented reform. This entails focusing on developing participatory, localized structures through which citizens are empowered to demand better results from government. This kind of institutional environment stimulates the incentive for governments to develop results-oriented institutions (rules and tools) themselves.

The citizen-centered governance framework combines common elements from reforms—results-oriented management, decentralization, and participation—with a new reform element, results-oriented evaluation. Through the selection of these elements as well as the synergy between them, the citizen-centered framework directly challenges the top-down governance models entrenched in the developing world. The bottom-up, results-oriented dimensions of citizen-centered governance focus public entities on outcomes and impacts rather than inputs and processes. They center attention on citizens as the ultimate principals of public entities. In so doing, the citizen-centered governance framework tackles the problems and weaknesses that plague governments in developing countries, providing both the focus and the incentives necessary for real governance improvement as well as the tools required to respond to such incentives.

The citizen-centered governance framework arises out of lessons learned from past reform failures. The main differences between citizen-centered reform and other common reform approaches are

- citizens' empowerment through a rights-based (citizen charter) approach.
- bottom-up accountability for results.
- evaluation of government performance by citizens as direct-users of public services.

The framework emphasizes reforms that strengthen citizen empowerment and bottom-up accountability (see table 6.3). In citizen-centered reform, citizen participation forms

- the basis of all government decisions (with public entities responding to citizen demands)
- the framework for government accountability (with citizens evaluating what government does and rewarding it or not)
- the central motivating factor for civil servants and politicians alike (with citizen evaluations driving their behavior)

TABLE 6.3 Key Elements of Citizen Centered Governance Reforms

- Citizens charter
  - Service standards
  - Requirements for citizens voice and choice
- Subsidiarity
- Citizen oriented output budgeting
  - Service delivery outputs and costs
  - Citizens report card on service delivery performance for the previous year
- Public sector as a purchaser through performance contracts but not necessarily provider of services
- Alternate Service Delivery Framework
- Benchmarking

▓ the foundation of government capacity (with governments drawing from their constituencies to achieve the capacity levels needed to meet demand)

Citizen empowerment is seen as central to the reform of governments in the literature (see Tiebout 1956, Hirchman 1970, Jackson 2000, Sartorius 2000, Peters 1996, Kaufmann 2000, Putnam 1993).[14] The prominent voices of social conscience, as expressed in the context of the struggle for development and growth in underdeveloped regions of the world, also increasingly emphasize participation. Expressing the importance of citizen involvement in government and society, and of social capital, Bishop Desmond Tutu says that, "to be . . . is to participate" (Krog 1998, 110).

Effective participation that actively results in citizen empowerment is difficult to achieve in large centralized governments. Thus the participatory concentration in the citizen-centered model is conceptualized at the local (or regional) level (Oates 1972). Governments at this level are small enough to facilitate citizen involvement. In this light, Vaughan (1995, 501) speaks of "the importance of sub-national environments where communities feel, breathe, and express themselves and thus, where development programmes are relevant." In decentralized governments citizens should have fairly ready access to political representatives and administrators alike, not just street-level bureaucrats. Living among constituents is assumed to be a most effective way of encouraging political and administrative officials to take such constituents seriously. Citizens have a direct and natural line of influence over officials who live alongside them.

Figure 6.3(a and b) shows the citizen-centered governance framework concisely. The direction of governance and reform influence is obvious. In contrast to the representation in figure 6.2 of common top-down reforms, citizen-centered systems are bottom-up. Citizens, in the bottom right corner, are the central role players in the governance and governance reform process.

Communication and interaction and participation take the form of implicit social and explicit political contracts between citizens and their representatives. These contracts are built on the social pressure that citizens can exert on public servants, as well as creative political and economic pressures that can be institutionalized through citizens' charters. Such contracts center on the provision, by government, of specific results—outputs, outcomes, reach, and impacts. An example could be an elected mayor being required, by law, to turn electoral promises into a contract for performance and management—spelling out what citizens can expect him/her to do in terms of providing water, education, roads, electricity, and so forth and enhancing civic participation in the evaluation of such performance.

Citizen empowerment is expected to lead to a natural results focus in the governance process. The rationale is simply that citizens are more interested in government outputs, outcomes, reach, and impacts than they are in controls over inputs. Citizens want to know what government does for them, not how it does it. The rationale extends to the simple argument that results-minded citizens, when empowered through clearer paths of access into the governance process (such as a contract provides) create pressure for their political representatives and administrators to be results oriented (hence the overlap between participatory decentralization and results-oriented management in the figure).

Figure 6.3(a and b) shows that the participatory decentralization element overlaps with the second and third reform elements of the citizen-centered framework: results-oriented management and results-oriented evaluations. These overlaps emphasize the fact that all reform elements revolve around the participatory decentralization component. It is citizen involvement in decentralized structures that creates the focus and provides the pressures that make the other elements both important and viable. The participatory decentralization holds citizen-centered reform together, with citizen demand providing the basis for a results-orientation and constituting the source for results identification and evaluation.

Results-oriented management arises in citizen-centered reform because of strengthened government accountability to citizens. Because citizens demand results from their political representatives (and when citizens are empowered through charter of rights as, for example, by the Clients' Charter in Malaysia), those politicians charged with running the administration (the executive) are pressured to deliver. In developing countries such pressure is problematic, however, because administrative processes are focused on inputs rather than results and because citizens are not empowered to demand accountability for service delivery performance. Results-oriented management reform as part of the citizen-centered governance reform can help resolve this problem. With the executive carrying the results-based demands of citizens (identified through participation mechanisms that facilitate citizen voice, and formalized in the political contract), it uses results-oriented management interventions to focus and enable the administration to achieve those demands. These interventions take a number of forms (see figure 6.4).

Program/ project	Inputs	Activities	Outputs	Reach	Outcomes	Impacts (goals)

Administration concerned with outputs.

Clear roles in the government production process, Bottom-up, Focused on managing for results, and Evaluated in terms of those results.

Output contract

Executive concerned with outcomes

Internal and external Results and process Evaluations

Outcome contract

Legislature

Citizens

E   V   A   L   U   A   T   I   O   N   S

Citizen evaluations

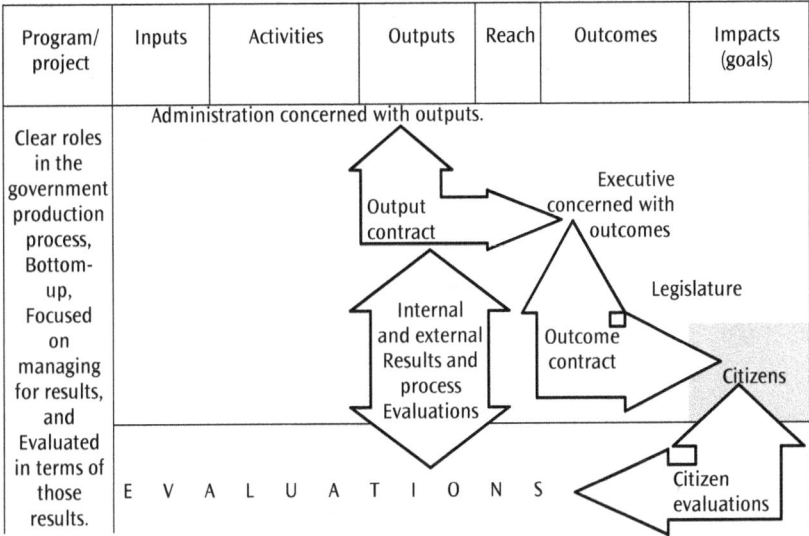

FIGURE 6.3(a) A Roadmap for Citizen-Centered Governance

Results-Oriented Management focuses on:

- Creating social contracts that link political representatives and administrators to citizens,
- Creating results-based relationships throughout government, and
- Introducing necessary tools to focus management on results.

Inputs   Activities   Outputs   Reach   Outcomes   Impacts (goals)

Administration Focusing management on results: Performance-based budgets, benchmarking, activity-based costing, balanced scorecard

Total Quality Management and other tools used to develop interaction between administration and citizens

Executive

Results-based relationship between executive/administration, accountable for outputs

Legislature

Results-based relationship between citizens and the executive, accountable for outcomes.

Political contracts link political representatives and the administration to Citizens

FIGURE 6.3(b) Citizen-Centered Reform—Formalizing the Results Focus

FIGURE 6.4 Citizen-Centered Reform Influences on Governance

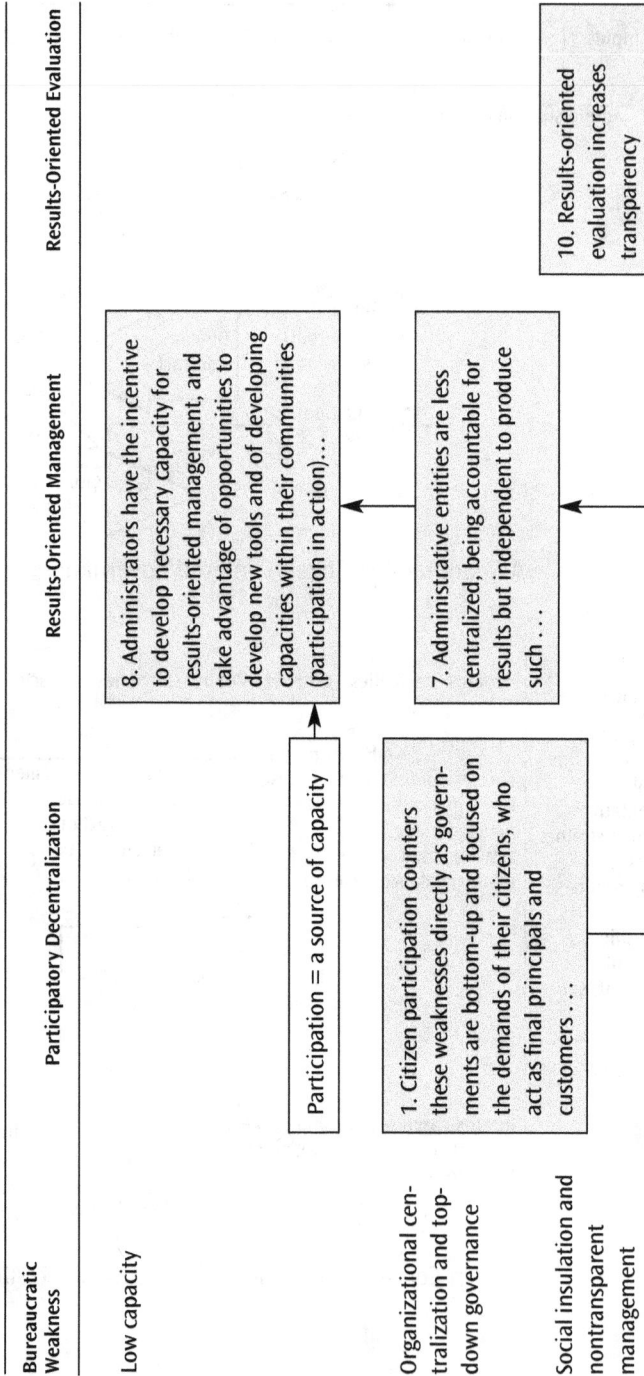

Bureaucratic Weakness	Participatory Decentralization	Results-Oriented Management	Results-Oriented Evaluation
Low capacity			
Organizational centralization and top-down governance			
Social insulation and nontransparent management			

Participation = a source of capacity

8. Administrators have the incentive to develop necessary capacity for results-oriented management, and take advantage of opportunities to develop new tools and of developing capacities within their communities (participation in action)…

1. Citizen participation counters these weaknesses directly as governments are bottom-up and focused on the demands of their citizens, who act as final principals and customers…

7. Administrative entities are less centralized, being accountable for results but independent to produce such …

10. Results-oriented evaluation increases transparency

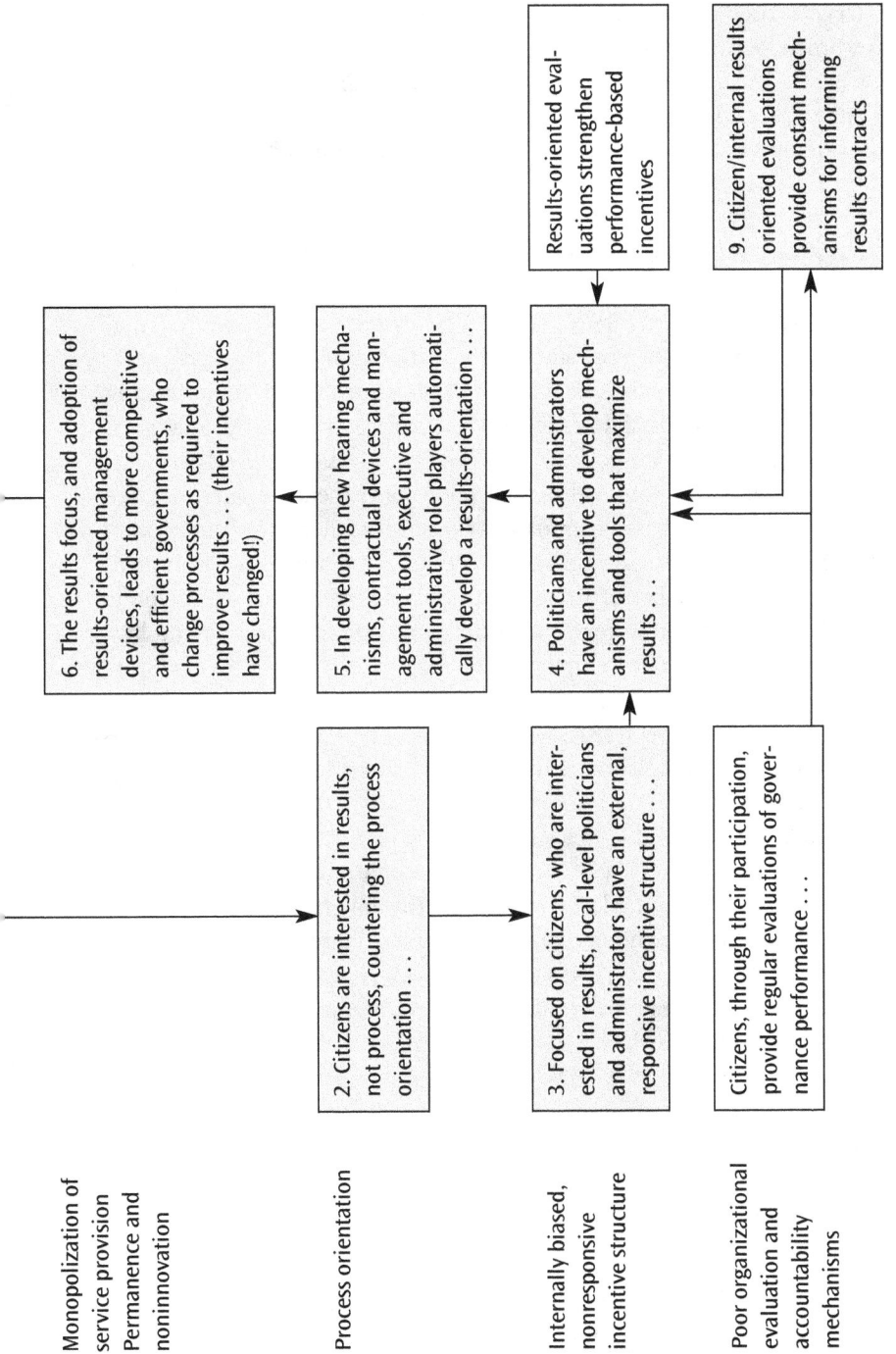

Monopolization of service provision
Permanence and noninnovation

Process orientation

Internally biased, nonresponsive incentive structure

Poor organizational evaluation and accountability mechanisms

6. The results focus, and adoption of results-oriented management devices, leads to more competitive and efficient governments, who change processes as required to improve results . . . (their incentives have changed!)

5. In developing new hearing mechanisms, contractual devices and management tools, executive and administrative role players automatically develop a results-orientation . . .

4. Politicians and administrators have an incentive to develop mechanisms and tools that maximize results . . .

2. Citizens are interested in results, not process, countering the process orientation . . .

3. Focused on citizens, who are interested in results, local-level politicians and administrators have an external, responsive incentive structure . . .

Citizens, through their participation, provide regular evaluations of governance performance . . .

Results-oriented evaluations strengthen performance-based incentives

9. Citizen/internal results oriented evaluations provide constant mechanisms for informing results contracts

- Devices used to effectively decipher citizen demands and hold the government accountable for service quality and standards, such as Clients' Charter and total quality management as used in Malaysia (Chiu 1997) and the "Serving the Community" booklet used in Hong Kong, "to raise awareness and understanding" of "serving the community" (Efficiency Unit, Hong Kong, China, Government 1999).
- Mechanisms creating performance contracts (particularly focused on output performance) between the executive and administration. These mechanisms have been adopted in some commonwealth countries and are described by Kaul (1997, 15) as "new management structures" that enhance accountability by tightening task definition and through "measurement of performance, devolution of resource control, strengthening monitoring, and clarifying incentives." Grindle (1997) finds that such structures differentiate governments she would classify as good performers from those she would classify as poor performers. In particular, she found that results-based planning and incentive schemes had a very positive effect on public organizations. Of the 26 case studies she examined, "12 out of 14 good performers set and applied performance expectations while 10 of 12 poor performers set no such standards for their employees. In these latter cases, employees were left to conform to the performance expectations for the public sector more generally—standards that were usually very low" (481).
- Tools used by administrators to transform their management processes from an input to an output and outcomes orientation (see figure 6.5). Various tools are used to this end, including performance-based budgeting, which Ammons (2002, 344) argues is important: "How can government be truly accountable if it only tracks the dollars moving through its system and barely mentions the services rendered through the use of these resources?" (See table 6.4.) Benchmarking is also an important tool used to orient management toward results—"essential because it provides a standard of reference by which a government entity can measure or judge performance" (Foltin 1999, 42). In Malaysia, benchmarking has been adopted to make comparisons with similar organizations that carry out the same functional activity, and in so doing to see how an agency's results measure up (Chiu 1997). Activity-based costing is a similarly relevant tool, needed to evaluate the costs of producing outputs and outcomes in order to evaluate performance and allocate resources (Rodriguez 1995).

The first two forms (mechanisms to decipher citizen demands and devices to entrench performance-based relationships) are considered the

Question for results-oriented management	Management tool	The entire process driven by a citizen focus:
Contract information—what is the final product we must produce and what do we receive to produce such product?	Performance-based budget	All these tools stress Total Quality Management and create a results-based accountability culture.
How do we know how we are doing in terms of the contract, and in terms of other producers from whom we can learn?	Benchmarking	
How much does it cost to produce such product (the complete cost)? How can we produce the product better so we can be sure of meeting and exceeding our contract obligation and receiving rewards?	Activity-Based Costing	
How do we report our results?	Full reporting using accrual accounting	
How do we manage the new reporting, production, and contract obligations we have, as well as run a citizen friendly administration?	Balanced Scorecard	

FIGURE 6.5 Tools for Results-Oriented Management—External, Citizen Focus

TABLE 6.4 Citizen-Centered budgeting

- Budget format to follow closely service delivery format and also to include a performance report and net worth assessment
- Citizens charter and sunshine rights
- Citizen inputs in budget process to be formalized at all stages
    - Formulation: Town Hall meeting on the previous year's performance and new proposals.
    - Review and execution: Formal process for complaints
    - Post: Compliance and feedback reports.

most important in citizen-centered governance. Devices to decipher citizen demands are the core instruments that administrators use to develop their results focus, while output contracts create the incentives for administrators to respond to demand. The management tools that help administrators in achieving results, such as planning tools and accounting tools, are of secondary importance and should be offered only as options for administrators to appropriate as they see fit (rather than as the basis of reform, as they often are presented). The rationale is that if administrators can identify the results they have to achieve, and if they have incentives to achieve those results, they will develop the necessary tools and processes themselves (or take advantage of capacity-building opportunities presented to them). The flip side of this rationale is that if results-oriented tools are introduced and capacity is developed without the mechanisms for identifying results and enhancing incentives, administrators will not use the newly acquired tools to serve citizens because they will have no reason to do so.

The final element of citizen-centered governance is results-oriented evaluation, which plays an important role in strengthening the results-oriented incentives facing politicians and administrators in the governance process. Figure 6.3(a) shows that this element is intertwined with participatory decentralization. The element also relates directly to results-oriented management within government structures.

This last element involves simply the evaluation of results. Such evaluation is important for the ongoing analysis of results-oriented contracts, between citizens and political leaders where the concentration is on outcomes and between political leaders and administrators where the concentration is on outputs. These evaluations constitute important accountability and transparency devices, which help to inform and enforce important behavior-binding and shaping influences in the citizen-centered reform system:

- Citizen evaluations of outcomes are necessary for ensuring that citizens have the ability to assess public sector performance in terms of negotiated outcome contracts. Political leaders are expected to take such contracts seriously only if citizens, either directly or represented by groups in civil society, actively and regularly force them to do so (by evaluating performance and holding political leaders accountable for it). An example of this in action comes from Mazdoor Kisan Shakti Sangathan (MKSS), a nongovernmental organization in Rajasthan, India. Here, community evaluation devices take a number of forms, including *jan sunwai*—public hearings—at which detailed accounts derived from public expenditure records and other documents are read aloud to assembled villagers. Local people are invited to give testimony that might highlight discrepancies between official records and their own experiences. Through this direct form of social audit discrepancies have been identified and public officials (politicians and administrators) have been brought to account. This "reinforces democratic notions regarding the obligations of government officials and elected representatives as public servants" (Jenkins and Goetz 1999, 605).
- Performance audits can also strengthen bottom-up accountability. Such audits—especially at the local level—are becoming increasingly popular in industrial countries. Niesner (1999) notes, "Local government auditors

are increasingly being recognized for their role in establishing accountability while improving government performance" (37).

▨ Citizen evaluations of outputs are necessary to strengthen the results orientation of administrators. Although the political-administrative output contract sets formal incentives for administrative behavior, citizen interaction with administrators is an often overlooked but powerful informal influence on administrative performance. If citizens actively evaluate outputs as well as outcomes, they can consistently engage with administrators (who live in their midst) about results, creating incentives for administrators to work hard at maximizing their performance.

The three types of results-oriented evaluations thus reinforce the citizen-focused results orientation in citizen-centered reform. They complete the citizen-centered reform model by consolidating new incentives in the public organization that not only support a new view of governance but also help facilitate reform itself: the more regular, focused, and participatory results-oriented evaluations are, the greater is the incentive to make change work and produce results.

Conclusion

The citizen-centered governance framework offers potential for responsive and accountable public governance in the developing world. This chapter has described common responses to public sector misgovernance and provided a number of reasons why reforms often prove ineffective in solving such problems. These reasons relate to the poor fit of reform elements to situations either conceptually or in implementation, the absence of any citizens' evaluations of elements in common reforms, and the adverse effects accompanying reform combinations.

The citizen-centered governance framework seeks to avoid such shortcomings by focusing on reform elements that have intuitive appeal in the context of developing countries (that is, empowering citizens to demand accountability from their governments). The impact of such reforms is captured in figure 6.4. The figure shows the basic argument of how citizen-centered reform counters administrative and governance weaknesses in the developing world. In the first instance participatory decentralization directly counters weaknesses related to top-down, centralized, and insular governance structures. This effect is achieved by focusing government on citizens (usually at the bottom of the governance hierarchy) and decentralizing public sector structures.

Participatory decentralization is also expected to stimulate changes in the organizational orientation and incentives in the public sector. Citizens empowered by a rights-based institutional framework demand accountability for results. As they express their preferences, it is expected that public organizations will divert their attention to outputs and outcomes, having explicit incentives to do so (the better their results are, the greater will be their citizen support).

Results-oriented management enters the equation to bolster the new incentives and results orientation. Political representatives, influencing administrators through output-based contracts, create incentives for these administrators to focus on results rather than processes. Beyond these incentive mechanisms, administrators also develop new tools for evaluating citizen demands and meeting them (see figure 6.5 and table 6.4). These tools facilitate the change to a results orientation and lead to government agencies being more creative, efficient, and competitive in their provision processes. New results-oriented management incentives and tools also lead to decreased centralization, as government entities are held accountable for results but given significant discretion over how results are produced. This discretion leaves capacity building in the hands of actual service producers. Administrators have an incentive to improve their capacity for service provision, can access results-oriented management tools, and also can lean on their participating communities for necessary skills and processes. Once again, the elements work together to counter the weaknesses of centralization and lack of technical capacity.

The final weakness, usually untreated in reforms, relates to the poor evaluation and monitoring devices in public sector entities. This weakness is addressed directly through results-oriented evaluations. As results are evaluated by citizens as consumers of government services, so governments are held accountable for service delivery performance. These accountability mechanisms bolster incentives created by results-oriented management tools.

Notes

1. Monopoly producers have no incentive to improve on performance. This incentive problem results in entrenched inefficiencies, in fact entrenching the status quo. Inefficient bureaucrats do everything they can to protect their production processes and inefficient project and input choices from facing competitive pressures (from other producers or from comparative statistics).
2. This argument is synthesized by Peters (1996).
3. Government cost statistics reflect this kind of monopoly power. They are often developed to limit the potential for comparison with private sector cost statistics. As public

administrators enjoy monopolies over this kind of information, they are unaccountable, unresponsive, and have no incentive to act efficiently (Niskanen 1971; Moe 1984; Kraan 1996).

4. The central importance of information in the development and governance process is most eloquently argued by Freire (1985).

5. Organizations concentrate on those aspects of their mandates that are actively evaluated (knowing that poor evaluations will have stinging consequences) (Feinstein and Picciotto 2000).

6. Many audit reports are performed on special political request, for example.

7. Although many audit offices in the developing world are building capacity, most still lack the resources to perform audits routinely for all administrative entities, for example.

8. Deficits (as a percentage of total expenditure) fell from an average of 15.86 between 1981 and 1993 to 11.25 between 1994 and 1999 (calculated from South African Reserve Bank data, July 2000).

9. Capital spending comprised 9 percent of spending between 1981 and 1993, but only 4 percent between 1994 and 1999. Fixed assets made up 2.94 percent of total expenditure up to 1993, but had a 1.49 percent share between 1994 and 1999 (South African Reserve Bank data, July 2000).

10. Strategic spending has dropped in real terms and there is a concern that departments are underspending their budgets, leading to inefficiencies and low levels of budgetary responsiveness. Can a reform be successful if it improves one outcome but not others? Is the decline in capital spending a manifestation of Alesina and Perotti's (1996) observation that medium-term budgeting allows creative accounting and the postponement of difficult projects?

11. Dollar and Svensson (1998) find that stabilization programs regularly faltered. They explain such experiences by saying that many countries simply were not ready for reform.

12. South African studies include the Foundation for Contemporary Research (1999); Oranje, Oosthuizen, and van Huyssteen (1999); Otzen and others (1999); PLANACT (1999); and Planning Initiative (1999).

13. Huther and Shah (1998) find that 38 percent of the variance in governance quality is explained by decentralization alone.

14. Peters (1996, 48) argues that participatory approaches in governance reform emerge because of the belief that "the hierarchical, rule-based organizations usually encountered in the public sector [are] severe impediments to effective management and governance."

References

Adamolekun, L., Noel Kulemeka, and Mouftaou Laleye. 1997. "Political Transition, Economic Liberalization, and Civil Service Reform in Malawi." *Public Administration and Development* 17: 209–22.

Alesina, Alberto, and Roberto Perotti. 1996. "Fiscal Discipline and the Budget Process." *American Economic Review* 86 (May): 401–7.

Ammons, David N. 2002. "Performance Measurement and Managerial Thinking." *Public Performance and Management Review* 25 (4): 344–47.

Andrews, Matthew. 2001. "Adjusting External Audits to Facilitate Results Oriented Management." *International Journal of Government Auditors*, (April): 10–14.

———. 2002. "A Theory-Based Approach to Evaluating Budget Reforms." *International Public Management Journal* 5 (2): 135–54.

———. Forthcoming. "Selecting and Sustaining Community Programs in Developing Countries." *Public Administration Quarterly.*

Atkinson, Sarah, Regianne Leila Roilm Medeiros, Paulo Henrique, Lima Oliviera, and Ricardo Dias de Almeida. 2000. "Going Down to the Local: Incorporating Social Organization and Political Culture into Assessments of Decentralized Health Care." *Social Science and Medicine* 51: 619–36.

Blair, Harry. 2000. "Participation and Accountability at the Periphery: Democratic Local Governance in Six Countries." *World Development* 28 (1): 21–39.

Brinkerhoff, Derek W. 2000. "Democratic Governance and Sectoral Policy Reform: Tracing Linkages and Exploring Synergies." *World Development* 28 (4): 601–15.

Brinkerhoff, Derek W., and Nicolas P. Kulibaba. 1996. "Perspective on Participation in Economic Policy Reform in Africa." *Studies in Comparative International Development* 31 (Fall): 131–51.

Chiu, Ng Kam. 1997. "Service Targets and Methods of Redress: The Impact of Accountability in Malaysia." *Public Administration and Development* 17: 175–80.

Coston, Jennifer M. 1998. "Administrative Avenues to Democratic Governance: The Balance of Supply and Demand." *Public Administration and Development* 18: 479–93.

de Merode, Louis, with Charles S. Thomas. 1994. "Implementing Civil Service Pay and Employment Reform in Africa: The Experiences of Ghana, the Gambia, and Guinea." In *Rehabilitating Government: Pay and Employment Reform in Africa*, ed. David L. Lindauer and Barbara Nunberg, 160–94. Washington, DC: World Bank.

Desai, Vandarda, and Rob Imrie. 1998. "The New Managerialism in Local Governance: North-South Dimensions." *Third World Quarterly* 19 (4): 635–50.

Dhesi, Autur S. 2000. "Social Capital and Community Development." *Community Development Journal* 35 (3): 199–214.

Dia, Mamadou. 1996. *Africa's Management in the 1990s and Beyond*. Washington, DC: World Bank.

DISHA (Developing Initiatives for Social and Human Action). 2000. "Presentation D." PREM Network, World Bank, Washington, DC.

Dollar, David, and Jakob Svensson. 1998. "What Explains the Success or Failure of Structural Adjustment Programs?" Policy Research Working Paper 1938, Development Research Group, World Bank, Washington, DC.

Easterly, William. 2000. "Can Institutions Resolve Ethnic Conflict?" World Bank Working Paper, World Bank, Washington, DC.

Efficiency Unit, Hong Kong, China, Government. 2000. "News, Information, and Views on Public Sector Reform." http://www.info.gov.hk/eu/psrhk/hist_con.htm.

Egeberg, Morten. 1995. "Bureaucrats as Public Policy-Makers and Their Self-Interest." *Journal of Theoretical Politics* 7: 157–67.

Feinstein, Osvaldo, and Robert Picciotto, eds. 2000. *Evaluation and Poverty Reduction: Proceedings from a World Bank Conference*. Operations Evaluation Department, World Bank, Washington, DC.

Foltin, Craig. 1999. "State and Local Government Performance: It's Time to Measure Up!" *Government Accountants Journal* 48 (1): 40–46.

Foundation for Contemporary Research. 1999. *A Review of Integrated Development Planning in the Western Cape.* Cape Town, South Africa.

Freire, Paulo. 1985. *The Politics of Education: Culture, Power, and Liberation.* Hadley, MA: Bergin & Garvey.

Grindle, Merilee S. 1997. "Divergent Cultures? When Public Organization Perform Well in Developing Countries." *World Development* 25 (4): 481–95.

Gurgur, Tugrul, and Anwar Shah, 2002. "Localization and Corruption: Panacea or Pandora's Box." In *Managing Fiscal Decentralization,* ed. Ehtisham Ahmad and Vito Tanzi, 46–67. London and New York: Routledge Press.

Hirschman, Albert O. 1970. *Exit, Voice, and Loyalty: Responses to Decline in Firms, Organizations, and States.* Cambridge, MA: Harvard University Press.

Huther, Jeff, and Anwar Shah. 1998. "Applying a Simple Measure of Good Governance to the Debate on Fiscal Decentralization." Policy Research Working Paper 1894, World Bank, Washington, DC.

Huther, Jeff, Sandra Roberts, and Anwar Shah. 1997. *Public Expenditure Reform under Adjustment Lending: Lessons from World Bank Experiences.* Washington, DC: World Bank.

Jackson, Edward T. 2000. "The Front-End Costs and Downstream Benefits of Participatory Evaluation." In *Evaluation and Poverty Reduction: Proceedings from a World Bank Conference,* ed. Osvaldo Feinstein and Robert Picciotto, 115–26. Operations Evaluation Department, World Bank, Washington, DC.

Jenkins, Rob, and Anne Marie Goetz. 1999. "Accounts and Accountability: Theoretical Implications of the Right-to-Information Movement in India." *Third World Quarterly* 20 (3): 602–22.

Kaufmann, Daniel. 2000. "Governance and Anticorruption: New Insights and Challenges." In *Evaluation and Poverty Reduction: Proceedings from a World Bank Conference,* ed. Osvaldo Feinstein and Robert Picciotto, 289–94. Operations Evaluation Department, World Bank, Washington, DC.

Kaul, Mohan. 1997. "The New Public Administration: Management Innovations in Government." *Public Administration and Development* 17: 13–26.

Kraan, Dirk-Jan. 1996. *Budgetary Decisions: A Public Choice Approach.* Cambridge, U.K.: Cambridge University Press.

Krog, Antjie. 1998. *Country of My Skull.* Cape Town, South Africa: Jonathan Cape.

Litvack, Jennie, Junaid Ahmad, and Richard Bird. 1998. *Rethinking Decentralization in Developing Countries.* Sector Studies Series, Poverty Reduction and Economic Management, World Bank, Washington, DC.

Melkers, Julia, and Katherine Willoughby. 1998. "The State of the States: Performance-Based Budgeting Requirements in Forty-Seven Out of Fifty." *Public Administration Review* 58: 66–73.

Moe, Terry. 1984. "The New Economics of Organization." *American Journal of Political Science* 28: 739–77.

Niesner, Helen. 1999. "Local Government Auditing—Improving the Performance of Government in the Next Century." *Government Accountants Journal* 48 (4): 32–38.

Niskanen, William. 1971. *Bureaucracy and Representative Government.* Chicago: Aldine-Atherton.

Oates, Wallace. 1972. *Fiscal Federalism.* New York: Harcourt Brace Jovanovich.

Oranje, Mark, Riette Oosthuizen, and Elsona van Huyssteen.1999. "An Investigation into the LDO-Endeavour in the Provinces of Gauteng and the North-West." Report prepared for the Department of Land Affairs, South Africa.

Otzen, Uwe, Ulrich Hoecker, Britta Menzel, Silke Pfeiffer, Heike Poerksen, and Vera Weik. 1999. "Integrated Development Planning: A New Task for Local Government in South Africa." Working Paper 9/1999, Deutsches Institut für Entwicklungspolitik, Bonn, Germany.

Peters, B. Guy. 1996. *The Future of Governing: Four Emerging Models.* Kansas City, KS: University Press of Kansas.

Peterson, Stephen B. 1998. "Saints, Demons, Wizards, and Systems: Why Information Technology Reforms Fail or Underperform in Public Bureaucracies in Africa." *Public Administration and Development* 18: 37–60.

PLANACT. 1999. "Towards a Social Approach to Integrated Development Planning." Integrated Development Planning Unit Study. PLANACT, South Africa.

Planning Initiative. 1999. "An Evaluation of the Integrated Development Planning in KwaZulu Natal." Report prepared for the Town and Regional Planning Commission, KwaZulu Natal, South Africa.

Polidano, Charles. 1998. "Public Sector Reform in Developing Countries: The State of Practice." *Journal of International Development* 10 (3): 373–75.

Prud'homme, Rémy. 1995. "On the Dangers of Decentralization." *World Bank Research Observer* (August): 201–10.

Putnam, Robert D. 1993. *Making Democracy Work: Civic Traditions in Modern Italy.* Princeton, NJ: Princeton University Press.

Qualman, Ann, and Joe Bolger. 1996. "Capacity Development: A Holistic Approach to Sustainable Development." CIDA International Development Information Centre, Gatineau, Quebec. http://www.acdi-cida.gc.ca/index-e.htm.

Rodriguez, Justine Farr. 1995. "The Usefulness of Cost Accounting in the Federal Government." *Government Accountants Journal* 44 (1): 31–35.

Sartorius, Rolf. 2000. "Building Local Capacity for Participatory Monitoring and Evaluation." In *Evaluation and Poverty Reduction: Proceedings from a World Bank Conference,* ed. Osvaldo Feinstein and Robert Picciotto, 133–43. Operations Evaluation Department, World Bank, Washington, DC.

Schick, Allen. 1998. "Why Most Developing Countries Should Not Try New Zealand Reforms." *World Bank Research Observer* 13 (1): 123–31.

Schneider, Hartmut. 1999. "Participatory Governance for Poverty Reduction." *Journal of International Development* 11: 521–34.

Shah, Anwar. 1994. *The Reform of Intergovernmental Fiscal Relations in Developing and Emerging Market Economies.* Policy and Research Series 23. Washington, DC: World Bank.

———. 1998. "Balance, Accountability, and Responsiveness: Lessons about Decentralization." Working Paper 2021, World Bank, Washington, DC.

———. 1999. "Governing for Results in a Globalised and Localised World." *Pakistan Development Review* 38 (4, part I): 385–431.

Shah, Anwar, and Mark Schacter. 2004. "Combating Corruption: Look before You Leap." *Finance and Development* 41 (4): 40–43.

Shah, Anwar, and Theresa M. Thompson. 2004. "Implementing Decentralized Local Governance: A Treacherous Road with Potholes, Detours, and Road Closures." In *Reforming Intergovernmental Fiscal Relations and the Rebuilding of Indonesia,* ed. James Alm, Jorge Martinez-Vazquez, and Sri Mulyani Indrawati, 301–37. Northampton, MA: Edward Elgar.

Shah, Anwar, Theresa Thompson, and Heng-fu Zou. 2004. "The Impact of Decentralization on Service Delivery, Corruption, Fiscal Management, and Growth in Developing and Emerging Market Economies: A Synthesis of Empirical Evidence." *CESifo Dice Report* 2 (Spring): 10–14.

South African Reserve Bank. 2000. *Quarterly Bulletin, July 2000.* Pretoria: South African Reserve Bank.

Stillman, Richard J. 1991. *A Preface to Public Administration.* New York: St. Martin's.

Tauxe, Caroline S. 1995. "Marginalizing Public Participation in Local Planning: An Ethnographic Account." *Journal of the American Planning Association* 61 (Autumn): 471–82.

Tiebout, William. 1956. "A Pure Theory of Local Expenditures." *Journal of Political Economy* 64 (5): 416–24.

Turner, Mark, and David Hulme. 1997. *Governance, Administration, and Development.* New Hartford, CT: Kumarian Press.

Vaughan, Olufemi. 1995. "Assessing Grassroots Politics and Community Development in Nigeria." *African Affairs* 94 (4): 501–19.

Walker, Laura, and Berhana Mengistu. 1999. *Spend and Deliver: A Guide to the Medium-Term Expenditure Framework.* Cape Town, South Africa: Institute for Democracy in South Africa.

World Bank. 1998. *Public Expenditure Management Handbook.* Washington, DC: World Bank.

Wunsch, James S., and Dele Olowu. 1996. "Regime Transformation from Below: Democratization, Local Governance, and Democratic Reform in Nigeria." *Studies in Comparative International Development* 31 (Winter): 66–82.

7

Toward Citizen-Centered Local-Level Budgets in Developing Countries

MATTHEW ANDREWS AND ANWAR SHAH

There is an extensive literature on public budgeting and financial management reform, especially as it pertains to developing countries. This literature tends to concentrate on central government budgeting issues and is often either overly technical (assessing the appropriateness of tools and mechanisms such as zero-based budgeting, performance-based budgeting, and the medium-term expenditure framework, for example) or conceptual (investigating the political or organizational complexities of budgeting processes, for example). This chapter considers the popular topic from a different perspective—that of the citizen served by the local government (contributing to and benefiting from the budget). It asks how well budgets and financial management processes serve citizens and how they could be structured to serve citizens better. This perspective is highly relevant to recent public sector reform movements, which variously emphasize civic participation, citizen accountability, or consumerism.

The first section considers how conventional budgeting processes and formats in place in developing countries frustrate citizens' abilities to contribute to the governance process, and to evaluate and respond to government performance. The second section proposes institutional adjustments in budgeting processes and a new budget format that orients budgets to citizens. This citizen-oriented budgeting approach is particularly relevant at the local level in developing countries, where citizens generally have close proximity but limited access and influence over those responsible for governing—especially those involved in the financial management and allocation process.

Citizens and the Common Approaches to Budgeting in Developing Countries

Local governments in developing countries typically provide services that are vital for development. These services tend to be highly visible as well, with citizens able to see whether roads are built or maintained, nurses are appointed and present in clinics, water is running through piping systems, or waste collected on a regular basis. Citizens lack any effective role in the budgeting and financial management process in such settings, however, limiting their ability to contribute to which roads are built, to inform representatives when clinics are not effectively staffed, or to seek redress when water is consistently dirty or waste is not collected. Citizens lack abilities to make such contributions partly because of the way in which budgeting and financial management processes are typically structured at the local level (and other levels) and partly because of the way in which budgets and financial statements (the actual documents detailing expenditures and revenues planned and recorded) are designed and formatted.

Implications of Common Budget and Financial Management Processes for Citizen Access

Budgeting processes differ substantially between governments, but most tend to involve five distinct stages: target development, bid and draft formulation, bid selection, bid implementation, and evaluation and control (see von Hagen and Harden 1996 and Andrews 2002, for similar process identification). These five stages are shown in table 7.1, which also provides details of the entities commonly involved in each stage. It also identifies the stages at which formal policy or legislation in developing countries typically requires citizen involvement in the budgeting process.

In the five stages of the budgeting process governments determine how much money to spend and how to spend it, actually spend the money on the items or activities or projects identified, and evaluate their performance on the job. The main players include internal financial entities (such as municipal accounts offices), local administrative entities charged with service pro-

TABLE 7.1 A Typical Budget Process and Time line for Local Governments in Developing Countries

Stage	Budget revenue and expenditure targets formulated	Budget bids and drafts formulated, reconciled and finalized into budget proposal	Political representatives debate, amend and approve budget	Budget is executed, with in-year changes made and execution monitored.	Ex post evaluation and control
Entity(ies) involved	Internal financial entities, higher-level government treasuries, potential citizen input	Internal financial entities and internal administrative entities (service providers), high-level government entities (providing related services), local representatives and potential citizen input	Internal financial entities, senior administrators, local representatives, sometimes high-level government representatives	Internal financial entities, Internal administrative entities, some local political input	Internal financial entities, local political representatives, external audit agencies, higher-level government entities (usually treasuries or dedicated local government ministries).
Where citizen input is intended					

vision (such as municipal roads or water departments), local representatives (elected at the municipal level or appointed by national or regional governments), and high-level government representatives and entities (national or regional government treasuries and departments or agencies providing services similar to the local government or operating in the jurisdiction, or political representatives of national or regional government or national-level audit and monitoring agencies).

Citizens have historically been excluded from all (or at least most) of the five stages, but recent legislation and policy reform in countries ranging from Bolivia to Paraguay, the Philippines, South Africa, Tanzania, Ukraine, and Vietnam have required local governments to involve citizens in the first two stages. Citizen participation is usually required in participatory planning processes at the local level, with governments required to adopt participatory mechanisms in their planning processes, develop plans through a participatory process, and base budget decisions and implementation on plans. Bolivia's Law of Popular Participation, for example, "stipulates that the local population participate in the planning . . . of social and economic projects at the municipal level" (Goudsmit and Blackburn 2001, 587). In South African municipalities, citizen participation in integrated development planning processes is intended to entrench the right of people to take responsibility for their own futures and to participate in the realization of the vision for their area (DCD 1998).

Evidence suggests that, even with legislative and policy participation requirements, citizens remain excluded from the budget and financial management process. Goudsmit and Blackburn (2001) write that local communities are still dominated by higher-level governments in the Bolivian budgeting process, saying that these communities "must adapt to plans that come 'from above' which have been designed with practically no participation outside the state bureaucracy" (590). A study in South Africa reflects on the fact that participatory mechanisms in the planning stage can actually lead to "a decline in participation related to a nonempowering way of involving people" (DCD-GTZ 1999, 6). In these and other examples, common problems associated with participation in the budgeting and financial management process (problems that limit citizen access and hinder a citizen orientation) include the following:

- Citizens are generally not empowered to participate, even when participatory mechanisms are provided. Citizens are commonly poorly informed about how the process works, what the public meeting agendas are, and what budgets actually involve (often citizens have no access to previous budgets, for example). Local governments seldom demystify their processes to enable citizen understanding, instead presenting technical documentation or using a technical tone in communications with participatory structures or through participatory mechanisms.

- Participatory mechanisms tend to be structurally flawed. Mechanisms such as public meetings (the most regularly used mechanism) are commonly poorly advertised, irregularly held, and managed in such a way as to limit civic input (either in an absolute sense or by allowing inputs from select groups only). They are also held as events separate from the formal budgeting process (introduced as an add-on or related event, rather than an intrinsic part of the process). These structural factors limit the value citizens derive from using the mechanisms, the influence citizens have over budgetary behavior and outcomes, the interest citizens have in participation, and the incentive officials have to develop a citizen orientation in their decisions and implementation activities.

- The products of participation are generally difficult to identify and are commonly ignored by budgeters and financial managers. Fundamentally, policy makers seldom conceptualize what these products will be, how they will be presented, where they will fit into the budget decision-making process (how plans developed through participatory processes should influence budgets, for example), how administrators will record such products, and who (administrators or representatives or citizens) will report on the way citizen inputs have affected budget decisions and outcomes. Legislation and policy, where it does require participation, usually lacks a focus on evidence of the influence of a participatory product in budget decisions and implementation, limiting officials' incentives to ensure that such influence occurs.

- Even where citizens are involved in developing budget proposals in the first two stages, the lack of citizen access or influence in the other three stages fatally limits the value of their contributions. There is no way to ensure that participatory products are taken seriously in budget decisions, implementation and monitoring, and evaluation. Without any ability to access these stages, citizens cannot press local officials to act on their demands and ideas or to hold officials to account for budget implementation. In most cases this problem is manifested in limited citizen influence over the incentives facing public officials at the local level—and consequently limited citizen influence over what public officials do at the local level.

Implications of Budget and Financial Statement Formats for Citizen Access

The format of the budget and financial statement is a major device limiting citizen influence over budget decisions and implementation performance. Even where citizens are invited to participate in plans, the influence of such plans on budget decisions and implementation is generally limited by the common format of the line-item budget and financial statement.

Citizens concerned about the poor condition of their roads might advocate spending on road maintenance in South African Integrated Development Plans, for example, or citizens attempting to ensure continued water supply to a district in Bolivia might plan for funds to replace leaky pipes. The same citizens may try to determine whether their interests, plans, and proposals were incorporated into budgets and implemented by spending agencies. They would have a difficult time doing so, however, because budgets and financial statements in local governments in the developing world typically arrange allocations by line-item inputs rather than by projects, activities, programs, or outputs (the kinds of items that are identified in plans and of interest to citizens). An example of such a budget format is provided in table 7.2.

The typical structure of the budget and financial reporting documents that local governments (and others) in the developing world produce is in fact very unhelpful for orienting governments to citizens or for answering the basic questions citizens ask of their governing authorities:

- What is government doing with the money it receives?
- What are the end goals of government interventions?
- Is government reaching its end goals, or at least moving toward their achievement?
- How much money is government spending, and is it spending more than is needed to achieve its goals?
- Are revenues sufficient to meet expenditures? If not, why not?
- Who is responsible for spending behavior and outcomes?

Citizens asking the first three questions are interested in seeing how money is being translated into services. The format of the budget and financial statement limits analysis to aggregated line items about inputs, typically arranged so as to hinder understanding of any connection to actual activities, projects, or services. Even where direct service expenditures might be disaggregated into electricity provision, water provision, and roads provision,

TABLE 7.2 A Typical Local Government Budget and Financial Statement in Developing Countries

Expenditure Item	Amount Budgeted $	Amount Spent $	Revenue Source	Amount Targeted in Budget $	Amount Received $
Direct service expenditures	100	100	Rates and taxes	150	130
General expenditures	80	75	User fees	50	40
Salaries, wages and allowances	150	140	Inter-governmental grants	300	330
Repairs and maintenance	25	25	Retained income	10	10
Capital costs (Interest and redemption)	40	40	Loans	30	30
Contribution to capital expenditure	35	35			
Working capital expenses	30	30			
Contribution to provisions and funds	30	30			
Contribution to bad debts	50	50			
Total Expenditure	**540**	**525**		**540**	**540**

for example, the direct expenditures on these services do not include portions of general expenditures; salaries, wages, and allowances; and other expenditures on each service type.

Citizens asking the fourth question are interested in spending efficiency, yet budget and financial statements provide no means of assessing how well money is spent. Citizens asking the fifth question are attempting to investigate the discipline of spenders, the performance of revenue-raising entities, and the match between revenue sources and expenditure requirements. Yet budget and financial statements provide only a broad measure of discipline (through comparison of budgeted and actual expenditures which, in aggregate, provide the much-vaunted deficit statistic). Citizens asking the final question are trying to identify an accountability structure, yet budget and financial statements typically provide none.

Citizens Analyzing Municipal Finances in Developing Countries: A New Approach

Budgeting and financial management processes at the local level in developing countries are typically unfriendly to citizens. Citizens have limited access to budgeting processes in such settings and face constraints in assessing government performance or holding government accountable on the basis of published budgets and financial statements that follow the line-item format. A move toward citizen-oriented local-level budgeting and financial management in developing countries requires adjusting both the institutions that structure the budgeting process and the budget or financial statement format.

Institutionalizing Citizen-Oriented Budgeting Processes

Budgeting processes are highly institutionalized; rules, laws, and norms have major effects on fiscal allocation and management behavior and outcomes. Institutions in all five stages of the budgeting process in developing countries typically entrench an anticitizen orientation at the local level, limiting citizen access and input into decisions and citizen comment and response on implementation and evaluations. To orient budgets and budgeting processes toward citizens and citizen interests requires effective institutional mechanisms that influence the budgeting process in general and at each of the five stages. To ensure that these changes are more effective than some of the legislated participatory planning requirements in place in numerous countries, it is important that "such changes do not only take place on paper but that new formal institutions truly affect the choice of actors within the rules," constituting "effective institutional reform . . . that has taken place both de jure and de facto" (Mummert 1999, 2).

In general, a citizen-oriented budgeting process requires some form of representative institutional structure and rules that ensure the right to information. Such processes further require institutions that facilitate (in a meaningful sense) the revelation of citizen demand, the opportunity for citizen reflection and resolution (in the budget decision or approval stage), the ability of citizens to report (on budget implementation), and avenues for citizen response and redress (that influence the incentives administrative and political officials face). These institutional mechanisms are shown in table 7.3. They

TABLE 7.3 Institutions Facilities: A Move Toward Citizen-Oriented Budgeting Processes

Stage	Budget targets formulated	Budget bids and drafts formulated, reconciled, and finalized into budget proposal	Political representatives debate, amend, and approve budget	Budget is executed, with in-year changes made and execution monitored	Ex post evaluation and control
Specific institutional requirements	Revelation institutions: Citizen input regarding resource availability	Revelation institutions: Citizen input required regarding service demand	Reflection and revelation institutions: Citizen access to debate, as well as institutionalized transparency of debate process and outcomes and citizen-based approval process	Reporting institutions: Citizen participation in projects, citizen monitoring and response mechanisms required	Response and redress institutions: Citizen evaluation and response mechanisms required
General institutional reforms required	Representative institutions *Right-to-information institutions*				

are expected to effect a citizen orientation most efficiently when introduced within structures that ensure local political representation and the right to information.

Representative Institutions

For local government budgets to be oriented to citizens, it is vital that there be some form of institutionalized representation in the local government. Local entities that are not created to represent local people at a political level (through some form of legislative entity, often called a council at this level) surely cannot be expected to have a local citizen orientation in a fiscal or administrative sense either. Many such local governments are typically accountable to higher-level governments (which delegate responsibilities to them and appoint officials to run them) rather than to local citizens. A citizen orientation for the budget is limited in these kinds of unrepresentative governments because decisions about spending amounts and direction (the "how much" and the "how" of spending) are the result of top-down intergovernmental delegation rather than local decision.

Governments seeking to orient their budgeting processes toward citizens' needs must of necessity have formal channels for citizen influence. These channels largely come in two shapes: formal, institutionalized forms of representation (and rules informing the work of local legislatures) and parallel, participatory mechanisms through which select citizens can attempt to channel their voices. The latter approach is reflected in the burgeoning participation literature, which identifies and details a variety of mechanisms used to this end around the world. It is argued that the formal representative local government is the most appropriate basis for citizen-oriented local government. The best option for developing a citizen orientation in the budget involves working within the political and administrative structures of representative local governments to institute such an approach (as opposed to a second option of creating parallel participatory structures). This argument has three strands, related to the issues of institutional influence, institutional adoption, and institutional cost:

- *Institutional influence:* Budgets are the result of highly institutionalized processes and systems that typically limit citizen influence and involvement. To change that, new institutions need to be introduced that are strong enough to influence the incentives officials face in the budgeting process and the culture of that process—introducing a new citizen focus, citizen-oriented questions and access points, and a citizen-friendly accountability structure in the budget. Such influences will be most effective when they are located within the system itself, and particularly when they are developed as rules within entrenched representative structures (so that they can influence incentives and culture from the inside out). Where participatory mechanisms are developed to run parallel to or in competition with established representative structures, experience suggests they have a limited positive influence on internal incentives and culture—and in many instances a negative influence as officials work to keep the new processes, such as participatory planning mechanisms, outside their established approach, thus limiting citizen influence on administrative incentives and culture (Andrews 2002).

▪ *Institutional adoption:* Official representative structures are considered the most appropriate place in which to adopt new rules and norms orienting governments toward citizens. Participatory mechanisms designed to institutionalize such an orientation from outside the established process are often seen to run in a parallel way to established processes. They are often only partially adopted, given that existing incentives within established structures tend to run in opposition to such adoption. If representative structures are not working, they need to be reformed to facilitate representation. Creating parallel participatory structures alongside faulty representative structures does not achieve this purpose. Doing so only creates a "representative" tension that ultimately threatens the effectiveness of both mechanisms.

▪ *Institutional cost:* Institutional reform is costly in many respects. The higher the cost is, the less likely it is that the reform will succeed. Creating new participatory channels is considered a more costly route to citizen-oriented budgeting than reforming existing representative mechanisms. New channels require high levels of social capital and civil society organization, and they stretch civic interest and time. To ensure that such channels are broadly representative, significant resource outlays are required as well. Reforming existing representative structures is considered less costly because such structures already have some kind of institutionalized status and operational standing, which can be improved upon to orient fiscal processes toward citizens.

Right-to-information institutions

The reality of reform is a blend of both changes in formal representative institutions (reforming councils to establish citizen-oriented budgets) and the development of participatory mechanisms (focused on the same goal). In both approaches, it is important to create rules by which citizens can access relevant information in a costless, accurate, and timely fashion—empowering their involvement in the various budgeting stages. One way of doing this involves following the U.S. approach of legislating information access and creating elaborate and costly paths of information provision. Another way is that followed in countries such as Malaysia and Uganda, whereby all government entities must publish their budgetary data (how much they are spending and on what, and how they are progressing in budget implementation) at their "storefront" (whether on billboards at the entrance of every welfare office, as in Malaysia, or on blackboards in every classroom, as in Uganda).

The aim of such institutionalized access to information is to provide documentary reference points (some kind of record of engagement) to empower citizen participation in the budgeting process and to ensure that citizen inputs work their way into budget documents and into the final evaluation and review. In this sense documentation itself becomes an institutional device designed to shape behavior and outcomes, with government entities held accountable for the performance they are required to disclose (in publicly accessible places).

Revelation institutions

Representative and right-to-information rules at every stage of the budgeting process are vital for the development of a citizen orientation. Various other rules and norms are also required at specific points in the process, including those that entrench rules and norms regarding civic revelation. The aim of revelation institutions is to enhance civic access to the budgeting stages at which targets are formulated and budget bids and drafts are formulated, reconciled, and finalized into proposals. It is in these stages that governments often determine how much they will spend and where (generally) demand exists for monies to be spent. Both activities are of obvious interest to citizens, who not only bear the fiscal burden for their governments (in one form or another) but are also the ones with the legitimate demands and claims on funds. Because of such obvious citizen interest in these activities, channels for citizens to express their voices need to be institutionalized into these stages if budgets are to be citizen oriented. This requires creating stage rules and norms that entrench incentives for government officials to facilitate and respond to citizens' revelation of demands (in targeting revenues and expenditures).

One approach to institutionalizing this revelation involves incorporating it into representative structures—requiring directly elected representatives to elicit budget demands from their constituents, in written form, during the targeting and draft formulation stages. National legislation could also require that local councilors hold specific (highly publicized) meetings during these stages, at strategic points in jurisdictions (notably giving the poor easy access), to elicit budget demands and revenue-related suggestions (which legislation should require to be recorded). Legislation could also require that councilors focus agency and department budget drafting on citizens' output require-ments. It could also require that the process of identifying outputs be both transparent (open to citizens) and directly linked to citizen demands (as could be verified by requiring councils to publish exactly where requests came from, in document form for a higher-level government and in local media for civic analysis)—so that people in the jurisdiction can see exactly how their contri-bution influenced the final outputs that are targeted. The institutionalization of a budget office and political budget subcommittee could also help facilitate citizen access to the budgeting process (they would know who to approach with suggestions) and store, organize, and respond to citizens' revelation.

The participation movement posits institutionalizing channels for civic revelation apart from the general representative process, which is typically considered representative only at election time and in regard to general issues (Blair 2000). It suggests that municipal entities develop participatory mech-anisms such as public meetings and even budget-related community boards to facilitate the expression of citizens' voices. In Belo Horizonte and Porto Alegre, Brazil, citizen groups meet in the city's various regions to voice their demands, which are then carried by representatives to smaller budget hear-ings. In Asunción and Villa Elisa, Paraguay, budget hearings are held through which citizens voice their demands to local councils (linking the participa-tory mechanisms to the representative institutions).

In both cases the institutionalization of civic revelation has resulted in changes to budget allocations. Regarding Belo Horizonte, Nadia de Villefort reflects on the improvement in municipal responsiveness to the poor: "Although I still do not have the exact statistics about less poverty, I do know that life conditions of those living on the slopes, regarding housing, sanita-tion, paving of roads, and slope containment have really improved" (ESSET 2000, 4). Similarly, the voice effect of public budget hearings in Villa Elisa, Paraguay, has led to significant adjustments in budget allocations (in line with social demand): "Of the 98 petitions submitted, 55 percent received a favorable response and were included in the projects slated for fiscal year 1998" (Domecq 1998, 6).

However civic revelation is institutionalized, it is vital that there be some way of ensuring that civic input is taken seriously as the foundation of budget requests. One such way is to publish demands and to show how such demands equate with the general focal points of the government budget. An example of such an approach is shown in table 7.4.

TABLE 7.4 Citizen-Oriented Revelation Records: An Example

Citizen Demands, Registered as Issues Requiring Attention and Interpreted into Outputs Identified for Production	General outputs identified for production (based on citizen input through institutionalized voice channels, decided at the special budget demand council meeting on December 11)	Revenue-Raising Suggestions from Citizen Interaction with Council
Issues requiring attention (based on citizen input through institutionalized voice channels)		Revenue and resource targets, by source (based on citizen interaction with political representatives at public meeting on December 12)
1. Issue: Increased population in Zone A. Insufficient infrastructure in the zone, which is also inhabited by mostly poor households. *Demand Source:* Letter of budget recommendation from C. Stiles, October 23, received by councilwomen Ross. Further raised at initial public meeting on November 18 in Zone A. Recorded by A. Buys. Further raised by nongovernmental organization ABfree through NGO Forum on November 20. Recorded by A. Buys.	Increased residential-type infrastructure in Zone A, particularly roads opening new areas for development	*Rates and taxes* Water pipe tax at 10¢ per mile, expected to yield $30. Road tax at 10¢ per mile, expected to yield $20. Residence tax at 1¢ per hectare, expected to yield $100. *User fees* Water use fee at 1/liter expected to yield $50. *Intergovernmental grants* As per equitable share grant = $300. *Retained income* As per year 2001 budget = $10
2. Issue: Business expanding in Zone B has very poor infrastructure for expansion. *Demand Source:* Visit by Zone B business delegation to open council meeting on October 10 (as recorded by A. Buys). Further raised at Zone B public meeting November 10 (as recorded by A. Buys) and through letter of budget recommendation from G. Giles on November 12, as received by Councilman Goss.	Increased business-type infrastructure in Zone B, particularly roads facilitating business expansion in the area.	*Loans* As per civic recommendations, council will attempt to obtain a loan for $30 from development Bank 1. *Community input* As per community suggestion, and individual and neighborhood commitments, 200 community labor hours available per month for labor intensive projects.

3. Issue: Streets in town very dirty

Demand source: Various citizen complaints at public meetings on October 12 and November 1 (as recorded by A. Buys). Letters of complaint by various citizens to Councilmen Goss and Foss and Councilwoman Ross. Business delegations to council meeting on October 10. Local ratepayers association budget request through Budget Hearing Center, October 23. Thirty citizen requests for extra street cleaning activities registered at Budget Hearing Center between October 23 and November 10 (as registered with the center).

More regular and efficient road sweeping in residential and commercial areas

Sources of revenue targets
Citizen inputs through Budget Hearing Center, NGO forum, Council Meeting agreements on October 10 and November 5.

4. Issue: Urgent requirement for rural road development. Two peri-urban communities have sprung up alongside Zone C and have no roads developed in them as yet. This is posing a major problem for inhabitation of the area, as there is no access ability for potential residents. Zone C inhabitants are against road development in the communities, however, concerned about the development of peri-urban communities. Groups representing Zone C residents have suggested that the new inhabitants of the peri-urban communities be re-settled in the Zone A extension proposed as demand 1.

Rural roads system in peri-urban area alongside Zone C

Demand source: One hundred and twenty individual petitions in favor of the rural road development were received at the Budget hearing Center between October 10 and November 23 (as registered with the center). The NGO R1 presented the case in favor of such development at the October 1 Council meeting (as recorded by A. Buys). As there is no ward council member for the peri-urban area, there have been no petitions by individuals to councilors. There have, however, been two petitions by potential residents to the official opposition party in the council (as submitted to the November 5 council meeting by that party). Two hundred petitions in opposition to the development were presented by citizens to the ward councilor Goss. The Zone C ratepayers voiced their opposition as a group at the public budget meeting on November 1.

The left-hand side of the table shows issues that require attention, as identified by citizens. The demand sources listed suggest a mix of council-based and participatory mechanisms. The second column indicates the general outputs identified for production (at a special council meeting). The third column shows the general revenue targets decided on. This kind of document would serve as the basis for formulating a draft budget (with agencies and departments required to suggest programs and projects through which to produce the outputs identified) and a transparency-enhancing publication (that citizens could access to see how their suggestions were taken up).

Reflection and resolution institutions

Citizens have a role in ensuring that their demands are realized in the budget formulation and decision-making stage. It is thus necessary to institutionalize mechanisms that facilitate civic reflection of actual spending alternatives, and resolutions about final spending allocations, in order to achieve the objective of a citizen-oriented budget process. This is a fairly complex undertaking because the budget formulation and decision-making stages are usually highly technical and internalized, with administrators from budget offices and administrators from service-providing agencies often dominating the process of identifying claims and making decisions. Even with complexity, however, it is vital and possible to involve citizens in the process.

The decision-making stage can be automatically oriented toward citizens by carrying output requirements through from the revelation stage as the basis of budget bids—as in column 1 of table 7.4. The budgeting guidelines set forth in legislation could require that all agencies and departments make bids that focus on producing these outputs (and disallow fund allocations that are not focused on them). Rules could also require that departments make more than one proposal as to how outputs could be produced, which would enhance the decision-making process, and disclose the specific performance criteria they would be willing to commit to (based on the specific output by quantity, location, and date and the benchmarked targets by total cost, cost per unit, and quality).

In this way citizens determine the general outputs but administrators determine the specific outputs that they will be held accountable for (and the budget is based on agreed-upon, measurable outputs, which citizens get to evaluate). If budgeting process rules regarding timing are well considered and adhered to, the project proposals could be published (in the media, at public places, and in council buildings, for example) to facilitate transparency.

Councils could also hold special meetings to make the proposed projects known and to elicit civic comment. These meetings could also be the basis of budgeting decisions regarding particular project allocations. In Villa Elisa and Asunción, public hearings at this point in the budgeting process are broadly attended and yield specific, project-based civic budgets that are forwarded for consideration by the council. In Naga City, the Philippines, a law called the Empowerment Ordinance created a specific entity, the Naga City People's Council, which is composed of civil society organizations (such as nongovernmental organizations). The council votes and participates in the deliberations on projects and programs (Jacob 2000). In both cases the city council makes final decisions but it is easily held accountable for those decisions because of the transparency of the process and the ease of civic participation in the process (through mechanisms connected to the council itself). Consider, for example, evidence regarding Asunción's budget hearings:

> Promoting transparency and citizen participation in this way opens channels of communication between city officials and the public, and creates a genuine forum for participation. As a result, citizens are better informed on public affairs and finances, they have an opportunity to air their own views, and the forum provides a way for public budget decisions to be explained. As a consequence of greater transparency, there is less room for corruption and citizens find that their opinions actually can influence government. (Pope 2000, 116)

Other devices to enable citizen influence in the decision process include referendums on entire budgets (as used in Porto Alegre) and citizen initiative votes on specific proposals (that could be controversial or just significant in size). These mechanisms could be used in conjunction with existing legislative structures, with the legislature required to hold such votes and accountable for implementing budgets as voted. As with revelation, institutionalizing civic reflection and resolution requires creating more than just opportunities for participation. It also requires ensuring that traditionally powerful decision makers have the necessary incentive to take civic interests seriously. One way of ensuring this involves requiring constant transparency in the budgeting process, through active documentation and publication of budget proposals or bids, output and efficiency targets, and final decisions. Table 7.5 is an example of such documentation, which could be required by law. In the table it is apparent that

- Output targets are carried forward from the revelation stage (in the first column).
- There are multiple project proposals related to each general output target.
- Output and efficiency goals listed in a specified, straightforward fashion.
- Final allocations (actual decisions) are clearly specified.

TABLE 7.5   Citizen-Oriented Reflection and Resolution Records: An Example

General Outputs Identified for Production (from revelation stage)	Proposed Projects/Activities (by administrative entity)	Proposed Outputs, Quantity, Location, Date (to be the basis of contract)	Benchmark Targets: Total Cost, Cost per Unit, Quality (to be the basis of contract)	Allocations by Department, Program or Project
Increased residential-type infrastructure in Zone A, particularly roads opening in new areas for development	Roads department	10 km road, clinic to school, May 1	Total cost = $50	$100
				Roads
				A. Construction
	Zone A residential street extension proposal 1.1		Cost of 5 per km for high-quality 1-lane concrete roads	1. Zone A residential street extension proposals 1.1 and 1.2
	Roads department	10 km road, lake to church, May 10	Total cost = $50	
	Zone A residential street extension proposal 1.2		Cost of $5 per km for high-quality 1-lane concrete roads	
	Roads department	18 km road, school to town hall, via lake	Total cost = $90	
	Zone A residential street extension proposal 1.3		Cost of $5 per km for high-quality 1-lane concrete roads	
Increased business-type infrastructure in Zone B, particularly roads facilitating business expansion in the area	Roads department	5 km highway, market to mines, May 1	Total cost = $65	$90
	Zone B commercial street building proposal 1.1		Cost of $13 per km for high-quality 2-lane concrete roads	Roads
				A. Construction

	Roads department Zone B commercial street building proposal 1.2	5 km highway, city hall to station, May 3	Total cost = $65 Cost of $13 per km for high-quality 2 lane concrete roads	2. Zone B commercial street building proposals 1.3 and 1.4
	Roads department Zone B commercial street building proposal 1.3	5 km road, market to mines, May 1	Total cost = $45 Cost of $9 per km for high-quality 1-lane concrete roads	
	Roads department Zone B commercial street building proposal 1.4	5 km road, city hall to station, May 3	Total cost = $45 Cost of $9 per km for high-quality 1-lane concrete roads	
More regular and efficient road sweeping in residential and commercial areas.	Roads department Residential street cleaning proposal 1.1	1 manual sweep per residential road per year (total = 400 km)	Total cost = $40 Cost of $0.10 per km for manual sweep	$80
	Roads department Residential street cleaning proposal 1.2	1 tractor sweep per residential road per year (total = 400 km)	Total cost = $200 Cost of $0.50 per km for tractor sweep	Roads
	Roads department commercial street cleaning proposal 1.1	1 tractor sweep per commercial road per annum (total = 160 km)	Total cost = $80 Cost of $0.50 per km for tractor sweep	B. Maintenance 1. Residential street cleaning proposal 1.1 2. Commercial street cleaning proposal 1.2

(continued)

TABLE 7.5   Citizen-Oriented Reflection and Resolution Records: An Example (*Continued*)

General Outputs Identified for Production (from revelation stage)	Proposed Projects/Activities (by administrative entity)	Proposed Outputs, Quantity, Location, Date (to be the basis of contract)	Benchmark Targets: Total Cost, Cost per Unit, Quality (to be the basis of contract)	Allocations by Department, Program or Project
	Roads department Commercial street cleaning proposal 1.2	2 manual sweeps per commercial road per year (total = 320 km)	Total cost = $40 Cost of $0.13 per km for manual sweep	
Rural roads system in peri-urban area alongside Zone C	Roads department Peri-urban rural road building proposal 1.1	20 km road system around Mt. High, and into Zone C	Total cost = $180 Cost of $9 per km for 1-lane reinforced gravel roads	None for 2002
Other	Roads department Peri-urban rural road building proposal 1.1	20 km broad path system around Mt. High, and into Zone C	Total cost = $45 Cost of $2.50 per km for reinforced sand pathways	

Reading such a document, citizens can see exactly which projects were chosen (and what they can expect from such projects) and which ones were not chosen. They can ask why certain projects were chosen and others not, identify which general outputs are being addressed and which are not (and ask why), and determine exactly what kind of standards departments should adhere to during implementation (to facilitate monitoring and evaluation).

In keeping with the example developed in this chapter, the table alludes only to new spending in one year. The model could easily be expanded to incorporate concern for base spending (established projects) and for multiyear projects and programs. In both instances established and multiyear programs and projects could (and should) be publicly evaluated on a regular basis for effectiveness, efficiency, and relevance (to citizen-identified goals). This could be done by requiring that project managers identify annual output and efficiency goals (as set out in the table) to be used as the basis for evaluation. Apart from the annual evaluations, these projects should be examined on a medium-term basis for performance and continued relevance to the council's citizen-identified mission.

Reporting institutions

Budget execution or implementation is often a problematic stage in the local budgeting process (Cameron and Tapscott 2000). This is partly because the stage tends to be considered a postdecision stage in which administrators and technical experts should be left to their own devices to implement the decisions made. Without oversight these administrators face little pressure (or incentive) to adopt the budget in an effective, efficient, and true-to-form manner. As a result, administrators are often criticized for spending more than budgeted, producing goods and services other than those requested in the budget allocations, using production and provision techniques that guarantee neither competitive production nor acceptable quality levels, or losing a great deal of money to corruption. These kinds of budget execution issues are major issues in countries throughout the developing world from Bolivia to India, Pakistan, South Africa, and others. Naturally this is an area of interest to citizens who have an interest in the type, quantity, and quality of services they receive. It is of particular interest in situations where citizens have some influence on the early budget decision stages but then face the prospect of never seeing their decisions implemented (or when implemented, see them done inefficiently).

Citizen reporting in the budget execution or implementation stage is vital if budget decisions are to be implemented in a manner that is responsive to civic demands (and true to citizen-based decisions). Institutionalizing reporting in this stage entails making civic comments on implementation the rule rather than the exception, the expected normalcy rather than the unexpected rarity. Approaches to such institutionalization come in a number of forms, some related to established representative and administrative structures and other developed on parallel paths (through nongovernmental organizations and such). Examples of the latter include the Public Affairs Center in Bangalore, India, which elicits citizen comments on service quality through its report card process, and the Vigilance Committee's role in Bolivian local governments. Examples of the formal, representative type include Malaysia's Public Complaints Bureaus, ombudsmen offices in various Eastern European and Latin American countries, and the help desks in certain South African municipalities (which are required, in some instances, to keep records of citizen queries and complaints and to ensure that all queries and complaints are responded to).

Reporting appears more influential when it comes through formal structures emerging from within representative government (such as the Malaysian Public Complaints Bureaus), because the civic reports are focused directly on service providers (with clear and appropriate lines of responsibility and accountability in place). In the Malaysian case and other examples where citizen reporting appears effective, the basis of the reports is service results, which are well known, of interest to citizens, and highly observable. Reporting influence is also enhanced when reporting is tied to a record and response system—whereby administrators are required to record civic reports and respond to them in a timely fashion. When this is the rule, administrators have every incentive to respond efficiently and appropriately, and budget implementation becomes a transparent and accountable stage of the budgeting process. Reporting can go beyond a concern with the implementation stage to issues regarding access in general. When this is the case, citizens can comment on whether they are accorded access to various budgeting processes, creating an incentive for administrators to facilitate such access.

Table 7.6 shows the kind of documentation that can be required to evaluate the level of civic reporting. The table reflects an example in which a grievance committee (located within the town council) or public complaints bureau offers a report, for all budget items (as carried through in the department, program, and project classification), on (a) the financial results reported on by the municipal administration (as shown in the second three columns) and (b) performance and access issues not reflected in financial statements but reported on by citizens.

TABLE 7.6 Citizen-Oriented Reporting Records: An Example

Department Program Project/Activity	Information from Internal Financial Statements			Grievance Committee or Public Complaints Bureau Report		External Audit Report
	Surplus (Deficit) $	Output Performance $	Efficiency Performance	Comment on Information from Basic Financial Statements	Comment on Performance and Access Issues not Reflected in Financial Statements	Overall Comment on Government Performance
Roads *A. Construction*	25 35			The fiscal reporting is correct.	Citizens routinely complained about access to information about roads construction. There were also complaints about the way projects were chosen with rural roads requests ignored in the decision stage.	The program ran a surplus but there are concerns about performance, citizen information access, and the verifiability of final output data. **Close inspection ordered; manager called for interview.**
1. Zone A residential street extension	40	5 km of 10 km clinic to school road complete, May 1 All of 10 km lake to church road complete, May 5	Under cost of $5 per km (actual = $4) for high quality 1 lane concrete roads	The fiscal and performance report are supported by citizen reports.	Citizens routinely complained about access to information about roads construction.	The program ran a surplus but there are concerns about performance and citizen information access, **Close inspection ordered; manager called for interview.**

(continued)

TABLE 7.6 Citizen-Oriented Reporting Records: An Example (*Continued*)

| Department Program Project/Activity | Surplus (Deficit) | Information from Internal Financial Statements | | Comment on Information from Basic Financial Statements | Comment on Performance and Access Issues not Reflected in Financial Statements | Overall Comment on Government Performance |
		Output Performance	Efficiency Performance	Grievance Committee or Public Complaints Bureau Report		External Audit Report
2. Zone B commercial street building	(5)	All of 5 km market to mines road complete, May 1 All 5 km city hall to station road complete, April 27	Exceeded cost of $7 per km (actual = $9.50) for high-quality 2-lane concrete roads	The fiscal report is supported by citizen reports. Ten citizen reports conflict with the output performance report regarding the city hall to station road, suggesting it is not complete (as claimed).	Citizens routinely complained about access to information about roads construction. Final output information was hotly disputed.	The program ran a surplus but there are concerns about performance, citizen information access and the verifiability of final output data. **Close inspection ordered; manager called for interview.**

B. Maintenance	0		The fiscal reporting is correct.	Citizen reports were generally positive regarding access to information about road maintenance and responses to queries by the program manager.	The program budget was balanced and performance reached all targets. **Future budgetary reward proposed.**
1. Residential street cleaning	0	Total = 200 km of 400 km roads swept in year. Average 0.5 sweeps per road	Exceeded manual sweep cost of $0.10 per km (actual = $0.20)	The fiscal and performance report are supported by citizen reports.	Citizen reports were generally positive.	The program budget was balanced and performance reached all targets. **Future budgetary reward proposed.**
2. Commercial street cleaning	0	Total = 240 km of 320 km roads swept in year. Average of 1.5 sweeps per road	Exceeded cost of $0.13 per km (actual = $0.17) for manual sweep	The fiscal and performance report are supported by citizen reports.	Citizen reports were generally positive.	The program budget was balanced and performance reached all targets. **Future budgetary reward proposed.**

Response and redress institutions

Table 7.6 also facilitates the institutionalization of redress and response in the local government budgeting process. By including a report of financial performance alongside one on civic access in the example, an auditor general can see very quickly whether a municipality has adopted a citizen orientation. Where it has not, an appropriately charged and empowered auditor general can require response in the next budgeting period (response either to poor performance or to poor civic access) or impose measures to ensure effective reward or redress (such as higher budgetary awards in the future or gain sharing as rewards, and closer auditing scrutiny, manager interviews, or even staff replacements for redress).

Few local governments produce documents such as that outlined in table 7.6, however, or have any means of identifying poorly performing departments, programs, or projects. Fewer governments have any set approach to ensuring that budget performance in one year earns some kind of response or redress in the next (such as an appropriate intervention by an auditor general). Money tends to follow existing projects rather than effective projects (resulting in the importance of the budget base in many developing countries). This is especially the case with recurring items or services, many of which are commonly provided at the local level (including water and electricity, road building and maintenance, and sewerage and sanitation services). Citizens are not served by such a budgeting blind spot, and citizens could hold the key to removing it—if effective response and redress mechanisms are institutionalized into the final evaluation and control stage of the budgeting process.

Institutionalizing response and redress in the budgeting process ensures that all other forms of citizen input are taken seriously, because it creates a rule or norm requiring a response to civic revelation, reflection, and resolution (decision) and reporting. According to such rules or norms, political representatives or administrators are held accountable for the degree to which they take citizen inputs seriously. Citizens often lack the ability to enforce their wishes (thus forcing a response or redress), however. Institutionalizing response and redress in the budgeting process thus requires that the expression of citizens' voices be enforced within existing social or representative systems (with the most obvious being established governance structures).

Examples of such mechanisms developed within representative structures include ombudsmen working with courts, and local-level budgeting committees (with members drawn from local councils and perhaps also from prominent citizen-based organizations and nongovernmental organizations). These entities could also have their influence underscored by having to file reports to the auditor general, who gives negative audit reports to all municipalities that have unresolved citizen complaints or lack evidence of citizen reporting (as in the table 7.6 example). Successful nongovernmental entities that are institutionalizing a demystified budgeting process and effective response and redress include MKSS in Rajasthan, which holds jun sunwais (or public meetings) to allow civic evaluation of government performance. As with the mechanisms located within government and deriving their influence through representative structures, the experience in Rajasthan is facilitated by the political representativeness in the Indian government, the right to budgetary information in the state, and the general ability of citizens (through civil society institutions, in this instance) to adjust the budget to a format that facilitates legibility.

A new budget and financial statement format

Budgeting process change is vital if budgets are to become citizen oriented. New institutions in the various budgeting stages create new incentives or entrench new cultural values that facilitate a citizen-oriented and responsive approach to budgeting. If such new orientation is not developed in the presence of such institutions, officials will be found out and held accountable, making responsiveness a norm. But even with institutionalized access, a major impediment to such incentive and culture change remains: the format of the budget document. Budgets are typically structured in a way that makes them illegible, leaving even the most astute citizen helpless when trying to assess budgetary performance. Consider budgets in the form of the one in table 7.2, and the lack of clarity it offers for basic citizen questions (as posed earlier). The budget "is like a mystery. There is no way an ordinary individual (or even a councillor) will be able to understand this 'language.' Budgets have been written like this for decades, and a 'language' is developed that officials learn. New councillors are often at a loss" (ESSET 2000, 1).

Budget demystification is required to solve this problem. Information needs to be provided in a more coherent way, in the spirit of tables 7.4, 7.5, and 7.6, which presented budget data in a citizen-friendly way at various points of the budgeting process. The principles guiding such reporting include relevance, readability, responsibility, and reportability. These principles drive the budget and financial statement format, as presented in table 7.7.

- *Relevance:* The reporting principle of relevance requires that budgets be classified in meaningful ways (that are of interest to citizens). Relevant budget formats and financial reporting should answer the major questions citizens ask: What is government doing with the money it receives?

TABLE 7.7 Citizen-Oriented Budget Format

Department Program Project/Activity	Budget and Targets			Financial and Performance Report			
	Budget $	Output Target: Quantity, Location, Date	Benchmark Targets: Cost per Unit, Quality	Outlay $	Surplus (def) $	Output Results: Quantity, Location, Date	Results against Benchmarks: Cost per Unit, Quality	Official Responsible
Roads	300			275	25			C. Biyela
A. Construction	190			175	35			A. Vase
1. Zone A residential street extension	100	10 km road, clinic to school, May 1 10 km road, lake to church, May 10	Cost of $5 per km for high-quality 1-lane concrete roads	40	60	5km of 10km clinic to school road complete, May 1 All of 10 km lake to church road complete, May 5	Under cost of $5 per km (actual =$4) for high-quality 1-lane concrete roads	P. Gumede
2. Zone B commercial street building	90	5 km road, market to mines, May 1 5 km road, city hall to station, May 3	Cost of $9 per km for high-quality 1-lane concrete roads	95	(5)	All of 5 km market to mines road complete, May 1 All 5 km city hall to station road complete, April 27	Exceeded cost of $7 per km (actual = $9.50) for high-quality 2-lane concrete roads	G. Peters
B. Maintenance	110			120	(10)			G. Bese

continued

TABLE 7.7 Citizen Oriented Budget Format (*Continued*)

	Budget and Targets			Financial and Performance Report				
Department Program Project/Activity	Budget $	Output Target: Quantity, Location, Date	Benchmark Targets: Cost per Unit, Quality	Outlay $	Surplus (def) $	Output Results: Quantity, Location, Date	Results against Benchmarks: Cost per Unit, Quality	Official Responsible
1. Residential street cleaning	40	1 manual sweep per residential road per year (total = 400 km)	Cost of $0.10 per km for manual sweep	40	0	Total = 200 km of 400 km roads swept in year. Average 0.5 sweeps per road	Exceeded manual sweep cost of $0.10 per km (actual = $0.20)	C. Phelp
2. Commercial street cleaning	40	2 manual sweeps per commercial road per year (total = 320 km)	Cost of $0.13 per km for manual sweep	40	0	Total = 240 km of 320 km roads swept in year. Average of 1.5 sweeps per road	Exceeded cost of $0.13 per km (actual = $0.17) for manual sweep	C. Phelp
3. Pothole filling	30	Estimate 98 potholes year. Target 80% fill within 3 days notice, rest within 7 days.	Cost of $0.3 per pothole for high quality asphalt filling	40	(10)	Exceeded response. Total = 106 potholes filled in year. 92% (97) filled within 3 days notice, 8% (9) within 7 days.	Exceeded cost of $0.3 per pothole. High quality fill for 300 potholes, sand filling for 200 potholes	G. Abers
Water	190				0			
A. Residential	*110*			*190*	0			P. Ramfete
1. Pipe maintenance	50	50 km pipes replaced in Mbo, May 1	Cost of $0.4 per km for pvc pipe	*110*	10	40 of 50 km pipes replaced in Mbo by May 1	Achieved cost of $0.4 per km for pvc pipes	P. Byers
		300 km town wide pipes serviced once	Cost of $0.1 per km for service	*40*		250 km of town wide pipes serviced once, 50 km serviced twice	Under cost of $0.1 per km for pipe service	P. Byers

Activity	Budget	Objective	Output / unit cost	Actual	(Var.)	Actual output	Result	Responsible
2. Water purchases	60	Average of 90 liters water provided daily to all 90 households, for 365 days	Cost of $0.01 per l for high chloride water	70	(10)	Average 70 liters (of 90l target) provided daily to all 90 households for 360 days (5 days no service)	Exceeded Cost of $0.01 per liter (actual = $0.03) for high chloride water	G. Jones
B. Commercial	80			80	0		Achieved cost of	A. Nabo
1. Pipe maintenance	15	150 km business sector pipes serviced once	Cost of $0.1 per km for pipe service	15	0	150km business sector pipes serviced once	$0.1 per km for pipe service	A. Nabo
2. Water purchases	65	Average of 1 kl water provided daily to all 20 businesses for 365 days	Cost of $0.01 per liter for high chloride water	65	0	Average 1kl water provided daily to 20 businesses for 360 days (5 days no service)	Achieved cost of $0.01 per l for high chloride water	V. Cram
Finance	**50**			**50**	**0**			G. Mayo
A. Accounts	*50*			*50*	*0*			G. Mayo
1. Internal auditing and monitoring	10 / 40 / 540	2 performance audits Dec 1 and May 1 May 1 annual statement	$3 each per published audits, $4 per published statement	10	0 / 0 / 25	Performance audits published Dec 1, May 1. Annual statement published May 1	Achieved costs $3 each per published audits, $4 per published statement	G. Mayo
2. Municipal debt mgt.	40	Pay off 7% debt (30), manage other debt, ensure AAA rating, May 1	Decrease debt payments to 2%, AAA rated instruments only	40		Paid off 7% debt (30), managed other debt, AAA rating assured, by May 1	Decreased debt payments to 2%, AAA rated instruments used only	G. Mayo
Mayor Office	515	All of the above	All of the above	515		All of the above	All of the above	Mayor Bee

What are the end goals of government interventions? Is government reaching its end goals, or at least moving toward their achievement? How much money is government spending, and is it spending more than is needed to achieve its goals? Are revenues sufficient to meet expenditures? If not, why not? Who is responsible for spending behavior and outcomes?

These questions require that governments report on information related to the basics of how much is spent as well as how money is spent (that is, the performance of agreed-on output goals). This kind of reporting should be detailed enough for citizens to see what government was meant to provide, where, in what quantity, and by what date, as well as what costs and quality promises were made. These requirements drive the format of the budget and financial statement in table 7.7, which shows first (by column, starting at the left) the government entity providing a service (by department, program, and project). The format then presents highly relevant information about where money was allocated (following planning, budget hearings, and decisions). Such information includes the budgeted amount (by department, program, and project) and the stated performance targets (in terms of outputs broken down by quantity, location, and date, and the more detailed cost and quality parameters driving the work). Third, the format shows relevant information regarding financial performance, in a way that allows easy comparison with targets: The real outlay is shown, with a simple deficit figure alongside, and columns that show outputs provided and costs and quality performance. The final piece of immediately relevant information provided here is the official responsible for the project. The budget allows citizens to answer all the questions asked above, facilitating civic engagement and interest.

Readability: To promote a citizen orientation, budgets must be formatted in a way that is accessible to citizens with at least a medium literacy level, allowing easy understanding of the crucial information and easy comparison of targets and performance. This is seldom the kind of financial reporting one encounters in developing or developed country governments, reporting which is typically complex, open only to technocratic understanding and interpretation. Budgets and budget plans are often formatted according to internally meaningful (but externally confusing) line-item categorizations. In addition, they are structured and formatted differently than financial statements, creating a budget opacity that prohibits meaningful civic influence.

Improving budget readability requires simplifying budgets and ensuring relevant reporting is made in restricted space, with easy comparison of goals and performance (as in table 7.7). This kind of simplification necessitates a move away from some of the technical detail usually considered vital in a financial report (such as line-item classifications). One can expect this kind of change to meet resistance from parties that favor the technocratic substance of traditional budgets, and the supposed internal control orientation it facilitates. Such resistance is akin to the normal professionalism that Chambers (1983) discusses as a major impediment to participatory reform—whereby professionals create processes that they control and understand and invite only other professionals to participate. In such instances a citizen orientation requires a de-technocraticzation of the budget format, and a move from internal, input-based controls (as reflected in the line-item budget) to an external, results-oriented reporting protocol that, because of its readability, facilitates external evaluation and control (by citizens). In this kind of model, administrators gain discretion over how they achieve a task but lose discretion over the final product (its output, cost, and quality).

Responsibility: Budgets and financial documents communicate the core responsibilities in a public organization (Mikesell 1995). The important questions about accountability and responsibility, however, are by whom? to whom? and for what? The principle of responsibility, as it pertains to the citizen-oriented budget format, is simply that the budget and financial reporting format must communicate and facilitate a responsibility by officials to citizens for things that matter to citizens.

Traditional budget and financial report formats favor an internal accountability orientation based on process and rule adherence, whereby government entities are held accountable for their adherence to strict procedural rules. Entities that spend an allotted amount on each line item are seen to be accountable, without any question of how efficient or effective that spending has been. This creates an inward-looking culture that lacks any kind of citizen-oriented bottom line and thus lacks incentives for citizen-oriented spending.

Table 7.7, and the process leading up to the information shown in it, encourages a different kind of accountability and responsibility relationship—by government, to citizens, for how much money government spends as well as how government spends its money. This new responsibility relationship is founded on the information reported on in the table—clear data on how much is spent and what spending achieves, as well as the identities of those officials entrusted with spending (for cost centers at different levels of the public organization, from individual projects, to programs, to departments). With this information officials can expect to be held accountable, and citizens are empowered to hold them accountable. The final line of the table indicates that the mayor's office is ultimately responsible for all that is done on her watch—a key principle of representative government and a bottom line worthy of any organization.

■ *Reportability:* The final principle informing the structure of table 7.7 is reportability, which is similar to relevance and readability. In terms of the principle the budget format must facilitate easy reportability, by citizens, in all stages of the budgeting process. For this to be the case, budget commitments should be clearly shown, with descriptions written in simple, layperson's language. Outlays should also be clearly shown, and deficits and surpluses indicated in an easy-to-identify way. Budget performance should also be clearly shown, with citizens able to compare outputs, outlays, costs, and quality performance with commitments. The ability to compare enables citizens to identify shortcomings in financial reports, facilitating reporting of questionable reports and performance. This principle not only guarantees citizens' budget literacy and interest but also constitutes a cost-effective way of reporting—without the complexities of a detailed accounting draft that only select, highly qualified technocrats have mastered.

Conclusion

This chapter started by asserting the view that budgeting processes and documents are not citizen friendly. This is a major impediment to reform and good governance, because the budgeting and financial management and reporting process is at the core of how government business is conducted. The chapter then proposed modifications to the common budgeting process and format that should facilitate a greater orientation toward citizens (through institutionalizing incentives and making appropriate budgeting approaches that are citizen friendly).

On a practical level many may ask how possible this kind of model is or argue that it is a radical approach that goes too far for the development community to embrace. In reality the approach merges two accepted budget reform streams, performance-based budgeting and participatory budgeting, with the new element arising from the synergy between the two. This synergy institutionalizes accountability more effectively than the two approaches have done alone, with the approach offering a practical and direct path to citizen-oriented and responsive budgeting. This path is offered in response to calls in the literature, such as the following by Chan (2001): "The emphasis on public accountability through popular reporting is consistent with [the] call for a type of budgeting that is also responsive to direct citizens' control" (81).

References

Andrews, Matthew. 2002. "Fiscal Institutions Adoption in South African Municipalities." Paper presented at the Center for Science and Industrial Research, Pretoria, 15 March.

Blair, Harry. 2000. "Participation and Accountability at the Periphery: Democratic Local Governance in Six Countries." *World Development* 28 (1): 21–39.

Cameron, R., and Chris Tapscott. 2000. "The Challenges of State Transformation in South Africa." *Public Administration and Development* 20: 81–86.

Chambers, Robert. 1983. *Rural Development: Putting the Last First.* London: Longman.

Chan, James L. 2001. "The Implications of GASB Statement No. 34 for Public Budgeting." *Public Budgeting and Finance* 21 (3): 79–87.

DCD (Department of Constitutional Development). 1998. *White Paper on Local Government.* Pretoria: Department of Provincial and Local Government.

DCD-GTZ (Department of Constitutional Development and German Technical Corporation). 1999. *Integrated Development Planning Pilot Projects Assessment Study.* Pretoria: South African Department of Constitutional Development.

Domecq, Raul F. Monet. 1998. "Paraguay's Public Budget Hearings: A Path to Transparency." *Accountability* 16: 6–7.

ESSET (Ecumenical Service for Socio-economic Transformation). 2000. "Brazil's Participatory Budgeting Process." *Economic Justice Update* 4 (3): 3.

Goudsmit, Into A., and James Blackburn. 2001. Participatory Municipal Planning in Bolivia: an ambiguous experience. *Development in Practice* 11 (5): 587–96. http://www.developmentinpractice.org.

Jacob, Jaime. D. 2000. "Empowering the Local Government: The Naga City Experience." *Asian Review of Public Administration* 12: 182–89.

Mikesell, John L. 1995. *Fiscal Administration: Analysis and Applications for the Public Sector.* 4th ed. Belmont, CA: Wadsworth.

Mummert, Uwe. 1999. "Informal Institutions and Institutional Policy—Shedding Light on the Myth of Institutional Conflict." Discussion paper 02-99, Max Planck Institute for Research into Economic Systems, Jena, Germany.

Pope, Jeremy. 2000. "Local Government." In *TI Source Book,* ed. Jeremy Pope, 115–18. Berlin: Transparency International.

von Hagen, Jürgen, and Ian Harden. 1996. "Budget Processes and Commitment to Fiscal Discipline." IMF Working Paper 96/78, International Monetary Fund, Washington, DC.

8

Voice Mechanisms and Local Government Fiscal Outcomes

How Do Civic Pressure and Participation Influence Public Accountability?

MATTHEW ANDREWS

Accountability "has been a dominant, if not the dominant, concern for the designers of democratic political systems" (Peters 1996, 112). It is also arguably the main concern in structuring public sector administrative systems and has been the driving focus of many development initiatives. Such initiatives increasingly emphasize the role of civic voice in ensuring the accountability of public officials to the public. This emphasis is especially evident in local-level reforms and decentralization initiatives, where policy makers see local voice—or the participation of citizens in various aspects of the governance process—as a potential source of discipline, guidance, and demand in the process.

Many national governments and international development organizations have recently attempted to facilitate voice expression with such influence in mind, hoping that enhanced voice in local and regional governments will promote greater accountability (with voice having a positive accountability effect). This chapter asks a pertinent question related to these reforms: Are the many voice mechanisms introduced by reformers making governments more accountable and responsive to citizens?

The first section raises this question in the context of relevant literature and reform experience in the developing world. The second section discusses the research method adopted to address the question. This method merges an analysis of more than 50 literature-based cases of adoption of voice mechanisms around the developing world[1] with the analysis of first-hand cases of such reform in South African local governments[2]—experiences that are generalizable to other developing country settings.[3] The third section presents observations from the literature-based and South African cases, which suggest a high degree of variation in the accountability effects of reforms involving the adoption of voice mechanisms:

- In many instances voice mechanisms had no impact on accountability at all.
- In other instances voice mechanisms facilitated improved accountability of government to narrow interest groups.
- In yet other instances voice mechanisms facilitated improved accountability of government to society as a whole.

The fourth section develops these initial observations to suggest why different reforms have had different accountability effects. On the basis of evidence from the literature-based cases, the section argues that different accountability effects arise because of differences in the focus and influence of voice expression through reform-based mechanisms:

- No accountability effect was in evidence in cases where voice mechanisms failed to facilitate the influential expression of civic voice.
- A narrow accountability effect was evident in cases where voice mechanisms facilitated influential expression of civic voice, but those expressing their voices were from a narrow (or highly focused) social segment.
- A broad accountability effect was evident in cases where voice mechanisms facilitated influential expression of civic voice, and those expressing their voices were from a broad section of society.

These differences are explained in terms of identifiable variation in the voice mechanism characteristics and in the environments where such mechanisms are adopted.

Background

Accountability has always been emphasized as a primary goal of governance and of governance reform. The concept has many meanings, however, and is thus difficult to evaluate or discuss in a clear sense:

▪ In the typical Weberian model of government (which traditionally has pre-vailed in developing countries), accountability involves adherence to a set of process requirements and rules. According to this model, governments are accountable if they adhere to established processes when governing.

▪ In the market and participation models responsible for new public man-agement and democratic decentralization reforms, accountability has a different meaning, focused more directly on how government interacts with (and what government provides for) citizens. In this approach gov-ernments are considered accountable if they engage with citizens in a transparent way and are responsive to citizen needs (Peters 1996).[4]

Recent definitions of accountability tend to combine these two approaches, suggesting that accountability should involve both conformance and performance dimensions. Manasan, Gonzalez, and Gaffud merge the tra-ditional process orientation with a citizen focus in describing accountability as a multifaceted concept involving the need for responsibility "for govern-ment behavior," especially related to resource use, and responsiveness "to the needs of the citizenry" (Manasan, Gonzalez, and Gaffud 1999, 152–53). Describing accountability as "the central and perhaps most powerful ele-ment of good governance," Schneider (1999, 523) suggests a similarly broad approach to the concept, involving "political, administrative, and legal dimen-sions" that "form a rather complex web of accountability which relies on clear rules of transparency, and on the threat of legal, administrative, or political sanction in case of noncompliance."

These definitions help illustrate what accountability is and facilitate identification of questions relevant for accountability evaluation:

▪ Are governments operating within the bounds of legislation?
▪ Are governments being responsible in their resource use?
▪ Do governments maintain high levels of procedural transparency?
▪ Are political officials responsible for the mandate they receive from constituents?
▪ Do governments allocate resources to priorities identified by citizens?
▪ Do governments report reliably and accurately on resource use?
▪ Do governments have channels set up for citizen interaction and for potential discipline of political and administrative officials?

The Link between Public Sector Accountability and Civic Voice

These questions relate to both procedural and outcome aspects of gover-nance. Both aspects have received attention in reforms aimed at enhancing accountability in developing countries. The role of citizens in the governance process has been a prominent focus of such reforms, with the intention of getting citizens involved in the procedures of governance and making citizens' interests the basis of governance outcomes. Blair (2000), for example, states, "Accountability means that people will be able to hold local government accountable for how it is affecting them" (22).

It is believed that people will be best positioned to hold government accountable if they have a strong potential to voice their demands, displeasures, and directives to governing officials. The importance of voice is widely recognized, with Hirschmann (1970) describing it as one of the main tools consumers have to deal with problems of performance deterioration in the private production of goods and services. Samuel Paul and others extend the application to the public sector, with the argument that the force of public voice is imperative in influencing public organizations to be accountable, responsive, and efficient in their service provision. Paul (1992, 1048) defines voice as "the degree to which they [the public] can influence the final outcome of a service through some form of participation or articulation of protest/feedback." Following on this research, "an awareness" has developed in many countries and development organizations "that the 'voice' of the people should inform and influence the decisions, actions, and accountability of government" (Paul 1996, 37).

The importance of voice and participation focused on enhancing voice is often emphasized in areas of the governance process where decisions are made regarding which services are provided and how they are provided, areas such as the budgeting and planning processes. Paul (1996) argues that increased participation and voice—public influence—in such areas will facilitate the attainment of higher levels of citizen-oriented accountability, a better knowledge of demand, and thus more effective and efficient use of resources and improved public sector responsiveness to citizen needs. Voice is also seen as a centrally important factor in the move toward performance-based government (and citizen-oriented accountability). In making such a connection, Gopakumar (1997, 282) states, "There could be no better way to gauge performance than the 'voice' provided by the end user." Voice is also considered a key check on public organizations, and a vital tool—one that is required if developing countries are to meet their area-specific service demands, which generally are shaped by the peculiar and often highly localized influences of poverty.[5]

Reforms Focused on Enhancing Voice and Accountability

Buoyed by apparent links between voice and one or another dimension of the expanded version of accountability, governments in developing and transitional countries have been challenged to free the expression of social voice in their governance process. To this end, a developmental approach has emerged that concentrates on developing mechanisms and tools that facilitate voice expression at the local and regional levels.[6] In this concentration, "A wide range of mechanisms" is seen to "serve as [potential] agents of accountability" (Blair 2000, 27). Paul (1992) presents these voice mechanisms as important "options available to improve public accountability" (1054). Such mechanisms are designed to provide regular channels, "windows," or "dedicated bodies" through which citizens can access governments (Schneider 1999, 530). In keeping with this work, voice mechanisms are presented as policy options available to governments or development agencies that are looking to enhance citizen influence over public entities. The reform logic is shown in figure 8.1, which represents the argument that voice mechanisms facilitate voice expression, which enhances accountability in the governance process.

Particular references to voice mechanisms are evident in the participation literature, with its emphasis on "strengthening public accountability through participation" (Paul 1996, 37). This literature stresses the importance of various tools and techniques in enhancing civic influence over the governance process, especially focused on identifying "ways of improving the capacity of marginal people to participate in governmental processes" (Desai 1996, 218). Three literature-based examples of such mechanisms are the citizen committees characterizing the healthy cities program in Léon, Nicaragua; the 300 community-based management committees in the environment and development programs in Ilo, Peru; and the participatory budgeting initiative in Belo Horizonte, Brazil. In all three examples, "The extent to which poor groups can influence urban government structures [the extent of their 'voice expression'] obviously influences the extent and nature of "pro-poor" policies and activities" (Mitlin 2000, 7).

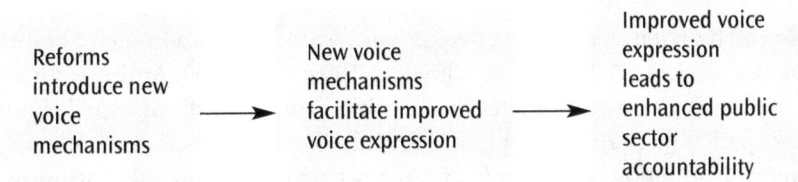

| Reforms introduce new voice mechanisms | → | New voice mechanisms facilitate improved voice expression | → | Improved voice expression leads to enhanced public sector accountability |

FIGURE 8.1   Voice Mechanisms, Voice Expression, and Accountability

A research question: Do voice mechanisms always facilitate improved accountability? The effect Mitlin points to is generally the one hoped for (and publicized) when voice mechanisms are introduced into governance processes (and shown in figure 8.1). Reforms introduce voice mechanisms, which facilitate improved voice expression, which then leads to enhanced public sector accountability and responsiveness. Reflecting the general expectation of such a "positive accountability effect," Awio (2001) writes, of participatory budgeting reforms in Uganda, "It was hoped that increased participation by local communities under decentralized management structures would enhance the efficiency and effectiveness of budgeting, with priorities better reflecting the needs of the local community" (80).

The literature suggests that this hope or expectation is not always met, however. Various authors point out that reforms involving the adoption of voice mechanisms have varying effects on community empowerment and different implications for the voice effect in the governance process (Desai 1996; Mohan and Stokke 2000; Souza 2001; Andrews forthcoming).[7] This line of critique suggests that the connection between participation, voice, and accountability in developing countries remains questionable. Manor and Crook (1998) find, for example, that reforms focused on decentralization and voice creation in Ghana and Côte d'Ivoire do not appear to have increased responsiveness or accountability. Charlick (2001), in his comment on recent studies, states, "Limited data suggest that even if participation [and the voice expressed through it] does expand with the reform of local government, the opportunities for participation do remain very unevenly distributed and local governments may not become more responsive and accountable" (150).

The comment raises important questions: Are the many voice mechanisms introduced by reformers making governments more accountable and responsive to citizens? If not, why does participation (and voice expression) emerging from reform not always enhance responsiveness and accountability?

A Research Approach

Research on participation and voice typically focuses on a limited number of case studies (Pelling 1998; Schneider 1999; Blair 2000; Andrews forthcoming). This focus facilitates the identification of significant detail about the specific mechanisms in place in specific situations, the factors influencing their adoption, and the influences they have on accountability. Its weakness lies in the difficulty of generalizing from specific to universal experience (although cases in the literature might provide interesting comparisons with other experiences, it is very difficult to transfer findings from a limited study to a general population).

To retain the strength of this approach but also promote generalizability beyond individual cases, this chapter involved analysis of two information sources:

- First, more than 50 literature-based cases were analyzed. This meta-analysis approach facilitated both a general view (across cases) and a specific view (within selected cases) of experience with voice and the adoption of voice mechanisms in developing countries.
- Second, the literature-based analysis was supplemented with a study of the adoption of participation and voice mechanism in South Africa between 1995 and 2000.[8] A national survey indicated which kinds of participation mechanisms municipalities adopted during this period.[9] The sample of 273 municipalities allowed for a general view of the kinds of mechanisms in place and also facilitated the identification of specific municipal experiences warranting further study. These experiences were examined using cases conducted by the German development agency GTZ and first-hand e-mail correspondence and site visits.

The research approach is fairly novel in that it combines secondary analysis (the case studies) with primary analysis (the South African study), as well as large sample analysis (of the cases and the South African survey) with specific analysis (of individual literature-based and South African cases). This research method is considered appropriate for addressing the questions at hand in a reliable way, reflecting a form of triangulation needed to investigate complex social situations. This triangulation of different means of data collection increases the reliability of the information reported on and of inferences based on that information (Yin 1998; Miles and Huberman 1994).

Observations about the Link between Voice, Voice Mechanisms, and Accountability

To address the research questions, this study sought to examine whether accountability effects associated with different reforms were as variable as papers such as those by Mohan and Stokke (2000) and Charlick (2001) represent them to be. The first step in this search involved identifying ways in which voice can be expected to improve accountability. On the basis of such accountability indicators, cases were examined for evidence of any influence that voice, as expressed through the new voice mechanisms, may have had on accountability.

Identifying Accountability Indicators

Broad sets of measures were identified as indicators of accountability effects, reflecting the broad accountability definitions discussed earlier (which merge considerations of conformance and performance, and procedure and outcomes). General indicators, with examples of experience, are as follows:

- *Changes in resource responsibility:* Fiscal responsibility is a key aspect of accountability and involves official concern for public revenues and for behavior within codified fiscal processes. Feld and Kirchgassner (1999) argue that direct democracies in which strong voice expression is allowed tend to be more fiscally responsible than weak or indirect democracies (in which weak voice expression is evident).[10] Social voice expressed through Participatory Poverty Assessments in Uganda appears to have had a positive effect on this accountability aspect, increasing the quality of money management in the education sector (Reinikka 1999; Robb 2000). In Cebu City, the Philippines, business has been effective in using voice mechanisms to influence government spending behavior, so as to control tax and debt burdens (Etamadi 2000).
- *Changes in responsiveness and performance:* Within a context of fiscal responsibility, public sector accountability also has a dimension of responsiveness. Governments should be accountable for how they spend as well as how much they spend. Andrews (2002) uses a measure of service expenditure allocations to indicate whether South African municipalities adopting new participation mechanisms are more responsive to citizens and accountable for the developmental mandate embodied in legislation.[11] Faguet (2000) uses this approach in evaluating the contribution of decentralization and voice mechanisms such as the Popular Participation Law in Bolivia. The voice effect of the participatory budgeting initiative in Belo Horizonte is seen to facilitate accountable government in this light (ESSET 2000, 4). Similarly, the voice effect of public budget hearings in Villa Elisa, Paraguay, has led to significant budget allocation adjustments (Domecq 1998, 6).
- *Changes in process transparency: Accountability* and *transparency* are generally used as interchangeable terms in the reform literature. If voice mechanisms increase transparency in governance processes, they are also understood to have a positive effect on accountability. This was not the

case in the South African municipality of Lichtenburg, where participants in public meetings and committees were still isolated from decision-making processes and were not even given feedback on their own interactions (DCD-GTZ 1999, North-West study). In Tlalmanalco, Mexico, the municipal-level participatory planning process led to "the people of Tlalmanalco" developing a new Municipal Development Plan in April 1997 (Moctezuma 2001, 128). The plan, embodying civic voice, did not enhance transparency in the early years: "Unfortunately, after the plan was approved, the municipal authorities were reluctant to implement it and not only failed to meet the commitments they had made but even secretly changed the document and produced a new version." The transparency of the process was then radically enhanced, as the community developed monitoring and evaluation processes to ensure accurate provision of information.[12]

▪ *Changes in corruption:* The reform literature also suggests a link between accountability and corruption, arguing that governments with high levels of accountability are less corrupt. As an indicator of accountability, therefore, reported reductions in corruption in districts in Rajasthan, India, suggest a positive accountability effect of social auditing mechanisms in those districts (with the literature showing links between the operation of the mechanisms and the reduction in corruption) (Jenkins and Goetz 1999). As regards Uganda's participatory budgeting initiative, however, evidence suggests that "this participatory process is sometimes undermined by the reports of corruption, including embezzlement and fraud, that are reported regularly by the Public Accounts Committee of Parliament . . . , the Auditor General's reports, and the Inspector General of Government" (Gariyo 2000, 2).

▪ *Changes in political and administrative accountability:* A final area in which accountability effects were identified involves political and administrative accountability. Officials are expected to be more accountable, in this line of thought, where they are forced to relate to citizens in a responsive way. Voice mechanisms that facilitated the development of relational links and reward and redress avenues that tied officials more closely to citizens were seen to enhance accountability. District-level democracy and the Participatory District Development Programme in Nepal had a positive effect on such accountability, bringing political representatives closer to their constituencies and forcing them to be more responsive. "The accountability of elected officials and local institutions" (Dixit 2000, 16) is seen to be the most important success factor arising from increased civic voice (through elections and the Programme). In the words of one political representative: "They (citizens) will not vote for us again, unless I earn the total trust of the people, unless they believe that what I am doing

benefits them, and makes their lives easier, and unless we show integrity
and commitment" (Dixit 2000, 16).

Observed Difference in Accountability Effects

When these indicators were combined, and evidence collected on their
strength,[13] it became apparent that experiences varied as far as the accountability effect of voice and reforms involving the adoption of voice mechanisms were concerned. This finding confirms the comments from Charlick
and others cited earlier, as well as research. Andrews (2002) shows that different South African municipalities adjusted their fiscal allocation behavior
differently after adopting voice mechanisms. Schneider (1999) finds that
some voice mechanisms (such as the Malaysian Public Complaints Bureau)
have a positive effect on accountability,[14] while others (such as Bangladesh
nongovernmental organizations [NGOs] and new election laws preserving
seats for women in local government to facilitate their voice) rarely have an
impact on government. The study conducted here led to the identification
of three types of accountability effect associated with the adoption of voice
mechanisms: no (or negative) accountability effects, narrow accountability
effects, and broad accountability effects.

Experiences Where Voice and Voice Mechanisms
Have No Accountability Effect

The first kind of accountability effect identified from the sample of cases and
the South African experience is where voice mechanisms have no effect or a
negative effect on accountability. Such effects are difficult to find in the
broad literature on participation and voice-based reform, because they generally suggest reform failure. The literature is largely focused on disseminating what could be called best practices and thus seldom provides evidence
of failure (in many cases little evidence is provided of actively positive results
either, which makes it difficult to provide any kind of assessment of the
effects that voice mechanisms have had on governance systems and accountability). The South African study provides a good counter to the literature
in this sense. Without the best-practice bias, the study reveals that many
cases of voice expression through voice mechanisms adopted in local governments do not improve accountability (and in some cases could lead to
less accountability).

A general econometric analysis suggests that any effort to incorporate
citizens in budgeting and planning processes in South African municipali-

ties enhances the accountability of local governments to the national mandate for service expansion (and their responsiveness to local service demand).[15] More detailed study of individual cases shows that voice and participation mechanisms do not always have positive accountability effects. Evidence from detailed cases of participatory reform linked to the planning-budgeting initiative called the Integrated Development Plan shows that participatory mechanisms are "not affecting the outcomes of the plans being prepared" (Planning Initiative 1999, 11). In some cases the Plan-related participatory reforms, focused on technical planning, could actually be reducing the accountability effects of civic voice. This is suggested in a multiple-case study that finds "a decline in participation related to a nonempowering way of involving people" (DCD-GTZ 1999, 6). It appears that, because the planning reforms were "viewed as highly technical," they facilitated a process by which technical experts could decrease planning and budgeting transparency (in the name of doing the plan correctly) and limit "participation to certain [and immaterial] parts of the process—leaving other crucial elements to the dictates of technocrats" (PLANACT 1999, 3).

This evidence relates to many cases in which new voice mechanisms did not improve accountability in South African municipalities, measured in any of the dimensions. In the Uthungulu municipality, for example, the council held workshops in which "women, youths, and the poorer strata of society were not adequately represented" (DCD-GTZ 1999, KwaZulu-Natal study, 10). The new workshops did not have a systematic effect on budgets or spending activities (either how much was spent or how money was allocated), transparency, corruption, or citizen-government relationships. Explicitly negative comments relate to the allocations, transparency, and relational dimensions of accountability. Instead of voices from workshops influencing allocations, for example, the participatory approach is described as "mere rhetoric" with dominant interest groups able to exert their influence "without checks and balances"—even though voice mechanisms were in" (DCD-GTZ 1999, KwaZulu-Natal study, 14 and 16). The process is further described as having no transparent methodology. The case report states explicitly that the participation mechanism did nothing to change the way government related to its citizens: "Neither scanning people's priorities nor involving people in the decision-making process (and allowing them to take over responsibilities) were conceptualized (as part of) how participation was organized."

Another example of adoption of a voice mechanism that had a low accountability effect is the mixture of public meetings and planning committees in Cradock. Case reports indicate that civic voices emanating from the meetings and committees have had little effect on the budgeting process:

"The poor link between technical planning components and community contributions jeopardize the extent to which communities would influence the planning outcome" (DCD-GTZ 1999, Eastern Cape study, 24–25). The following quotation provides further evidence that the council still relates to its citizens in a top-down, controlling manner, largely ignoring their voice (DCD-GTZ 1999, Eastern Cape study, 24):

The lack of recognizing and using information generated in workshops can be illustrated by the following examples:

- Workshop participants raised a concern regarding influx from farming community. This emphasized the need for cooperative planning . . . Unfortunately this was not explored.
- The lack of participation in the planning process is mentioned in the workshop. This would have provided an excellent opportunity to explore the reasons and develop possible solutions but such opportunity was not taken.

An example of a similar accountability effect in the broader international literature is Pelling's description (1998) of participatory planning and project implementation in Guyanese local authorities. Voice mechanisms in this case facilitated the participation of specific groups offering expertise or support to the ruling party or controlling administrators. This meant that, "despite a rhetoric of limited but inclusive participation in decision making the national framework for participation continued to exclude large sectors of the population" (Pelling 1998, 478). The participation program focused on engaging communities only where they were seen to contribute to the functioning of status quo administrative and political processes. Contributions (even by invited groups) had no material influence on who governed or how they governed, however, as officials tended to value and consider contributions only where they reflected established interests (which were already driving the governance process). Pelling implies that, despite the rhetoric about participation and voice, the decentralized governments were neither bottom-up nor inclusive: there was no community accountability as a result, a lack of transparency characterized decision making, and there was an absence of community-level information dissemination and decision making.

A second example of a reform in which voice mechanisms have been adopted with limited accountability gains comes from Bolivia, where a local participatory planning reform was developed in response to the Law of Popular Participation in the early 1990s. According to this law, "all municipal governments were legally obliged to prepare five-year Municipal Development Plans (MDPs) in accordance with the government Manual of Participatory Municipal Planning" (Goudsmit and Blackburn 2001, 588). The mechanism was introduced in conjunction with others, such as the vigilance committees. In an econometric analysis similar to that done by Andrews in the South African case, Faguet (2000) finds that such new localized voice mechanisms did generally affect public spending outcomes (an important accountability indicator) in Bolivia: "Decentralization did change local and national investment patterns in Bolivia, and . . . local preferences and needs are key to understanding these changes" (31). As with the South African example, however, case-based research shows that this general result fails to capture the variation in specific experiences:

- Goudsmit and Blackburn (2001) found, for example, that the new voice mechanisms often had no effect on fiscal outcomes (which were instead determined through negotiations between national and district governments).
- They also question the degree to which citizen voice mechanisms have effected improved transparency: "Planning teams have preferred to work behind closed doors (i.e., to get the job done as quickly as possible)" (Goudsmit and Blackburn 2001, 593), limiting civic voice in planning decisions, and transparency regarding the decision-making processes.

The general idea in such situations is that voice mechanisms adopted with the publicized intention of improving accountability do not always have such an effect. It is possible for governments to introduce participatory planning mechanisms, public meeting agendas, or citizen committees without such mechanisms facilitating the kind of voice expression that enhances accountability in the governance process.

Experiences Where Voice and Voice Mechanisms Have a Narrow Accountability Effect

The second kind of accountability effect identified from the sample of cases and South African experience is where voice mechanisms have a positive, though narrow, effect on accountability. What this means is that, on balance, the mechanism has a marked positive effect on accountability but not for society as a whole. Rather, mechanisms in these situations focus governments on narrow segments of society. The mechanism has the effect of increasing the responsibility or responsiveness of public organizations to certain social voices, for example, or of enhancing transparency in the budgeting process for specific groups.

About 60 percent of the literature-based cases can be placed in this category. An example is the participatory budgeting mechanism in Uganda, in which district budget conferences are held to elicit comment about government budgets. These mechanisms have effected improved fiscal accountability in governments, as evidenced through allocation adjustments and implementation improvements. In this light Gariyo (2000, 1) simply states, "We can claim that there has been some impact on the budgetary policy formulation." There is evidence of an increased incidence of opportunity for corruption associated with the adoption of the mechanism, which tempers the positive effect on accountability. On balance, however, it appears that the mechanism has opened the governance process to social voices, improved fiscal accountability and transparency, and facilitated a new citizen orientation in some areas of government—generally, a positive accountability effect.

The voices speaking through the budget conferences and representing the parties to which government now finds itself accountable are limited, however:

> The majority of the citizens of Uganda do not influence budgetary processes and policy formulation. This is because while they have a direct interest as taxpayers in the benefits, the mechanisms for constructing budgets are too complex and require skills and knowledge for this to happen. Thus only a small section of the elite has to date been able to influence the budgetary process and policy formulation in Uganda. These are drawn from the NGO sector, the academicians and researchers, the influential large business concerns through the Uganda Manufacturers' Association. (Gariyo 2000, 1).

The general impression of the participatory budgeting voice mechanism in Uganda is thus that it has made government more accountable to select social groups, influential NGOs, academics, and leading business interests. This is a positive, though narrow, accountability effect.

This accountability effect is also in evidence in a small subset of South African municipalities, including Bothaville in the Free State. In this town a "Representative Structure" and a "Management Team" facilitate participation by select members representing established community-based organizations (which appear to be related to political parties or to business). Participation in this case is explicitly described as narrow, because of the reliance on organized channels rather than more open forms of public access (DCD-GTZ 1999, Free State study). The Representative Structure is proving influential in transmitting the narrow voices, however, serving as "an effective base for information flows and participation" (DCD-GTZ 1999, Free State study, 25). The voices expressed through the mechanism appear to be influencing fiscal accountability, because decisions made by the Representative Structure are fed back to the council and have a defined and marked effect on planning outcomes. The mechanisms also seem to have enhanced access for specific community representatives (the narrow group participating in the process) to the budgeting process—a transparency improvement. The narrow accountability effect is evident in the municipality's new development plan, which reflects the voice of the Representative Structure, especially its specific interests and focus, providing "very little information . . . on issues of poverty, health education, and access to services" (DCD-GTZ 1999, Free State study, 28–29).

Such voice mechanisms facilitate some civic influence over governing officials and make governments accountable to parties outside the public structure. The fact that the groups to which governments are held accountable are so narrowly defined raises some interesting questions, however. In the first place, one has to ask whether the formal voice mechanisms (the participatory planning processes in Bolivia and Representative Structures in Bothaville) are really necessary to facilitate the kinds of voice expression that they do. In many instances the groups expressing themselves through such mechanisms (the wealthy, the powerful, the educated, and the politically connected) could reasonably be expected to develop their own informal channels of voice expression and influence (without the costs of a reform or the time needed to develop a complex mechanism). In the second place, there are concerns that narrow accountability relationships developed through such mechanisms facilitate government capture. This is an especially important consideration at the local level in developing countries, where social inequalities often create the conditions for such capture (by educated, wealthy elites, for example) (Oates 1993). Voice mechanisms that fail to counter such inequalities can easily lead to municipal capture and ultimately stimulate a governance system in which there are low levels of accountability to vulnerable groups.[16]

The Howick municipality in South Africa is an example of a positive, though narrow, accountability effect associated with the adoption of a voice mechanism in which signs of capture are apparent. The voice mechanism introduced in the setting is focused on the planning process. Attendance at community meetings is by invitation only and business leaders dominate, with a member of the National Business Initiative actually facilitating the process.[17] Business leaders in the planning committee elected through such meetings appear to have set the planning agenda and determined whose voices would be heard in plenary and in private. The narrow business voice has proved influential through the mechanism, with the municipality being active in developing tourism-related infrastructure (worth R 15 billion) while decreasing spending on other areas (such as direct services in poor areas)[18] (DCD-GTZ 1999, KwaZulu-Natal study). Although the new voice mechanism has enhanced government accountability in this case and many others, the group that government finds itself accountable to is extremely limited in size and interest. The narrow interests are having a significant effect on governance processes and outcomes, while other perspectives and voices remain unheard (and government has no accountability link to those other constituencies).

Experiences Where Voice and Voice Mechanisms Have a Broad Accountability Effect

The third kind of accountability effect identified from the sample of cases and South African experience is where voice mechanisms facilitate broad social accountability. What this means is that, on balance, the mechanisms have a marked positive effect on the accountability of government structures to society as a whole. The mechanisms have the effect of increasing the responsibility or responsiveness of public organizations to society in general, for example, or of generally enhancing transparency in the budgeting process (so that all citizens have an improved ability to observe and evaluate government processes, behavior, and outcomes).

This accountability type is often touted in the literature and is a hallmark of the democratic ideal (Peters 1996). It is also the basic form of accountability envisaged in decentralized systems, where a large number of localized governments are considered more likely to be accountable to broad social voice than are a small number of centralized (and distant) governments. The literature's best-practice bias reflects this belief, with at least a third of the prominent cases telling tales of adoptions of voice mechanism that lead to broad, influential voice expression and a broad accountability effect.

An example is Nepal's new district-level democracy and Participatory District Development Programme. The mixture of a local democratic system and a participatory program focused on the planning and budgeting process has facilitated broad accountability. This is evident in changes in expenditure allocations in many districts (in favor of poverty reduction initiatives), increased transparency, and a greater ability of citizens to hold officials responsible for their behavior (Dixit 2000; UNDP 2000). Another example is the participatory budgeting (or budget hearing) initiative in Villa

Elisa, Paraguay. This initiative involved setting up 64 budget committees in different regions of this city of 48,000. The large number of committees ensures broad representation (across geographic and demographic boundaries). The accountability effects are evident in changes in expenditure patterns, enhanced transparency, reduced corruption opportunities, and a new social ability to monitor the mayor (Domecq 1998). Pope (2000) discusses these accountability effects with regard to similar experience in Asunción:

> Promoting transparency and citizen participation in this way opens channels of communication between city officials and the public, and creates a genuine forum for participation. As a result, citizens are better informed on public affairs and finances, they have an opportunity to air their own views, and the forum provides a way for public budget decisions to be explained. As a consequence of greater transparency, there is less room for corruption and citizens find that their opinions actually can influence government.[19] (116)

In contrast to the large group of cases in which the literature shows that adoption of voice mechanisms stimulates broad accountability, there are no specific experiences in the South African case that could fit this category. This lack suggests the difficulty of facilitating broad accountability. However, some observers argue that the successful local government election process in South Africa generally facilitated increased, broad-based accountability. Elections are often assumed to constitute effective mechanisms for broad voice expression and social accountability. Blair (2000, 27) writes of this: "Free, fair, regularly scheduled elections and universal suffrage are the most direct mechanism for ensuring that those who govern are accountable to the citizens." Such thinking is foremost in the minds of those commentators who argue that the elections materially influenced accountability in South African municipalities. The counterargument is that the elections and local government structures did not effect significant administrative change or change in service provision, or enhance transparency in the budgeting process, particularly in the period between elections (the five years between 1995 and 2000) (Swilling 1997, 1998; Africa 1999; Andrews 2002).

Looking beyond South Africa, it is apparent that local-level elections are not a guarantee of broad accountability. In Nepal, local elections enhanced the responsiveness of local officials to citizens largely because they were complemented by mechanisms that facilitated voice between elections (the Participatory District Development Programme). In countries where local elections have not been partnered with such mechanisms they are arguably not seen to facilitate broad accountability (at least not beyond any form of basic, temporal political accountability). Côte d'Ivoire is a good example.

Local elections in that country are based on a list system, which results in the council being "a team put together by a powerful entrepreneur and his faction" (Manor and Crook 1998, 159). The electoral mechanism has not facilitated broad accountability relationships because of a lack of supporting mechanisms to consolidate political constituency ties between elections: "The evidence suggests that the lack of institutionalized constituency relationships and the lack of formal accountability mechanisms had a . . . serious impact on the accessibility of councillors" (Manor and Crook 1998, 163).

Factors Influencing Accountability Effects

In related research two constructs, voice focus and voice influence, were identified to help differentiate between the types of voice expression resulting from the adoption of voice mechanisms (Andrews and Shah 2002). Analyzing evidence of accountability effects indicates that these constructs are also useful in identifying different accountability outcomes associated with the adoption of voice mechanisms:

- Voice influence relates to the degree to which voice, as expressed through a voice mechanism, affects who governs (the formal governance representatives), how they govern (the governance process), what they consider (the governance agenda), and what they produce (governance outcomes). Cases in which influence is high also appear to be the cases in which positive accountability effects are observed. Cases in which influence is low also appear to be the cases in which accountability effects are absent.
- Voice focus relates to whose voice is expressed through a given voice mechanism. In some cases, voice focus is broad, and members of large segments of society are given the opportunity to express themselves. In other instances, voice focus is narrow, and only members of small segments of society are able to express their needs. The voice focus determines whom governments are held accountable to (if there is an accountability effect) when voice is expressed.

Figure 8.2 combines the voice influence and voice focus constructs to show how their various combinations relate to the types of accountability effects observed.

Figure 8.2 captures variation observed in the focus of experiences with adoption of voice mechanisms on the horizontal axis. In some experiences, the mechanisms facilitated narrow voice, while in others the mechanisms facilitated broad voice (with many experiences falling in the middle, indicating some degree of narrowness in focus or preference expression).[20] The figure

Voice influence	High		
		Narrow accountability effect (risk of capture) Narrow focus, High influence	Broad accountability effect (representative) Broad focus, High influence
		No accountability effect Narrow focus, Low influence	No accountability effect Broad focus, Low influence
	Low		
		Narrow	**Broad**

Voice focus

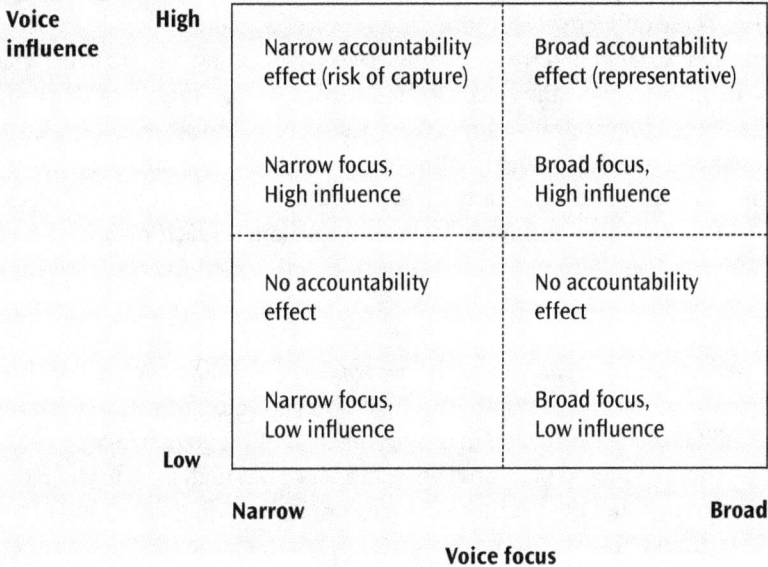

FIGURE 8.2 Voice Expression and Accountability Effects
of Mechanism Adoption

captures the variation observed in voice influence on the vertical axis: in
some cases the mechanisms facilitated no voice influence, whereas in others
mechanisms facilitated high voice influence (with mechanisms facilitating
only some influence in other cases).

In most instances, the experience of voice expression can be identified
as falling into one of four quadrants in the space created to show the interaction of focus and influence: narrow focus, low influence; broad focus, low
influence; narrow focus, high influence; and broad focus, high influence. The
three accountability effects can be located in the quadrants as well, with no
effect in the bottom two quadrants (where influence is low). The narrow
effect is located in the top left-hand quadrant, where influence is high but
focus is narrow. Where voice mechanisms facilitate this kind of expression
and accountability effect, there is a danger of capture (as discussed and as
noted in the figure). The broad effect is located in the top right-hand quadrant, where influence is high and focus is broad. This kind of accountability
effect is generally the stated goal of participatory and voice-based reforms,
especially those related to democratic decentralization initiatives.

In terms of the figure, it is apparent that a high voice influence is a necessary condition for a positive accountability effect. Similarly, a broad voice

focus is a necessary condition for a broad (and representative) accountability effect. These different voice influence and voice focus outcomes are explained in related research in terms of various factors, including the particular voice mechanism adopted, the voice mechanism design, mediums for voice transmission, the political and administrative structure, and socioeconomic conditions and social structure (Andrews and Shah 2002). In affecting the voice influence and voice focus outcomes related to adoption of a voice mechanism, these factors are also seen to have important impacts on accountability effects emerging from voice expression. Specific effects observed in the current research include the following:

- *Voices expressed in budgets and plans tend to be influential:* A general observation is that mechanisms yield high levels of voice influence when they facilitate voice expression in important areas of the governance process—like budgeting and planning. Voice influence was high in all participatory budgeting initiatives examined, for example, including the popular Porto Alegre and Belo Horizonte cases, the less-examined South American cases of Asunción, Villa Elisa and Cabo de Santo Agostinho, and the international cases of Kwaukuza (KwaZulu-Natal, South Africa), Uganda, and Ukraine. Other new mechanisms, such as participatory planning and report cards, are either difficult to evaluate (because the literature fails to provide information to assess accountability effects) or yield varied accountability effects in different situations (with planning-participation reforms in Tlalmanalco, Mexico, and in Bolivia yielding different results) (Moctezuma 2001; Goudsmit and Blackburn 2001). Where voice mechanisms designed to facilitate civic expression into planning processes actually did so (as in Mexico) accountability improved, while accountability was not improved in situations where voices were kept separate from actual planning decisions (as in Bolivia, Tanzania, and many of South Africa's municipalities). As in the Bolivian case, simply saying one is adopting a participatory budget or participatory plan and then not engaging citizens in these processes does not ensure influential voice and positive accountability effects.
- *Voice focus is narrowed where mechanism designs limit voice access:* Devices incorporated into the design of a voice mechanism to regulate access to the mechanism (and thus to the governance process) affect voice expression, particularly voice focus. Cases of voice mechanisms in which voice focus can be classed as narrow invariably had some kind of device controlling and limiting the voice focus of the mechanism. Narrow focus cases

from the South African study illustrate the point: In KwaDukuza Stanger groups and citizens had to preregister to attend workshops. In uThungula the strategic selection of meeting locations automatically limited the size of attendance and the identities of attendees. In Cradock and Howick, meeting and committee attendance was by invitation only (DCD-GTZ 1999). The influence of access devices on voice expression is also evident when considering cases of broad focus, where voice mechanism designs facilitated openness. In Thabanchu, South Africa, public planning meetings and workshops were announced in the media, which is also used to announce meetings in Uganda, Malaysia, and Nepal, where governments also stimulate access by placing announcements on public notice boards at the point of service.

Highly technical processes yield low voice influence and narrow voice focus: A common problem in participatory reforms relates to the highly technical nature of governance procedures. In many of the South African municipalities, and in Bolivia, Tanzania, and Uganda, government planning processes were simply too complex and technical to allow broad or influential voice contributions. Voice mechanisms in these situations were not designed to bridge the gap between civic expression and technical process. In Cradock, South Africa, for example, "The linkages between community participation and technical knowledge were not successfully integrated" to facilitate influential voice (DCD-GTZ 1999, Eastern Cape study, 24). In Uganda the influence of civic participation was limited by the complex language of the budget, which was "too abstract for ordinary citizens to comprehend" (Gariyo 2000, 4), and documents relating to the budgetary process, which were "only accessible by donors, academic institutions and some non-government organizations" (5). The failure to attend to these design issues has led to narrow participation in participatory budget reforms. Where voice mechanism design fails to enable citizen participation it hinders the influence on governance of the voices expressed through the mechanism. An example comes from Thabanchu, South Africa, where design issues hindered the ability of citizens to affect planning and budgeting decisions. Individuals were seen to "lose confidence because of a lack of understanding of concepts" (DCD-GTZ 1999, Free State study, 18) and hence withheld their voices. At the same time, officials were quick to ignore contributions from those with poor information or communication difficulties: "Where individuals articulate issues that don't fit in with the process consultant's definition of the session, the information (mostly useful) becomes lost in the process" (18).

▪ *Experimentation with varied mechanisms yields influential, broad voice:* Experience shows that reforms yielding broad and influential voice expression and a strong positive accountability effect are characterized by experimental designs (involving various voice mechanism types and simplified processes). This approach reflects Robert Chambers' principle of the so-called open manual, in which all parties in the participation process have "the opportunity to experiment with participatory methodologies and techniques" (Goudsmit and Blackburn 2001, 590). This process facilitates identification of technical and other voice impediments and allows the development of accountability-enhancing voice mechanisms.

▪ *Built-in evaluation devices stimulate voice influence:* Many of the experiences where voice mechanisms facilitated influential expression were designed with a defined monitoring or evaluating device in place. In Tlalmanalco's participatory planning mechanism, for example, participatory monitoring was introduced partly so that NGOs could evaluate the effect of voice on accountability and responsiveness, as is evident in Moctezuma's comment that, "the PUCSN [collaborative entity] . . . hopes to measure the efficacy of its interventions" (2001, 131).[21]

▪ *Voice influence is low where there is no medium for voice transmission:* Voice transmission mediums are devices that transmit ideas, feedback, and criticism voiced by citizens through participatory budgeting forums, public meetings, and the like to governing officials who actually make decisions. These mediums have a particularly important impact on the influence of the voices expressed through a voice mechanism, and thus on the accountability effect (or lack thereof) of such mechanisms. They can be built into voice mechanisms or they can be separate from them. There is evidence that suggests voice influence is lower, and accountability effects absent, where voices are not transmitted from the point of expression (through the voice mechanism) to decision makers. In Nelspruit, South Africa, for example, public workshop results are considered "hardly any use" (that is, uninfluential) because they are not processed, interpreted, translated, and transported into the planning process (DCD-GTZ 1999, Mpumalanga study, 12). In the Kentani municipality, voice has no apparent influence or accountability effect largely because "feedback structures/systems have not been formulated" (DCD-GTZ 1999, Eastern Cape study, 20). In the Eastern Cape town of Cradock the lack of transmission medium is again seen to limit influence and accountability effects, with no medium to ensure "in-departmental analysis" of citizen contributions in workshops (DCD-GTZ 1999, Eastern Cape study, 24). Where mediums exist to ensure that voices, once expressed through participation mechanisms, are transmitted to decision makers, these voices tend to be influential and accountability effects are evident.[22]

Centralizing political structures limits voice influence and narrows focus: Paul (1992, 1050) observed the importance political structures could have on voice expression when he commented that, "legal and institutional barriers to voice may exist in a country," which "could be traced to the nature of the larger political system or ideology." This perspective is well reflected in the literature and in evidence of voice expression, which suggests that political systems institutionalize "opportunity structures that can facilitate or hamper collective action" (Mohan and Stokke 2000, 260) and that higher-level political and administrative appointments create hierarchical responsive structures that are difficult to break (or to open to social influence). Evidence from the cases shows that, if the existing political process is undemocratic, centralized, or unrepresentative, disadvantaged citizens are more likely to be disenfranchised in the governance process, and voice mechanisms tend to facilitate narrower, less influential voice expression. Centralized political systems tend to tilt power and influence toward central political leaders and technical administrators. Voice expression through mechanisms adopted in South Africa (as in many similar countries) has been negatively affected by political structures even though the nation is both democratic and decentralized, however (Andrews 2002).[23] A major issue in such newly decentralized settings is the intergovernmental political and fiscal structure, which often focuses local representatives on national-level party agendas or high-level government policies rather than the voices of their constituencies. Beall (2001) writes of the national-level influence of a quasi-political group (SANCO) supposedly providing a voice mechanism in Johannesburg: "When local-level concerns become subverted to national-level ambitions . . . [the local level concerns] . . . have to balance their accountability downwards towards their membership of local residents, alongside their accountability upwards towards the broader aims and objectives of the national organization" (365). In light of this, Domecq (1998, 6) comments that, "decentralization of power and resources, political will to make government transparent, and citizen participation are the three pillars underlying public budget hearings."

Closed administrative systems limit voice influence and narrow voice focus: Technical administrators and administrative culture also affect governance processes and the possibility of voice expression in many developing countries (Brinkerhoff and Kulibaba 1996, 131). Where administrative decision making is centralized, administrative processes are complex, and information is unavailable—that is, where the administrative process is closed—citizen voice tends to have low influence and be narrowly focused. In such situations, technical administrators enjoy a powerful influence, which exceeds that of street-level administrators, political leaders, and community members (particularly where these other role players lack technical skills and information access, as is the case in most developing countries). The dominant influence of administrators in such cases drowns out other voices, leaving them without influence. Cases of low voice influence (such as in Tanzania's participatory planning mechanisms) show that administrative inertia certainly prohibits the kind of openness in the governance process that is required for effective voice influence (Eriksen 1997). In another negative case from Guyana, participation was limited to those whom administrators thought would contribute positively to the governance process (without effecting unsettling change) (Pelling 1998). This administrative impact is commonly called *normal professionalism,* where administrative officials invite participation only from those with whom they have a professional understanding (Chambers 1983). Such an administrative effect is observed in a comment regarding participatory reform in the Free State province, in South Africa, where social leaders (such as business leaders) were engaged in the planning process but "there was little appreciation of the possible direct contribution of other actors in the governance process" (DCD-GTZ 1999, Free State study, 28).

   In poor areas, voices are often ignored, or voice mechanisms captured: Experience shows that the poor are less likely to participate in public sector decision making than are the wealthy.[24] This effect is particularly manifested where participation has a large relative cost for the poor (Johnston and Clarke 1982). The poorer the society is, the more likely it is that participation costs outweigh potential benefits (especially where social capital is underdeveloped) and the less influence disadvantaged citizens have in decision making (Bryant and White 1982). Experience shows that technical administrators, advantaged citizens, and central-minded politicians enjoy influence in such poor, high-problem, and heterogeneous governments. Benjamin (2000) emphasizes the complex relational influences on poverty alleviation programs that emerge in such situations, arguing that many poor groups create partnerships of dependence with higher-income groups to overcome their socioeconomic voice constraints. Etamadi (2000) implicitly suggests similar collaboration in arguing that nonprofessional, marginalized groups have had their voice heard by partnering with professionals in the participation process: "Advocacy supported by hard data, not just rhetoric, is more likely to gain the support of the administration and the public" (69). Unfortunately, these partnerships could lead to co-optation of the voice expression process and the narrow expression of voice by wealthier subgroups.

■ *Weak social structures limit voice influence and narrow voice focus:* Where social organization is weak, experience reveals that the interests of technical administrators and advantaged citizens dominate the governance process—typically manifest in limited and often uninfluential voice expression through reform-based voice mechanisms. An example is Alice in South Africa, where public meetings and committees are not seen to facilitate broad or influential voice expression and "participation is complicated by poorly organized civil society in the isolated rural villages. Very few development/community committees function effectively" (DCD-GTZ 1999, Eastern Cape study, 27). Similarly, in the South African town of Kentani participatory structures are focused only on those communities that are organized: "The extent to which less organized communities, specific reference to isolated rural communities, are represented by the current structure is questionable" (DCD-GTZ 1999, Eastern Cape study, 20). Finally, the narrow voice focus in Uganda's participatory budgeting reforms is partly explained by weak social structures:

> The lack of a strong civil society is partly responsible for the influence donors have over policy planning in a country like Uganda. Citizens' participation in the budgetary process and policy formulation is limited by lack of strong civil society organizations/institutions to mobilize them and act as lead agencies to involve citizens in policy dialogue. (Gariyo 2000, 7)

Conclusion

The central research question of this chapter is, "Do voice mechanisms make governments more accountable and responsive?" The answer given in the title is plain: Not always. When considering experience in the literature and a study of South African municipal reform, it is apparent that voice mechanisms have different effects on accountability. In some cases accountability is not enhanced at all when voice mechanisms are adopted. In some cases accountability is enhanced, with governments called to account to narrow interest groups. In other cases accountability is enhanced, with governments called to account to broad constituencies.

The variation in accountability effects arising from the adoption of voice mechanisms reflects different forms of voice expression facilitated by new mechanisms. This is shown in figure 8.3, an adaptation of figure 8.1.

| Reforms introduce new voice mechanisms | → | New voice mechanisms alter voice expression, but in different ways, with some facilitating influential voice expression, others not, some facilitating narrow voice expression, and others facilitating broad voice expression | → | Altered voice expression leads to public sector accountability effects: Where voice expression lacks influence, there is no accountability effect Where voice expression has influence but focus is narrow, accountability is enhanced—to a narrow social segment Where voice expression has influence and focus is broad, accountability is enhanced—to a broad social segment |

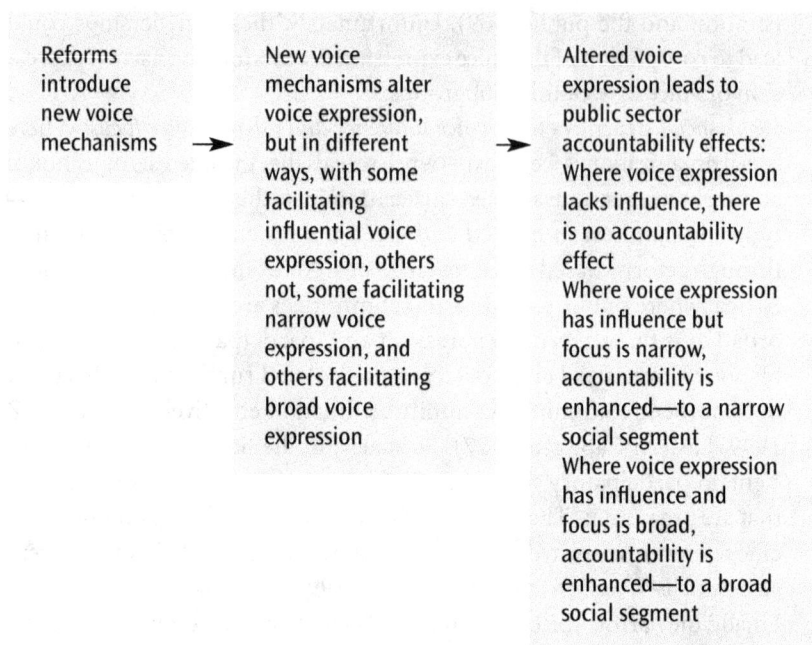

FIGURE 8.3. Voice Mechanisms, Voice Expression, and Accountability (Observed Experience)

Figure 8.3 reflects the observed experience that

- in those cases where voice expression lacks any kind of influence, voice mechanisms do not lead to improved accountability
- where voice expression is influential, but voice focus is narrow, accountability relationships are developed—but these are narrow and can facilitate government capture
- where voice expression is influential and voice focus is broad, resulting accountability relationships are also broad

This last kind of accountability relationship is the one generally intended in literature and reforms touting democratic decentralization (and the power of voice in such settings)—as was shown in figure 8.1. Through analysis of cases of participatory or voice-based reform, this chapter has shown that voice mechanisms do not always have this positive kind of accountability effect, however. This finding should re-focus analysts and policy makers on assessing and managing factors that facilitate influential, broad accountability effects. The various factors identified as affecting voice influence, focus, and accountability outcomes are intended to provide a first area of investigation for such research. These factors are also intended to guide policy makers who aim to develop voice mechanisms that facilitate broad accountability links between governing officials and the public.

Notes

1. Cases were selected in the desk study to reflect the broad patterns of voice and participation mechanism adoption at the subnational level throughout the developing world since the early 1990s.
2. The South African study involved the analysis of a national government survey, the Project Viability survey of July 2000, 19 case studies of planning reform (that included a participation concentration) conducted by the German development agency GTZ in 1999, and primary case study research conducted on selected municipalities using semistructured e-mail-based interviews in 2001 and 2002.
3. South Africa was selected for specific study to facilitate comparison of the desk analysis and to allow for detailed investigation of the adoption of voice mechanisms. The subject governments in this study, small urban governments existing in South Africa between 1995 and 2000 (called Transitional Local Councils or TLCs), are widely representative of urban governments throughout the developing world, in terms of both their demographics and their governance challenges. A national survey conducted in 2000, asking about participation at the local level (among other things), yielded a sample of 273 TLCs (62 percent of the total population) that displays the kind of variation common in developing countries—municipalities differ significantly in size (from fewer than 500 constituents to more than 500,000) as well as in socioeconomic standing and service provision performance. The TLCs all faced a common legislated mandate to develop participation mechanisms in their governance processes—also similar to situations faced in developing countries from Bolivia to the Philippines to Tanzania.
4. Both approaches have been interpreted in the institutional literature. In the Weberian model accountability involves conformance to formal rules of procedure and legislation, while in the market model accountability involves adherence to the less formal social rules of performance.
5. Mitlin (2000) argues that influences such as voice are vitally important in facilitating responsiveness and accountability in local governments, and a pro-poor attitude in service provision.
6. Evidence of this new concentration is available in national legislation throughout the developing world, which increasingly requires municipalities and the like to adopt such mechanisms. Countries with such legislation in place include Bolivia, India, Malaysia, the Philippines, South Africa, and Uganda.
7. Much research assumes that participation is about empowerment (Blair 2000). On the contrary, Mohan and Stokke (2000) argue that governments often use the concept of participation and local government for ends other than real social development. They suggest that research into participation should "examine the use of 'the local' by various actors" (254). Hyden and Bratton (1992, 158) emphasize that much of the policy talk about participation is mere rhetoric.

8. This situation relates well to that in countries throughout the developing world, characterized by transition, decentralization, and an accountability focus (with local governments required to increase their citizen emphasis and to manage resources effectively and efficiently) (Africa 1999).

9. The Project Viability Survey was conduced by the national Department of Provincial and Local Government.

10. Their argument is that voice creates a social disciplinary device that forces government officials to consider the revenues they raise seriously, and ensures that government officials behave within the socially determined and agreed-on code of fiscal management (including accounting rules). In relating to public choice theory, the argument is that "the principal-agent problem inherent in (more or less) representative democracies becomes less severe" when citizen participation and access is institutionalized and governments are made more accountable to local citizens (Feld and Kirchgassner 1999, 153).

11. This mandate required local governments to provide high-class services to an expanded constituency in a short period of time.

12. Participatory monitoring was introduced partly so that NGOs leading the participatory planning process could evaluate the effect of voice on accountability and responsiveness, as evident in Moctezuma's comment that, "the PUCSN (collaborative entity) . . . hopes to measure the efficacy of its interventions" (2001, 131).

13. With the authors making subjective judgments based on case and other evidence.

14. Schneider (1999) says that the Public Complaints Bureau had an effect of increasing "transparency and accountability in the public sector" (529), as well as improving responsiveness and enhancing public awareness of governance reforms.

15. In Andrews (2002) an index variable representing the strength of the participatory mechanism developed at the local level (a composite of answers to questions about adoption of participation paths in budgeting processes, facilitation of help desks, provision of response mechanisms associated with help desks, and so on) was found to have a positive and significant effect on the degree to which municipalities expanded their real service expenditures in the 1995–2000 period. Service expansion was a key focus of the developmental mandate incorporated in national and local government policy and legislation. Responsiveness to service need and to this mandate is a central factor in overall municipal accountability.

16. The potential for reforms involving citizen participation and voice enhancement to facilitate government capture is reflected in concerns Dolny (2001) expresses regarding work with cooperatives in Mozambique. Dolny attempted to improve accounting and financial literacy among members of agricultural cooperatives, to enhance their ability to interact and communicate (and voice their presence) to district and provincial administrators. Dolny explains that she "was committed to the idea that each cooperative would have a group of members who understood their own accounts" such that the people could be "in charge of their own affairs" (27). She emphasized training a group of people in each cooperative so that individuals would not be empowered to the point that they could capture the entity: "The quest to create a group who had shared knowledge was also an insurance attempt to make rip-offs more difficult. There were too many stories about the corruption that had harmed many of the Ujamaa cooperatives in Tanzania a decade earlier" (27). Dolny's implicit warning is an important one: reforms that are designed to empower the disem-

powered can create skewed accountability and responsiveness relationships (and facilitate government capture) if they empower voices of individuals within groups (or cooperatives) rather then empowering groups themselves.

17. The GTZ case cites the major involvement of the National Business Initiative in the town. This involvement included facilitating community meetings and an active partnership with the council, focused on garnering a casino license for the jurisdiction and developing tourism infrastructure. The Steering Committee is described as gender and poverty insensitive.

18. Andrews (2002) finds that Howick had a 10 percent decline in real service-related expenditures in the 1996–2000 period, when the national average showed a 2 percent increase in such expenditures (as calculated from the 273-municipality Project Viability database).

19. Rosenbaum (1999) analyzes this experience and finds similar positive accountability effects.

20. Even electoral systems in openly democratic countries fail to facilitate the expression of all social voices. The youth, a large portion of society in developing countries that is usually unevenly affected by poverty, is generally given no voice through such mechanisms.

21. The combination of local elections and the Participatory District Development Programme in Nepal is another example of a voice mechanism facilitating a broad, high-influence form of voice expression. In this case, assessment and evaluation devices were also used to effect change and ensure that voice had influence (UNDP 2000).

22. In Naga City, the Philippines, for example, local governments were entrenched in national law (constituting a supportive context for local government) and the council developed an appropriate internal medium for voice consideration (the Empowerment Ordinance, which made consideration of civic voice an integral part of the hierarchical governing process). In combination, the effective medium and supportive context helped facilitate highly influential voice expression through the Naga council. Accountability gains in this city have already been alluded to, and relate broadly to fiscal changes, transparency, and political accountability.

23. Andrews (2002) finds that local governments led by the African National Congress, which also ruled nationally and in seven of the nine provinces in the 1995–2000 period, had systematically lower levels of adoption of voice mechanisms. They were more likely to host undirected civic meetings than to host help desks with direct connections to planning processes.

24. Atkinson and others (2000) showed that socioeconomic influences also play out in participation levels according to specific classes and gender.

References

Africa, Elroy. 1999. *Developmental Local Government and Integrated Development Planning (IDP) in South Africa.* Pretoria: South African Department of Constitutional Development.

Andrews, Matthew. 2002. "Fiscal Institutions Adoption in South African Municipalities." Paper presented at the Center for Science and Industrial Research, Pretoria, 15 March.

———. Forthcoming. "Selecting and Sustaining Community Programs in Developing Countries." *Public Administration Quarterly.*

Andrews, Matthew, and Anwar Shah. 2002. "Voice and Local Governance in the Developing World: What Is Done, to What Effect, and Why?" Unpublished manuscript, World Bank, Washington, DC.

Atkinson, Sarah, Regianne Leila Rolim Medeiros, Paulo Henrique Lima Oliviera, and Ricardo Dias de Almeida. 2000. "Going Down to the Local: Incorporating Social Organization and Political Culture into Assessments of Decentralized Health Care." *Social Science and Medicine* 51: 619–36.

Awio, Godwin. 2001. "Decentralization and Budgeting: The Uganda Health Sector Experience." *International Journal of Public Sector Management* 14 (1): 75–88.

Beall, Jo. 2001. "Valuing Social Resources or Capitalizing on Them?" *International Planning Studies* 6 (4): 357–75.

Benjamin, Solomon. 2000. "Governance, Economic Settings and Poverty in Bangalore." *Environment and Urbanization* 12 (1): 35–56.

Blair, Harry. 2000. "Participation and Accountability at the Periphery: Democratic Local Governance in Six Countries." *World Development* 28 (1): 21–39.

Brinkerhoff, Derick W., and Nicolas P. Kulibaba. 1996. "Perspectives on Participation in Economic Policy Reform in Africa." *Studies in Comparative International Development* 31 (Fall): 131–51.

Bryant, Coralie, and Louise G. White. 1982. *Managing Development in the Third World.* Boulder, CO: Westview Press.

Chambers, Robert. 1983. *Rural Development: Putting the Last First.* London: Longman.

Charlick, Robert B. 2001. "Popular Participation and Local Government Reform." *Public Administration and Development* 21: 149–57.

DCD-GTZ (Department of Constitutional Development and German Technical Corporation). 1999. *Integrated Development Planning Pilot Projects Assessment Study.* Pretoria: South African Department of Constitutional Development.

Desai, Vandana. 1996. "Access to Power and Participation." *Third World Planning Review* 18 (2): 217–42.

Dixit, Kunda. 2000. "Nepal's Quiet Revolution." *Choices* (March): 16–17.

Dolny, Helena. 2001. *Banking on Change.* Johannesburg, South Africa: Viking.

Domecq, Raul F. Monet. 1998. "Paraguay's Public Budget Hearings: A Path to Transparency." *Accountability* 16: 6–7.

Eriksen, Stein S. 1997. "Development Planning in Tanzanian Local Governments." *Third World Planning Review* 3: 251–69.

ESSET (Ecumenical Service for Socio-Economic Transformation). 2000. "Brazil's Participatory Budgeting Process." *Economic Justice Update* 4 (3): 3.

Etamadi, Felisa U. 2000. "Civil Society Participation in City Governance in Cebu City." *Environment and Urbanization* 12 (1): 57–72.

Faguet, Jean-Paul. 2000. "Does Decentralization Increase Responsiveness to Local Needs? Evidence from Bolivia." Unpublished manuscript, World Bank, Washington, DC.

Feld, Lars P., and Gerhard Kirchgassner. 1999. "Public Debt and Budgetary Procedures: Top Down of Bottom Up? Some Evidence from Swiss Municipalities." In *Fiscal Institutions and Fiscal Performance*, ed. James M. Poterba, and Jürgen von Hagen, 151–80. Chicago: University of Chicago Press.

Gariyo, Zie. 2000. "Citizen Involvement in the Budgetary Process in Uganda." Paper presented at the Conference on Civil Society and Donor Policy in Glasgow, Scotland, May 24–26.

Gopakumar, K. 1997. "Public Feedback as an Aid to Public Accountability: Reflections on an Alternate Approach." *Public Administration and Development* 17: 281–82.

Goudsmit, Into A., and James Blackburn. 2001. "Participatory Municipal Planning in Bolivia: An Ambiguous Experience." *Development in Practice* 11 (5): 587–96. http://www.developmentinpractice.org.

Hirschmann, Albert O. 1970. *Exit, Voice and Loyalty: Responses to Decline in Firms, Organizations and States.* Cambridge, MA: Harvard University Press.

Hyden, Goran, and Michael Bratton. 1992. *Governance and Politics in Africa.* Boulder, CO: Lynne Rienner Publishers.

Jenkins, Rob, and Anne-Marie Goetz. 1999. "Accounts and Accountability: Theoretical Implications of the Right-to-Information Movement in India." *Third World Quarterly* 20 (3): 603–22.

Johnston, B. F., and W. C. Clarke. 1982. *Redesigning Rural Development: A Strategic Perspective.* Baltimore, MD: Johns Hopkins University Press.

Manasan, R., E. Gonzalez, and R. Gaffud. 1999. *Towards Better Government. Developing Indicators of Good Governance for Local Government.* Pasig City, Philippines: NEDA (National Economic Development Authority) and United Nations Development Programme.

Manor, J., and R. Crook. 1998. *Democracy and Decentralization in South Asia and West Africa: Participation, Accountability and Performance.* Cambridge, MA, and New York: Cambridge University Press.

Miles, M. B., and A. M. Huberman. 1994. *Qualitative Data Analysis.* 2nd ed. Thousand Oaks, CA: Sage Publications.

Mitlin, Diana. 2000. "Towards More Pro-Poor Local Governments in Urban Areas." *Environment and Urbanization* 12 (1): 3–11.

Moctezuma, Pedro. 2001. "Community-Based Organization and Participatory Planning in South-East Mexico City." *Environment and Urbanization* 13 (2): 117–34.

Mohan, G., and K. Stokke. 2000. "Participatory Development and Empowerment: The Dangers of Localism." *Third World Quarterly* 21 (2): 247–68.

Oates, Wallace. 1993. "Fiscal Decentralization and Economic Development." *National Tax Journal* 46: 237–43.

Paul, Samuel. 1992. "Accountability in Public Services: Exit, Voice and Control." *World Development* 20: 1047–60.

———. 1996. "Strengthening Public Accountability through Participation." In *Participation in Practice,* ed. Jennifer Rietbergen-McCracken, World Bank Discussion Paper 333, World Bank, Washington, DC.

Pelling, Mark. 1998. "Participation, Social Capital, and Vulnerability to Urban Flooding in Guyana." *Journal of International Development* 10: 469–86.

Peters, B. Guy. 1996. *The Future of Governing: Four Emerging Models.* Lawrence, KS: University Press of Kansas.

PLANACT (Planning in Action). 1999. *Towards a Social Approach to Integrated Development Planning: Integrated Development Planning Unit Study May 1999–August 1999.* Johannesburg, South Africa: PLANACT.

Planning Initiative. 1999. *An Evaluation of Integrated Development Planning in KwaZulu Natal: Report prepared for the Town and Regional Planning Commission.* Pietermaritzburg, South Africa: Planning Initiative.

Pope, Jeremy. 2000. "Local Government." In *TI Source Book,* ed. Jeremy Pope, 115–18. Berlin: Transparency International.

Reinikka, Ritva. 1999. "Using Surveys for Public Sector Reform." *World Bank PREMnotes* 23, World Bank, Washington, DC.

Rietbergen-McCracken, Jennifer, and Deepa Narayan. 1998. *Participation and Social Assessment: Tools and Techniques.* Washington, DC: World Bank.

Robb, Caroline M. 2000. "How the Poor Can Have a Voice in Government Policy." *Finance and Development* 37 (4): 22–25. http://www.imf.org/external/pubs/ft/fandd/2000/12/robb.htm.

Rosenbaum, Alan. 1999. "Good Governance, Accountability and the Public Servant." Institute for Public Management and Community Service, Florida International University, Miami.

Schneider, Hartmut. 1999. "Participatory Governance for Poverty Reduction." *Journal of International Development* 11 (4): 531–34.

Souza, Celine. 2001. "Participatory Budgeting in Brazilian Cities: Limits and Possibilities in Building Democratic Institutions, Urban Governance, Partnership and Poverty." Working Paper 28, University of Birmingham, Birmingham, U.K.

Swilling, Mark. 1997. "Building Democratic Local Urban Governance in Southern Africa." In *Governing Africa's Cities,* ed. Mark Swilling, 211–73. Johannesburg, South Africa: Witwatersrand University Press.

———. 1998. "Creative Vision for Local Government." *Weekly Mail and Guardian,* March 13.

UNDP (United Nations Development Programme). 2000. *Nepal Participatory District Development Programme.* http://www.undp.org/info.

Yin, Robert K. 1998. "The Abridged Version of Case Study Research: Design and Method." In *Handbook of Applied Social Research Methods,* ed. Leonard Bickman and Debra Rog, 229–59. Thousand Oaks, CA: Sage Publications.

Index

Access to pension assets, 102

Accountability of local governments, civic pressure/participation, reforms focused on enhancing, 220–22

Administrative costs, public pensions, 83

Adverse selection, public pension, 81–82

Age, grouping by, in public expenditure analysis, 10–11

Allocation of public expenditures, 15–25
  education, 21–22
  goods, purchases of, 20–22
  health care, 22
  in-kind transfers, 20
  services, purchases of, 20–22
  transfer payments, 19–20
    to business, 20
    to persons, 19–20

Analysis of government expenditure, 1–32

Annual analysis *vs.* lifetime analysis of public expenditures, 14–15

Atkinson's inequality measures, 40–42

Benefit incidence, in public expenditure analysis, 3

Benefits to individuals, costs of government, public expenditure analysis, compared, 15–16

Budget
  citizen-centered, 176
  local government, citizen-centered, financial statement, 189

Capital markets
  public pensions, 98–99
  underdeveloped, 86Capital taxes, 86

Citizen-centered budgeting, 176

Citizen-centered governance, 153–81
  conventional reform evaluation, 156–65
    legacy of, 156–58
  developing countries, common governance, administrative weakness in, 154
  limitation of reform effects, 158–65
    reform arrangement, 161–65
    reform elements, 158–61
  process bias, reform combinations, 161
  public sector reform in developing countries, 154–56
    accountability mechanisms, lack of, 156
    low capacity, 155
    organizational centralization, 155
    participation, lack of, 155–56
    service monopolies, 155
    social insulation, 155–56
    top-down governance, 155
    transparency, lack of, 155–56
  reform, citizen-centered framework guiding, 165–72
  weaknesses in reforms, evaluation of, 165

Citizen-centered local-level budgets, developing countries, 183–216
  budget format, 210–12

Citizen-centered local-level budgets,
developing countries, (*continued*)
budget process, 185
citizen access, 184–87
budget, financial statement formats
for, 188–90
citizen analysis of municipal finances,
190–215
institutional move toward, 191
budget, financial statement format,
209–15
institutional adoption, 183
institutional cost, 193
institutional influence, 192–93
reflection, resolution institutions, 198
reporting institutions, 203–7
representative institutions, 1932–215
response, redress institutions, 208–9
revelation institutions, 194–98
right-to-information institutions,
193–94
institutionalization of, 190–92
local government budget, financial
statement, 189
reflection, resolution records, 200–202
reporting records, 205–7
revelation records, citizen oriented,
196–97
Civic pressure/participation, local government fiscal outcomes, 217–48
accountability, 223–41
accountability effects, observed difference in, 226
accountability indicators, identifying,
224–26
broad accountability effect, 232–34
factors influencing accountability
effects, 234–41
narrow accountability effect, 229–32
no accountability effect, 226–29
reforms focused on enhancing, 220–22
research approach, 222–23
Classification of government expenditures, 17–19
Components of government expenditure,
5–6
Components of income, 12

Contributory pension schemes, 99–125
"Cost incurred on behalf of" approach to
public expenditure analysis, 16–17
Costs of government, benefits to individuals, public expenditure analysis,
compared, 15–16
Counterfactuals, in public expenditure
analysis, 4
Coverage of public pensions, 100

Database in public expenditure analysis,
6–7
Defined-benefit public pensions, *vs.*
defined-contribution, 109
Defined-contribution pension benefits,
vs. defined-benefit, 101
Design of public pensions, 100–103
Developing countries. *See also under* specific country
citizen-centered local-level budgets,
183–216
common approaches to budgeting in,
184–90
common governance, administrative
weakness in, 154
public sector reform in, 154–56
Direct effects of public expenditures, 3
Disability risk, public pension, 80
Disaggregated indexes, 27–28
Disaggregation by level of government, in
public expenditure analysis, 6
Distributional effects
basis for measuring, 61–62
public expenditures, 25–29

Earmarked payroll tax, pension funds, 109
Economic effects of, contributory pension schemes, 114–25
aggregate savings and investment,
120–23
backloading, 116
capital market development, 123
capital market effects, 117–23
earnings, 115
employment effects, 117
hiring, 117
human capital accumulation, 115–16
individual savings, 118–20

labor demand, 116–17
labor market effects, 114–23
labor mobility, 116
labor supply, 114–16
life-cycle hypothesis, 118
matching of workers to jobs, 117
overlapping generations model, 121
participation, 115
retirement age, 115
Ricardian equivalence hypothesis, 123
size of labor force, 124
transitional effects, 124–25
turnover, 116–17
Economic well-being overview, in public
    expenditure analysis, 14
Education, 21–22
Efficiency, market failure, 72–73
    free-rider problems, 72–73
Elderly
    public pensions, 88–99
    transfers to, 88–99
        economic effects of (*See* Public pen-
            sions)
Entropy measures of inequality, 39–40
Equity, 73–74
    blunt incentives, 74
    intergenerational, 24
    vertical, 14
Equivalence scales, in public expenditure
    analysis, 9
Expenditure incidence, 2–5
    allocation of expenditures, 19–22
        education, 21–22
        goods, purchases of, 20–22
        health care, 22
        in-kind transfers, 20
        services, purchases of, 20–22
        transfer payments, 19–20
            to business, 20
            to persons, 19–20
    allocation of public expenditures,
        15–25
    analysis of, 1–32
    annual analysis *vs.* lifetime analysis,
        14–15
    B classification of government expen-
        ditures, 18
    benefit incidence, 3

classification of government expendi-
    tures, 17–19
"cost incurred on behalf of" approach,
    16–17
costs of government *vs.* benefits to
    individuals, 15–16
counterfactuals, 4
database, 6–7
direct effects, 3
disaggregation, by level of government,
    6
distributional effects, 25–29
economic well-being, 14
equivalence scales, 9
expenditure incidence, 2–3
externalities, 17
general expenditures, 22–24
government expenditure, components
    of, 5–6
government expenditures, 14
government overview, 5–6
government spending, 17
groupings of government expenditure,
    26
income
    components of, 12
    overview, 11–14
indexes of expenditure incidence, 27
    disaggregated indexes, 27–28
    Gini coefficient, 28
        comparisons, 29
    global indexes, 28–29
    local measures of redistribution, 27
indirect effects, 3
perspective of vertical equity, 14
public debt, allocation of interest pay-
    ments, 24–25
    current expenditures, 25
    intergenerational equity, 24
in public expenditure analysis, 2–3
taxation, raising dollar through, 17
unit of analysis, 7–11
    age, grouping by, 10–11
    families, 7–9
    households, and families, 7–9
    income level, grouping by, 10–11
    individuals, 7–9
    size, adjustment for, 9–10

External, citizen focus tools for results-oriented management, 176

Financing public pensions, 96–97
Fund management, pensions, 107
Funded vs. unfunded public pensions, 100–101
Funding requirements
  pension, 106
  pensions, 107

Gender budget, 135–52. *See also* Gender in public expenditure analysis
Gender in public expenditure analysis, 135–52
  Barbados, gender budget document, 149–51
  budget statement, gender-aware, 140
  business support, gender balance in, 140
  changes in policy, 142–43
  child allowances, 144
  data, 141–42
  education, 144
  gender budgets, 135
  gender-disaggregated beneficiary assessments, 139
  gender-disaggregated public expenditure, incidence analysis, 139
  gender-sensitive budgetary analysis, examples of, 144–49
  health services, 144
  Israel, 144
  methodology of analysis, 139–41
  policy appraisal, gender-aware, 140
  public sector contracts, gender balance in, 140
  public sector employment, gender balance in, 140
  social affairs, 144
  South Africa, gender budget document, 145–48
  Sri Lanka, gender budget document, 148–49
  vocational training, 144
General expenditures, 22–24
Gini index, 36–39
  calculations, 37–38

Goods, purchases of, 20–22
Government expenditures by functional classification, Philippines, 60
Government guarantees, 107–8
  public pensions and, 107–8
Government intervention, rationale for, 72–88
Government regulation of pensions, 107–8
Government spending. *See* Public expenditure
Governmental system, overview of, 5–6
Groupings of government expenditures, 26

Health care, 22
Household, as unit, in public expenditure analysis, 7–9

Illness, risk of, public pension, 80
Illustration using Lao PDR data, 44–46
In-kind transfers, 20
  public pensions, 92
Incidence, expenditure. *See* Expenditure incidence
Income
  components of, 12
  overview, 11–14
Income earners, 109
Income level, grouping by, in public expenditure analysis, 10–11
Income transfers, women's priority, 140
Indexes of expenditure incidence, 27
  disaggregated indexes, 27–28
  Gini coefficient, 28
  comparisons, 29
  global indexes, 28–29
  local measures of redistribution, 27
Indirect effects of public expenditures, 3
Individual access to pension assets, 102
Inflation risk, public pension, 80
Institutional move toward citizen-centered local-level budgets
  budget, financial statement format, 209–15
  institutional adoption, 183
  institutional cost, 193
  institutional influence, 192–93

reflection, resolution institutions, 198
reporting institutions, 203–7
representative institutions, 1932–215
response, redress institutions, 208–9
revelation institutions, 194–98
right-to-information institutions,
193–94
Insurance, public pension, 80–85
Insured service, overuse by suppliers of, 83
Intergenerational equity, 24
Intergenerational inequality, transfers to
elderly, 77
Intragenerational inequality, transfers to
elderly, 76–77
home care, 76
OECD countries, 76
pharmaceuticals, 76
Investment and inflation risk, public pensions, 83
Investment risk, public pension, 80
Israel, gender in public expenditure
analysis, 144

Labor market effects, public pensions,
97–98
Limitation of reform effects in developing countries, 158–65
reform arrangement, 161–65
reform elements, 158–61
Local-level budgets in developing countries, citizen-centered, 183–216
budget format, 210–12
budget process, 185
citizen access, 184–87
budget, financial statement formats
for, 188–90
citizen analysis of municipal finances,
190–215
institutional move toward, 191
budget, financial statement format,
209–15
institutional adoption, 183
institutional cost, 193
institutional influence, 192–93
reflection, resolution institutions, 198
reporting institutions, 203–7
representative institutions, 1932–215
response, redress institutions, 208–9

revelation institutions, 194–98
right-to-information institutions,
193–94
institutionalization of, 190–92
local government budget, financial
statement, 189
reflection, resolution records, 200–202
reporting records, 205–7
revelation records, citizen oriented,
196–97
Longevity risk, public pension, 80
Lorenz curve, 35, 53
social welfare, 34–36

Macroeconomic policy management, 45
Mandatory retirement saving schemes,
112–14
Market failure, 72–73
information asymmetries, 73
market frictions, 73
underdeveloped markets, 73
Moral hazard, public pension, 82–83

Occupational private pension design
issues, 103–8
Overlapping generations model, pension
schemes, 121

Payroll tax, earmarked, pension funds, 109
Pensions. See Public pensions
Philippines, fiscal policy in, 49–68
distributional effects, basis for measuring, 61–62
government expenditures by functional classification, 60
indirect taxes, 56–57
Lorenz function, 53
Philippine fiscal system, 57–60
Price Reform Index for Expenditures,
66
subsidies, 56–57
welfare, income components, 52–55
welfare measures, 50–52
welfare reform index, 55–56
income effect, 55
inequality effect, 55
Welfare Reform Index for Income
Components, 63

Portability, pensions, 105–7
Portfolio restrictions, pensions, 107
Poverty measurement, 42–44
Poverty measures, 33–48
Price Reform Index for Expenditures, Philippines, 66
Private pension design, occupational issues, 103–8
Provident fund design issues, 112–14
Provident funds, 112
Public debt, allocation of interest payments, 24–25
    current expenditures, 25
    intergenerational equity, 24
Public expenditure incidence, 2–5
    allocation of expenditures, 19–22
        education, 21–22
        goods, purchases of, 20–22
        health care, 22
        in-kind transfers, 20
        services, purchases of, 20–22
        transfer payments, 19–20
            to business, 20
            to persons, 19–20
    allocation of public expenditures, 15–25
    analysis of, 1–32
    annual analysis vs. lifetime analysis, 14–15
    B classification of government expenditures, 18
    benefit incidence, 3
    classification of government expenditures, 17–19
    "cost incurred on behalf of" approach, 16–17
    costs of government vs. benefits to individuals, 15–16
    counterfactuals, 4
    database, 6–7
    direct effects, 3
    disaggregation, by level of government, 6
    distributional effects, 25–29
    economic well-being, 14
    equivalence scales, 9
    expenditure incidence, 2–3
    externalities, 17
    general expenditures, 22–24

    government expenditure, components of, 5–6
    government expenditures, 14
    government overview, 5–6
    government spending, 17
    groupings of government expenditure, 26
    income
        components of, 12
        overview, 11–14
    indexes of expenditure incidence, 27
        disaggregated indexes, 27–28
        Gini coefficient, 28
            comparisons, 29
        global indexes, 28–29
        local measures of redistribution, 27
    indirect effects, 3
    perspective of vertical equity, 14
    public debt, allocation of interest payments, 24–25
        current expenditures, 25
        intergenerational equity, 24
    taxation, raising dollar through, 17
    unit of analysis, 7–11
        age, grouping by, 10–11
        families, 7–9
        households, 7–9
        income level, grouping by, 10–11
        individuals, 7–9
        size, adjustment for, 9–10
Public pensions, 77
    administrative costs, 130
    aggregate savings and investment, 120–23
    backloading, 116
    capital market development, 123
    capital market effects, 117–23
    capital markets, development of, 129
    contributory pension schemes, economic effects, 114–25
    defined-benefit vs. defined-contribution, 109
    design, 108–12, 126–27
    earmarked payroll tax, 109
    earnings, 115
    economic effects, 127–28
    economic growth, 129
    employment effects, 117

evaluation, 69–134
  best practices, 69
  reform, imperative for, 69–72
extent of funding, 110–12
fiscal burdens, 129
fund management, 112
funded vs. unfunded, 131
hiring, 117
human capital accumulation, 115–16
income earners, 109
increase self-sufficiency of elderly, 128
increasing awareness, 126
individual savings, 118–20
labor demand, 116–17
labor market effects, 114–23
labor mobility, 116
labor supply, 114–16
life-cycle hypothesis, 118
mandatory retirement saving schemes,
  112–14
mandatory vs. voluntary, 131
matching of workers to jobs, 117
overlapping generations model, 121
participation, 115
provident fund design issues, 112–14
provident funds, 112
public sector inefficiency, 130
public vs. private role, 131
redistributional effects, 130
reduction in inequality, 129
retirement, voluntary provision for,
  125–28
retirement age, 115
Ricardian equivalence hypothesis, 123
savings rates, 125
size of labor force, 124
source of funds, 109–10
stable economic environment, 126
structure of, 132
tax incentives, 126–27
traditional forms of support, 127
transitional effects, 124–25
turnover, 116–17
university vs. targeting, 131
voluntary savings, provident funds for,
  127
Public sector reform in developing countries, 154–56
  accountability mechanisms, lack of, 156
  low capacity, 155
  organizational centralization, 155
  participation, lack of, 155–56
  service monopolies, 155
  social insulation, 155–56
  top-down governance, 155
  transparency, lack of, 155–56
Public services, women's priority, 140

Redistribution, 75–80
Redistributive instruments, scope of cov-
  erage, 89–91
Reflection, resolution records, citizen-
  oriented, 200–202
Reform, citizen-centered framework
  guiding, 165–72
Reporting records, citizen-oriented,
  205–7
Reporting requirements, pensions, 107
Results-oriented management, external,
  citizen focus tools, 176
Retirement
  undersaving for, public pensions,
    85–86
    myopia, 85
  voluntary provision for, 125–28
Revelation records, citizen oriented,
  196–97
Ricardian equivalence hypothesis, 123

Samaritan's dilemma, 86
Savings
  inadequacy of, public pensions, 85–88
  rates, public pensions, 86–87
Services, purchases of, 20–22
Social welfare, Lorenz curve, 34–36
South Africa, gender budget document,
  145–48
Sri Lanka, gender budget document,
  148–49

Taxation, 108
  capital, public pensions, 86
  payroll, earmarked, pension funds, 109
  pension contributions, benefits, 108
  raising dollar through, 17

Top-down governance, public sector reform in developing countries, 155
Transfer formula, public pensions, 93–95
Transfer payments, 19–20
Transfer-sensitivity axioms, 44
Transfers to elderly, economic effects of, 97–99. *See also* Public pensions

Undersaving for retirement, public pensions, 85–86
  income loss, 85
  incomes inadequate, 85
  myopia, 85
  Naivete, 85
  traditional forms of support, 85
Units of public expenditure analysis, 7–11
  age, grouping by, 10–11
  families, 7–9
  households, 7–9
  income level, grouping by, 10–11
  individuals, 7–9
  size, adjustment for, 9–10

Vertical equity, 14
Vesting
  pensions, 105–7
  public pensions, 105
Voice, 217–48. *See also* Civic pressure/participation
Voluntary forms of support, role of, 96
Voluntary provision for retirement, 125–28
  administrative costs, 130

capital markets, development of, 129
design issues, 126–27
economic effects, 127–28
economic growth, 129
fiscal burdens, 129
funded *vs.* unfunded, 131
incentive effects, 130
increasing awareness, 126
individual risks, reduction of, 129
inequality, reduction in, 129
mandatory *vs.* voluntary, 131
provident funds, 127
public sector inefficiency, 130
public *vs.* private role, 131
redistributional effects, 130
savings rates, 125
self-sufficiency of elderly, 128
stable economic environment, 126
structure, 132
tax incentives, 126–27
traditional forms of support, 127
university *vs.* targeting, 131

Weaknesses in reforms, evaluation of, 165
Welfare measures, 50–52
Welfare reform index, 55–56
  income effect, 55
  inequality effect, 55
Welfare Reform Index for Income Components, Philippines, 63
Welfarism, public pensions, 88–89
Women's budget, 135–52. *See also* Gender in public expenditure analysis

www.ingramcontent.com/pod-product-compliance
Lightning Source LLC
Chambersburg PA
CBHW071844270326
41929CB00013B/2101